A History of Psychology in Ten Questions

This student-friendly book on the history of psychology covers the key historical developments and controversies in all areas of psychology, linking history to the present by focusing on ten conceptual issues that are relevant today.

How did psychology become a science, and what kind of science did it become? How do psychologists measure and explain the fact that in some ways everyone is unique? Is psychoanalysis scientific? Why did cognitive science replace behaviorism? This book addresses all these questions and more, covering the whole range of psychology, from neuroscience and artificial intelligence to hermeneutics and qualitative research in the process. Drawing on the author's experience of how to make the subject interesting for students, the book is structured around ten key questions that engage with all the core areas of psychology and the main schools of thought. Showing how each of the different approaches or paradigms within psychology differ not based on data but on assumptions, Michael Hyland provides an engaging introduction to debates from history and in contemporary society.

Including boxed material on hot topics, historical figures, studies/experiments, and quirky facts, this is the ideal book for undergraduate students of psychology taking CHIPS and other history of psychology modules.

Michael Hyland was a lecturer and later professor of health psychology at the University of Plymouth, retiring in 2018 after 44 years teaching history and theory in psychology. He is currently a part-time professor of health psychology at Plymouth Marjon University.

A History of Psychology in Ten Questions

Michael Hyland

Routledge
Taylor & Francis Group

LONDON AND NEW YORK

First published 2020
by Routledge
2 Park Square, Milton Park, Abingdon, Oxon OX14 4RN

and by Routledge
52 Vanderbilt Avenue, New York, NY 10017

Routledge is an imprint of the Taylor & Francis Group, an informa business

© 2020 Michael Hyland

British Library Cataloguing-in-Publication Data
A catalogue record for this book is available from the British Library

Library of Congress Cataloging-in-Publication Data
A catalog record for this book has been requested

ISBN: 978-0-8153-6507-5 (hbk)
ISBN: 978-0-8153-8487-8 (pbk)
ISBN: 978-1-351-20303-6 (ebk)

Typeset in Sabon
by Apex CoVantage, LLC

Illustrations by Kate Hyland

To Orin and Theo

Contents

Preface

Student satisfaction ratings are now an important part of university life. They were not used when I started teaching 40 years ago, but if they had my ratings would have been poor. I had no interest in history, and my own recent experience as a student had been entirely negative. The course taught by a young lecturer when I was an undergraduate went something like this:

> There was Fechner, yeah, and he was early and then there was Wundt. Wundt was important. Yeah, yeah, really, really important. Then there was Watson, he was also important. He started behaviourism, like . . .

I am sure it wasn't that bad, but that is how I remember it. My early courses were only a little better. I taught history from a respected textbook on the history of psychology, but I had no love for the subject. Over time, things changed. In the year I retired from the University of Plymouth, the average overall satisfaction for my course was 4.7 out of 5, with an interest rating of 4.6. Freetext comments from students showed that many anticipated the course to be boring because of its title only to be surprised by how interesting they found it.

Some people find history interesting. The majority of psychology students do not. They have come to study modern psychology. They have not come to study history. When presented with the term 'conceptual issues,' most students don't know what it means and lack interest. However, students *will* find these topics interesting if they are presented in a way that is relevant to their understanding of modern psychology. To be successful in teaching historical and conceptual issues in psychology (CHIPS), the topic must be linked to existing concepts that students find interesting. This educational principle is not new!

There are two ways of teaching CHIPS. One way is to provide a historical introduction to each topic that makes up a psychology course. For example, social psychology courses start with a historical introduction to social psychology, and developmental psychology courses start with a historical introduction to development psychology. The advantage of this approach is that it avoids the negative ratings that can accompany CHIPS courses. There are two disadvantages. One is that students continue to perceive psychology as a set of disconnected topics rather than a whole that has evolved over time. A second is that this approach neglects the broader conceptual issues.

An alternative is to teach CHIPS as a separate course. If not done well, students will find it uninteresting, but if done well, this approach can cover the broader conceptual issues and provide a sense of psychology as a whole. In this book, conceptual issues are presented in the form of questions. This technique enables students to learn with a purpose – an idea that predates the founding of academic psychology in Leipzig (Parsons, 1873). Each chapter deals with a different conceptual issue, with a historical introduction, and then shows how that issue is relevant today. Many of these conceptual issues have to do with the different assumptions of different groups of psychologists, assumptions that have changed over time.

In writing this book I have been mindful of the fact that many students have studied psychology, including the history of psychology, at school or in some introductory course. Students find repetition tedious. The content of this book is selected to avoid repetition. For example, students will have a basic understanding of behaviourism and cognitive psychology but be unaware that each answers a different type of question using a different type of theory. Students will have been introduced to some of Freud's ideas but not know why some are true, some are false, and some are unfalsifiable. Students will know about the heredity-environment controversy but not that modern epigenetics shows that it is based on a false premise, nor will they know how it is informed by the person-situation debate. Students will know about neuroscience but have little understanding of biopsychosocial interactionism. Students will know about qualitative methods but not know the different assumptions of those who use qualitative methods in different ways.

The book is also suitable for anyone wanting to gain an overall understanding of the conceptual issues in psychology, and in particular for undergraduates taking a CHIPS course on a psychology degree. There is some advantage in having some experience of psychology before reading this book, for example having studied psychology at an advanced level in school or equivalent. The discipline of psychology is like a jigsaw puzzle made out of many pieces, and it is good to have at least some understanding of the pieces in order to see the picture as a whole. Some of the conceptual ideas are more challenging than others, but there is enough in each chapter to be of interest to all students.

This book does not provide the kind of historical detail that is more suited for a specialist course on the history of psychology. I have selected some personal historical detail, but only where it is useful or interesting for students. I refer to events in William James' life to show that even famous psychologists can have mental health problems. I refer to Watson's sacking from his university for the less good reason that students will find the gossip interesting. I mention that Wundt was a nice guy, because I like nice guys. I refer to racism in psychology because it tends to be airbrushed out, but it is relevant to the heredity-environment controversy. I refer to personal details if it is relevant to a person's theory or research or because it is pertinent in some other way. There is some historical detail along with the conceptual issues, but the historical details are not as thorough as will be found in proper histories of psychology, written by proper historians. I don't mention where Wundt was born, nor reports of his performance at school – interesting as those may be.

Any book reflects the personal interests of the author. My PhD was theoretical, and as a young lecturer I was instrumental in setting up the International Society for Theoretical psychology. However, I have spent most of my working life as a health psychologist trying to solve practical problems by using new theories or new applications of old theories. I developed an interest in the history of psychology through teaching the subject. Readers may detect a sympathy with applied psychology, a fascination with theory, and an interest in the quirkier aspects of history.

This book is written for a specific purpose: to show how conceptual issues that are relevant today have developed over the history of academic psychology. My hope is that this book will help other lecturers provide interesting and inspiring lectures, and for students to enjoy a subject that can inform their understanding of the subject they have chosen to study: the discipline of psychology.

1

What is science and what do scientists do?

This chapter covers two topics: the philosophy of science and the psychology of science.

How do you know if something is true? That question is particularly pertinent in a world where news is sometimes described as 'fake news.' To know whether something is true it is necessary to have criterion, a criterion that can distinguish truth from falsity. But how can you tell whether the criterion is true? The answer is that you cannot tell, because if there is a criterion for the criterion, then you don't know whether *that* criterion is true. Knowing whether a criterion is true or not is called the *problem of the criterion*. Although philosophers have discussed the problem of the criterion for at least two thousand years, in this book two criteria for knowledge will be assumed to be true. These are the logical criterion and the empirical criterion.

The science of psychology, like any other science, is based on the empirical criterion. However, the empirical criterion has a logical basis, so this chapter starts with a brief discussion of logic.

Logic

Imagine you have a pack of cards face down in front of you. You take the first card from the pack, and you find that it is the ace of hearts. Let me explain, in case there is any doubt, that this is an ordinary pack of cards, and there is only one ace of hearts in the whole pack. Now, consider the two following statements

The next card you draw will be the ace of hearts.
The next card you draw will not be the ace of hearts.

You, the student, will know straight away that the first sentence is false and the second sentence true, and you know this without having to look. You know this without empirical evidence. The reason is that you are applying a logical rule. The logical rule is this: Something cannot be in two places at the same time.

Logic is based on the application of rules, the rules of logic. There are many different logical rules and few will be discussed here. However, students will already have come across logical rules in statistics. Null hypothesis testing is based on the assumption that a hypothesis is either true or false – but not both true *and* false at the same time. Statistical tests give the probability that a hypothesis is not true (e.g., two groups are not equal); statistical tests apply the rule that a hypothesis can be either true *or* false, but not true *and* false. The process of science is a logical one; it is based on following certain accepted rules of practice.

What is the logic of science?

What is the logic of scientific enquiry? Philosophers and historians of science observe what scientists do and provide an answer, but that answer has changed over time. In the 19th century the view was that science was based on the logic of induction. In the 20th century the view was that science is based on the logic of deduction. Both types of logic will be examined separately before a psychological analysis will show how both types are used in science.

Induction and inductive laws

The logic of induction is based on the assumption that general laws can be 'induced' from facts, or, to use the more technical term, singular occurrences. Here is an example of how it works. Suppose you are travelling round the country and you see a white swan. The observation of the white swan is a singular occurrence. You go a little further and see another white swan. You keep on travelling seeing one white swan after another until you are ready to induce a general law:

All swans are white.

The rule of induction can be summed up as this:

If something has been observed to occur regularly in the past, the same will occur in the future.

Inductive rules are therefore useful for predicting and controlling the world in which we live. Inductive rules make practical sense.

In the example of the swans, induction has produced the statement 'all swans are white,' but is this statement true? In any group of psychology students, there will be some who know that not all swans are white – swans in (or originating from) Australia are black. So, after observing some black swans, it is possible to conclude that the original law – all swans are white – is false; it is now possible to write a new statement:

All swans are either black or white.

Again, it is possible to ask, is it possible to prove this statement true, in the sense that is known to be 100% true? The answer is no. It can never be proved with 100% certainty that all swans are either black or white as there may be some hiding away somewhere in the undergrowth that are not black or white. You may be interested to learn that the statement 'all swans are black or white' is in fact false. The reason is that in a far-away galaxy, on the planet Zog, there

Naughty green swan hiding from scientists on planet Zog.

are a group of swans that are pink with blue spots. You don't believe me? You cannot be sure that there are no pink and blue swans any more than I can be sure that there are.

OK, so now it is possible to generate another rule:

Some swans are white.

This rule can be proved true, but it cannot be proved false. The same applies to the following statement:

Some swans are green.

It is always possible that there are some green swans hiding away somewhere – not necessarily on the planet Zog, so this statement can never be shown to be false.

From a psychological perspective, the statement that 'some swans are white' is a lot less interesting than the statement 'all swans are white.' Imagine being told this:

After careful consideration and observation, I have come to the conclusion that it sometimes rains in England.

This conclusion would be true, but it is also obvious and therefore uninteresting. Thus, the type of inductive generalisation is important. One criticism of the assumption that science is based on induction is that scientists do not collect facts randomly. They collect the facts on the basis of 'ideas' about what is interesting. The collected facts should be important or interesting in some way. Some swans are white is a lot less informative than all swans are white – even though the latter is false.

Prediction and explanation

Inductive rules *describe* what happens in the world in which we live. They do not *explain* what happens. They describe the 'what' but not the 'why.' Because these rules describe regularities in things that happen, they can be used to predict the future. However, the prediction is limited to the rule of what has happened before. Explanations will be described in the next section and permit prediction of things that have not happened before. The early history of psychology was largely one of induction – of finding regularities but not providing explanations. The later history is one where greater emphasis is placed on explanation.

The logic of deduction and hypothesis testing

Karl Popper (and others) (Popper, 1935/1992, 1963) argued the logic of science is not based on induction. Even when scientists collect facts, they don't do so randomly. Data collection is always based on a hypothesis or *conjecture*. Instead of science being based on induction, Popper suggested that the logic of science was based on deduction.

In science, deduction is the process of making a prediction on the basis of a theory. The theory *explains* the regularities in things that happen. Again, it is best illustrated with an example. Instead of starting with an observation, let us start with a theory, the theory of gravity. It is possible to deduce from the theory of gravity that if I let go of my keys, they will fall to earth. This prediction is of a singular occurrence or fact. The next step is used to test whether the singular occurrence, predicted by the theory, actually occurs. I hold out my hand holding my keys. I let the keys go. They fall to earth showing that the prediction of the theory is true.

Deduction is a logical rule that can be summed up as this:

On the basis of these theoretical assumptions the following events will happen.

Has the simple fact of my dropping the keys proved the theory of gravity? The answer is no. Even if I keep dropping my keys and collect a sizeable pool of data supporting the theory, the theory of gravity can never be proved to be true, because there is an alternative explanation. The reason that keys keep falling to earth is nothing to do with this strange thing called gravity. There is a much simpler explanation. It is caused by a gravity monster who sits at the centre of the earth and waves its tail. Whenever the gravity monster waves its tail, it attracts objects to its tail. That is the real reason why things fall to earth. And the gravity monster is always waving its tail. Or is it?

The reality is that when data confirm a theory – i.e., when singular occurrences are consistent with the prediction of a theory – it is always possible that the same data can be explained by another theory. It is always possible that some data will be found in the future that cannot be explained by the theory. Therefore, theories can be confirmed but never proved to be true. Data do not *prove* theories. Scientists try to rule out competing hypotheses by setting up experiments where the competing hypotheses make different predictions. In principle, it takes only one observation that cannot be explained by the theory to show that a theory is false. Of course, as more and more data of different kinds are found to support the theory, the more the theory is corroborated by those data. So, some theories can be well confirmed, but they can never be proved to be true.

Popper suggested that science proceeds through a series of 'conjectures and refutations' – which is the title of one his books (Popper, 1963). Scientists have a hypothesis or conjecture. They test the hypothesis and for a while the data confirm (but never prove) the theory. Eventually data are found that falsify the theory and so it is necessary to develop a new conjecture or hypothesis. Science proceeds by a series of conjectures and refutations; each time the conjecture becomes more 'true' than the conjecture before. In practice, scientific advance is not quite the elegant process suggested by Popper. Disconfirming evidence usually leads to changes rather than the rejection of a theory, or simply rejection of the disconfirming evidence.

Theories that are eventually found false

Newton developed a mathematical theory to explain the relationship between force, mass and velocity. Newton's theory explains many things – from how cars move in collisions to the orbits of planets. Everyone was so convinced by this theory, and the way they predicted things accurately, that they became known as 'Newton's laws of motion.' However, when mass becomes very large or when it is very small, Newton's laws no longer apply. Einstein predicted that space was curved by mass, a theory first tested by observing the position of the sun during an eclipse. Other theories of classical physics have been shown to be false by quantum mechanics. Of course these classical physics theories are true in the sense that they apply under most conditions, but the fact that there are exceptions shows that they cannot be treated as the universal laws they once were.

The key difference between the earlier inductive view of science and the deductive/falsification model proposed by Popper is that the latter involves theories, and theories provide explanations as well as predictions. The theory provides an explanation of why something happens. The explanations have one key advantage over predictions based on inductive generalisations. They allow novel predictions. The ability of theories to make novel predictions is not something that is automatic. Humans are needed to make novel predictions. Science is a creative activity involving the insight of people.

Metaphysics versus science

Popper used his idea of conjectures and refutations to provide a logical criterion for science. An alternative is to use a social criterion, such as scientists are those perceived by ordinary people as scientists. Popper's criterion was based on the application of rule – i.e., on a logical rule. Popper's criterion of science is this:

Scientific statements are those that can be shown to be false through observation.

> *Statements that cannot be shown to be false through observation are not scientific statements but metaphysical statements.*

This criterion, known as the criterion of falsifiability, distinguishes what Popper called science from metaphysics. Metaphysics, according to Popper, consists of statements that cannot be shown to be false through observation, and therefore are outside the realm of science.

There are a number of different types of statement that cannot be shown to be false by observation, and one of these has been presented already. The statement 'some swans are green' cannot be shown to be false through observation, whereas the statement 'all swans are white' can be shown to be false. The latter sentence is therefore a scientific statement – but false – whereas the former is not even scientific according to Popper's criterion. There are many types of statement that are non-falsifiable. One particular type relates to religious beliefs.

Consider the following statement:

God exists.

What kind of evidence is there that God does not exist? It is possible to cite miracles and other kinds of evidence suggesting that God exists, but there is no type of evidence that could prove – i.e., show with 100% certainty – that God does not exist. So, the statement that 'God exists' is therefore unfalsifiable, and the statement is metaphysical rather than scientific. It is also, note, impossible to falsify the statement that 'somewhere there are swans with pink spots on a green background.' Statements that, on logical grounds, cannot be shown to be false are not scientific.

Science and religions

Religious beliefs are metaphysical beliefs and therefore outside the realm of science. Some scientists are religious, and believe in God. Some scientists are not religious and do not believe in God. Some scientists believe that religion is a dangerous illusion. Some scientists (and some psychologists) study how other people practise and believe in religion. Discussion of these different views is beyond the remit of this book but forms an interesting point of discussion as students themselves will have different views.

Falsifiability and the strength of prediction

Popper makes one additional point in relation to his criterion of falsifiability. The degree of falsifiability determines the *strength* of a theory. Again an example will illustrate how this works. Imagine that you are in England (where it rains a lot) and you want to do your washing and hang it on the line to dry. Consider the following two statements:

> *It will be dry on one day and only one day next week.*
> *It will be dry on Wednesday and only on Wednesday next week.*

Both statements are falsifiable. If it doesn't rain or if it rains on more than one day, then both statements are false. Both are scientific rather than metaphysical. Both show that washing is possible on one day next week. But the second sentence is a lot more useful in helping you decide when to do your washing. The second sentence is also *more* falsifiable, in the sense that it is more likely to be wrong if weather is random. The second sentence gives a more powerful prediction.

Popper distinguishes between strong theories that are highly falsifiable and weak theories that are falsifiable in principle, but difficult to show wrong. Note that the degree of falsifiability has nothing to do with whether the theory is actually false or not, which is something that is determined through observation. The strength of a theory is something that can be evaluated without observation. The degree of falsifiability or strength of the theory is an 'internal' property of a theory and not an 'external' property, which is a theory strength that can be determined independently of the observation that tests. Strong theories are easily shown to be false, but if they are not shown false then they provide more useful information than weak theories that are less likely to be shown false.

Some theories are falsifiable but so weak – so difficult to show false – that they are not very useful. The strength and therefore usefulness of psychological theories is something that will be discussed later in this book. One of the criticisms against Freud's theory is that it is almost completely unfalsifiable. Others have argued that his theory is in fact unfalsifiable, and therefore metaphysical. Both arguments cannot be true, but they certainly need consideration in relation to both psychoanalytic and other theories in psychology.

Prediction and explanation

Theories explain why things happen. They do this by introducing 'explanatory concepts' that then explain the regularities that have been detected through inductive inference. Explanatory concepts are also known as theoretical terms. In physics, examples of theoretical terms include molecules and electrons. In psychology, examples of theoretical terms include memory and cognitions. The theoretical terms explain why things happen in the way they do. However, explanatory terms can also be used to predict things that have not been observed before. So, theories enable scientists to predict – and therefore control – the world they know. Inductive rules also enable scientists to predict what happens next so long as it has happened in the past. Theories enable prediction of things that have not happened in the past.

One way in which theories differ is whether they make quantitative predictions. Compare the following two statements

It will rain tomorrow in my village.
Two inches of rain will fall tomorrow in my village.

The second statement makes a stronger prediction and it makes a quantitative prediction. If only one inch falls or three inches fall, then the prediction is false. Some sciences make quantitative predictions, some make (on the whole) qualitative predictions. Psychology and medicine fall into the latter category. Physics and chemistry in the former. Theories of physics are typically represented by an equation. For example, Boyle's law predicts *how much* a gas will expand when heated. Hooke's law predicts *how much* a spring expands with different weights. In medicine, theories typically predict change but not the amount of change. So, for example, antibiotics reduce infection, but there is no prediction about the rate of reduction of infection. In psychology, research shows that childhood trauma leads to behavioural problems, but the behavioural problems are not quantified.

Quantitative predictions in psychology

Although a minority, they do exist: in psychophysics (see Chapter 2, Weber's fraction and Fechner's law), in behaviourism (see Chapter 4, Hull's theory), and in mathematical psychology (see Chapter 4, Luce's choice axiom).

Theories that make qualitative predictions – such as those in psychology and medicine – use statistics to test whether the qualitative prediction occurs or not. As an example, imagine a qualitative prediction that exam performance is enhanced by a mind-altering drug. A study is conducted where students are

---

Effect size

The degree of difference is indicated by the statistic called *effect size*. A small effect size between two groups is more likely to be found to be statistically significant if the sample size is large than if it is small. Hence, studies that employ very large samples will reveal effects that are statistically significant, but may have little practical significance. Guidelines for psychological journals increasingly require authors to quote effect size along with statistical significance. This information is useful as it provides quantitative information.

randomly assigned to receive the drug or a placebo and their performance compared, statistically, to see if the probability of the drug and placebo having the same effect is sufficiently low (e.g., $p < 0.05\%$) for the alternative hypothesis to be accepted. Statistics are used to test whether a difference occurs or not, not to test the degree of difference.

Induction and deduction together: the psychology of scientific discovery

To sum up so far: Inductive rules are created from data; the logic of deduction is used for testing theories. One view puts the primary unit of science as data, the other the primary unit of science as theory. Both views can be supported by examples from the history of science. As a general rule, inductive inference is more common in less developed or historically older sciences. Explanatory theories – from which deductions can be made – are a feature of more advanced or more recent sciences (Royce & Powell, 1983).

Popper was a philosopher rather than a psychologist. He never provided an answer to the question, where do the conjectures or hypotheses come from? Hypotheses must come from the minds of scientists. So how are hypotheses formed?

Where do theories come from?

The following is a quote from Popper's *The Logic of Scientific Discovery* published in 1935 (Popper, 1935/1992):

> The question how it happens that a new idea occurs to a man – whether it is a musical theme, a dramatic conflict, or a scientific theory – may be of great interest to empirical psychology; but it is irrelevant to the logical analysis of scientific knowledge.
>
> (p. 7)

The story of the discovery of penicillin provides one possible insight into the creative process of hypothesis formation and the relationship between theory and data.

Alexander Fleming, a Scottish researcher, was growing bacteria on a petri dish. He came back from a two week holiday in 1928 to find that one of his dishes had been contaminated with what looked like mould, and no bacteria were growing where the mould had contaminated the petri dish. One possible reaction would be to say "bother, my petri dish has been contaminated."

Instead, Fleming made a connection with something outside his experiment. He hypothesised that the mould had killed the bacteria and the mould could therefore have therapeutic properties. This hypothesis was tested initially by Fleming and then by others. The stage of data collection took time. It wasn't until 1942 that the first patient was successfully treated with penicillin.

In this example, there is a chance discovery that creates an observation. Fleming then formed a mental link between that observation with other knowledge that he had but was irrelevant to the initial experiment. The creative process is one of forming links between ideas, of showing how existing ideas can be combined in novel ways to form entirely new ideas. Creativity is a synthesis of the many, and in science the many can come from many different sources. These include chance discoveries, data that are recently available, past data, past theories, past lived experience. The discovery of new theories is not a mechanical process that can be easily taught. New theories come from simply thinking about things. Testing of theories is also a creative process, because testable predictions require a person to deduce a prediction. Scientific development is not a purely logical process!

Data and theory are inextricably linked in the minds of scientists to the extent that inductive and deductive inference both feature in scientific discovery. An understanding of data helps determine what questions are asked, but the questions that are asked also depends on the scientist's prior knowledge and understanding of what is important and what is not. The modern view is that theories rather than data are the basic unit of science, but the development of those theories, and not only the testing of theories, is always linked to observation, observation that may occur over many years of a scientist's lifetime.

Where do rules of logic come from? For curious students only

Science is based on the logical rules in induction and deduction. Are logical rules independent of observation? Consider the example used at the beginning of this chapter where it was possible to tell that the next card in a deck of cards is not an ace of hearts if it has already been drawn.

In everyday life we observe that something cannot be in two different states at the same time. This rule can be applied to state of being alive versus being dead. An animal is either dead or alive, but not both. The rule is based on observation. However, in the world of the very small, the world of quantum mechanics, something very odd happens. The principle of quantum superposition makes it possible for something to be in two different states at the same time. The example often used to illustrate this principle is Schrödinger's cat. A cat is placed in a sealed box where at some random point in time a cyanide capsule will be released and the cat will die. Common sense tells us that *before* the box is opened, the cat must be either dead or alive. The principle of superposition says that before the box is opened the cat is both dead *and* alive. Neils Bohr, one of the fathers of quantum mechanics, said "If you are not shocked by quantum mechanics, you don't understand it." If we experienced the world like it is in the quantum world, perhaps our logical rules would be different! So logical rules are based on observations about the universe in which we live. Science is based on observation but the rules of science come, ultimately, from observation as well.

Metatheory, research programmes, and paradigms

The story so far goes like this. Scientists test their theories with data. The theories are constructed on the basis of a mix of prior theories and data, including chance observations, all informed by a lifetime of observation not necessarily related to science; it is observation and thought that enable scientists to make often intuitive guesses or 'conjectures' about how the world works.

The story continues like this. Although theories are tested by data, all theories are based on 'metatheoretical assumptions' that are never tested. These assumptions are not tested because they are (or assumed to be) so obvious that everyone thinks they must be true. Two historians of science have written about these assumptions and their work will be described below. They are Imre Lakatos (Lakatos, 1970, 1978) and Thomas Kuhn (Kuhn, 1962).

Lakatos' concept of research programmes

Science builds on previous knowledge. Read any psychology journal article and you will find a list of papers at the end. The article you are reading builds on previous research and the discussion section, in particular, makes the link with previous research explicit. In fact, if authors fail to reference any earlier research, then they are unlikely to get their papers accepted. Furthermore, the article you have selected to read is likely to be cited by other articles that are published subsequently, and those subsequent articles will also cite articles cited in the article you have selected. Sciences builds on the past.

Lakatos suggests that, within a discipline, there are several strands of research which he calls 'research programmes.' The research programme is based on assumptions. Lakatos calls these assumptions 'a positive heuristic.' The word *heuristic* means a useful tool for discovery. What the assumptions or positive heuristics do is to define what research questions should be asked within the particular research programme and how to go about researching those questions. The positive heuristic defines the underlying assumptions of the strand of research that makes up a research programme.

For example, in the research programme of 'early childhood trauma and later poor health,' the research programme defines that the area of interest as that linking early trauma of varying kinds with later health of varying kinds. The research programme also defines the different methodologies that investigate the underlying hypothesis that early child trauma has negative consequences.

Lakatos distinguishes two types of research programme, those with a progressive problem shift, where theory precedes data, and those with a degenerating problem shift, where data precedes theory. The relationship between these two types of problem shift, and inductive versus deductive approaches to science could not be clearer. In the progressive problem shift programme, research is based on hypotheses that are tested. Research follows the conjecture and refutation approach suggested by Popper, and the creative part of theory construction comes before data collection. In the degenerating problem shift, research is based on careful data collection that then generates theory – the approach suggested by the earlier inductive approach to science. The progressive problem shift relies on the creativity of scientists, the degenerating problem shift on their methodological rigour.

Lakatos was a historian of science. He provided evidence that the progressive problem shift tends to produce better results than the degenerating problem shift (and hence his choice of terminology). In the progressive problem shift, the discovery of new data doesn't lead to outright rejection of the theory but rather modification that is then tested with more data. The theory progresses with the data. The degenerating problem shift gets stuck in problems of methodology because the focus is on examining data without developing a new theory.

Stages of a scientific discipline

Joseph Royce (Royce & Powell, 1983, p. 19) suggested that sciences go through four stages of development "(a) prescientific philosophic speculation, (b) empirical exploration, (c) sophistication of methods of controlled observation and quantification, and (d) theoretical formalization and unification." Royce felt that psychology was between (b) and (c), but psychology may have moved on since 1983.

The distinction between progressive and degenerating problem shifts is based on whether research is theory-led or data-led. This distinction is not a binary one but a continuum. In evaluating research in psychology and other disciplines, the question to be asked is to what extent the research is theory-led versus data-led?

Are there examples of progressive and degenerating problem shifts in psychology? In Chapter 4, I shall suggest that one of the reasons for the decline of behaviourism was that it became a degenerating problem shift. Behaviourism was largely data-led. Lack of theoretical development and decline characterises other types of early psychology, such as the early German psychology of Wilhelm Wundt (see Chapter 2). By contrast, theory plays a much greater role in cognitive psychology, in neuroscience, and the more recent connectionist psychology (see Chapter 10).

Theoretical physics is a much respected part of physics where speculative theory plays a major part in empirical research. The Large Hadron Collider was built at a cost of more than six billion pounds to test theories developed by theoretical physicists. Theoretical psychologists lack that status in psychology. The Center for the Advanced Study of Theoretical Psychology was founded by Joseph Royce (1921–1989) in 1966 at the University of Alberta, Canada, and closed in 1990, shortly after his death. Royce's vision was to create the psychological equivalent of theoretical physics. The International Society for Theoretical Psychology, founded in 1985, has conferences every two years, but much of the focus is on critiquing mainstream psychology rather than presenting new theories. Royce's vision of a highly respected and influential theoretical psychology has not been achieved – but psychology is still a young science compared to physics. Who knows what changes will be brought about by the students of today?

Kuhn's concept of scientific revolutions

Kuhn (1962) uses the term *paradigm* to describe the meta-theoretical assumptions that underpin theories. According to Kuhn, sciences go through stages. When a science first develops there are often a number of competing meta-theoretical assumptions. Kuhn calls this the pre-paradigmatic stage, because no paradigm has become universally accepted. Then one or other of these competing sets of assumptions becomes dominant, and the science has its first paradigm. The paradigm defines the kind of theories that can explain the phenomena under consideration, as well as defining the kind of phenomena that require investigation.

Once the paradigm is settled, there is long period of *normal science* when scientists investigate the theories within the paradigm. At some point in time, the original assumptions are challenged in one way or another to the extent that they are replaced by another set of meta-theoretical assumptions – i.e., new types of theory and things to be investigated. This shift from one set of assumptions or paradigms to another set of assumptions or paradigms is called a paradigm shift. Researchers then work on the new paradigm until that paradigm is replaced by yet another. Science therefore proceeds by a series of paradigms and paradigm shifts.

When scientists are working within a paradigm, they are working within what Kuhn calls *normal science*. Normal science consists of a series of 'mopping up' studies to find out the answers to things that require an answer as defined by the particular paradigm. When a paradigm changes, then this is called a *scientific revolution.* So science proceeds by a series of periods of normal science followed by a short scientific revolution and then a new period of normal science.

Why do new paradigms occur? There are several possible reasons, but a common one is that there is a body of data that simply cannot be explained by any of the theories using the original paradigm. A good example of this is the paradigm shift that led to the development of quantum mechanics. Light sometimes behaves as though it were a wave. It sometimes behaves as though it were a particle. None of the explanations of classical physics could explain why light could behave in different ways at different times.

Kuhn's paradigms and Lakatos' research programmes are similar. Both refer to metatheoretical assumptions. The difference is that the paradigm involves a more fundamental sort of assumption than the programme, but this difference is best thought of as a continuum, rather than a dichotomy. The term *paradigm* is often used for units of research activity that Lakatos would describe as a research programme. The term *paradigm* will be used here in this more general sense. Lakatos' distinction of theory-led versus data-led research applies to both.

The psychology of scientific revolutions

One view is that science proceeds through the falsification and therefore improvement of theories. One might imagine that scientists are therefore happy for their theory to be proved false. Nothing could be further from the truth. When a scientist develops a theory and then tests it, they will be hoping that the results come back confirming the theory. Scientists *like* their theories. They like to find evidence to *support* theory, not find evidence that shows that they are wrong. Falsification of theories in psychology is surprisingly rare.

Falsification in psychology

Students reading this book might like to ask themselves what psychological theories have been shown to be false. The issue of falsification is related to the crisis of replication described later in this chapter.

However, when it comes to research paradigms, scientists are even more protective of what they have assumed in the past to be true. No one wants to find that they have invested years of their careers carrying out research – or practice – based on assumptions that are incorrect. So when paradigm shifts are proposed, there can be strong resistance from scientists working in the older paradigm. New paradigms are met with two kinds of response: enthusiasm from those who believe that the new paradigm provides a novel solution, and hostility from those who don't. If the latter camp is stronger, the new paradigm takes longer to become established.

The development of the paradigm of modern medicine is a good example of how people can respond to a change in paradigm. Since the time of the Greeks till the middle of the 17th century, medicine was based on assumptions that originated with Hippocrates. Illness was believed to be caused by an imbalance in four 'humours' that flowed round the body. The humours (in case you were wondering) were black bile, yellow bile, blood, and phlegm. An alternative paradigm became available during the middle ages, as clockwork and mechanical systems became more common. The body is a mechanical system and illness is caused by faults in that mechanical system. The mechanical paradigm was the new paradigm, and early evidence in favour of this new paradigm was published by William Harvey in 1628 who described how the heart was a pump that pumped blood round the body. Harvey wrote at the time that he expected his discovery to be met with scepticism and downright hostility and that is exactly what happened. The following (see text box) was written in 1647, shortly before Harvey's discovery became accepted.

Rejection of a new paradigm

The following is a translation of the original Latin written by Emilio Parisano in 1647. Parisono was an eminent physician of Venice.

> We have no problem to admit that, if the horse swallows water, we can perceive a movement and we can hear a sound. But that a pulse should arise in the breast that can be heard, when the blood is transported from the veins to the arteries, this we certainly can't perceive and we do not believe that this will ever happen, except Harvey lends us his hearing aid. But above all, we do not admit such a transport of the blood. . . . If blood is transported from the veins of the lung . . . into the branches of the arteries, how could a pulse be felt in the breast, how a sound? I am completely innocent of such subtle speculations. Above all, Harvey has it that a pulse should arise from the movement of the blood from the heart into the aorta – no matter from which ventricle. He also claims that this movement produces a pulse, and, moreover, a sound: that sound, however, we deaf people cannot hear, and there is no one in Venice who can. If he can in London, we wish him all the best. But we are writing in Venice.

There are two points to note about Parisano's criticism of what is now universally accepted as true – the heart does actually pump blood. The first is that the critics of the new paradigm deny that a pulse can be heard there. This point illustrates a general principle known in the philosophy of science as theory-ladenness of observables (Hanson, 1958). The principle of the theory-ladenness of observables means that observation is always coloured by expectations about what is being observed. People perceive only what they believe to be possible. Observation is not independent of theory. The principle of ladenness of observable is represented in psychological theory (see Chapter 10) as part of the gestalt movement – perception is based on hypotheses. The idea that science is based *only* on induction does not stack up. Not only are data selected for observation on the basis of theory, but what is seen is also informed by theory. The physicians of Venice could not hear a pulse because they 'knew' that no pulse existed!

The second point to note in this criticism is in the final sentence "but we are writing in Venice." In the 17th century, Venice was a magnificent city, looking very much as it looks today, and was a centre of learning and art. London was a hotchpotch of timber framed buildings, many of which burned down in the great fire of 1666. Parisano is, in effect, telling Harvey: "You come from an inferior place and should listen to us clever people from a superior place."

It is not unusual for paradigm shifts to be made from people working in less prestigious institutions or who, at the time of writing, are less well known, simply because they are less immersed in the old paradigm. Freud was responsible for a paradigm shift where mental illness was treated by a 'talking therapy' and his work and legacy will be discussed in Chapter 5. Albert Einstein published his theory of special relativity (and other ground-breaking papers) while employed at a patent office and in the same year that he was awarded his PhD in Zurich.

What paradigm does psychology have?

There are three possible views. One is that psychology as a discipline is pre-paradigmatic. Another is that it does have a paradigm. And a third is that it is a special case, and different from other sciences in having several 'complementary' (note, not spelt 'complimentary') forms of paradigm.

It cannot have escaped the notice of any attentive student of psychology that their lecturers have different views about psychology, and that lecturers do not always agree about the type of explanation psychologists should employ. Some lecturers believe that explanations should involve the words and the meaning of words that people speak. Explanations should be based on a description of discourse, and interpretation of what that discourse means. Another group, associated with cognitive psychology, believe that explanations should be based on the description of information processes. Yet another group believes that explanations should be based on the description of events in the brain. This multiplicity of types of explanation can be used to conclude that psychology has not formed an accepted paradigm, and is still pre-paradigmatic.

Disciplines shift from pre-paradigmatic to paradigmatic by one or other of the original paradigms becoming universally accepted. Although there is no universally accepted paradigm, some believe that there is a dominant paradigm, a paradigm that is so dominant that others will eventually fade away. That dominant paradigm is cognitive neuroscience. In cognitive neuroscience, information processing is explained in terms of the physiology of the brain. It is certainly the case that at the time of writing cognitive neuroscience is the paradigm of psychology with the highest status. Papers in cognitive neuroscience are often cited by other researchers and in public newspapers, and some psychology departments have prioritised appointments in cognitive neuroscience – even though the popularity of this topic varies somewhat between students.

A third view is that psychology is special. The nature of psychology means that it is impossible to explain all phenomena using a single type of explanation and so complementary explanations are needed. That is, psychology is a science that differs from others in that it requires multi-paradigmatic explanations as a mature science, not as an immature, pre-paradigmatic science (further detail about complementarity is found in Chapter 6).

Each of these three views has its adherents. At the end of this book, the student should be able to form a view about psychology: Whether it is pre-paradigmatic, paradigmatic, or necessarily multi-paradigmatic. And of course, it is always necessary to remember that the answer to this question attracts strongly held views – and strongly held criticism – so whatever conclusion you come to will be both wrong and right according to other people!

What do scientific psychologists do?

Karl Popper paints a noble picture of what scientists do. Scientists come up with conjectures or hypotheses. They then test these hypotheses rigorously, trying to falsify them. Eventually the hypothesis is shown to be false and a new hypothesis is proposed. Is this really what happens? The answer is, no.

Scientists, and that includes psychologists engaged in scientific enquiry, are human. They have the same psychological characteristics as other humans. One of these characteristics is confirmation bias. Confirmation bias means that people tend to accept information confirming their existing hypothesis and ignore or discount disconfirming information. This bias is compounded by another factor. Psychologists, like other scientists, have an emotional attachment to theories they are working on. Just as football enthusiasts will support 'their' team, so psychologists and other scientists will support 'their' theory. The result is that evidence contrary to a theory may have less impact in developing new theory than might otherwise be thought. If evidence is found contrary to a theory, then a possible response is to doubt the replicability of the data – which is not necessarily a bad thing to do, as will be shown later. Another response is to find a way of modifying the theory to explain what is considered an exception. Yet another response is to simply ignore the data.

Here are two examples that illustrate this point. Both examples come from theories that inform current practice:

> *Example 1*. The serotoninergic theory of depression is that depression is caused by low levels of serotonin in the brain and that drugs that increase serotonin levels (antidepressants) reduce depression. Irving Kirsch (Kirsch, 2010) and colleagues has shown that at least 80% of the effect of antidepressants in clinical practice is due to placebo. These results have been confirmed independently by other authors and, coupled with data showing that antidepressants do not always resolve depression, this finding provides evidence inconsistent with the serotoninergic theory of depression.

> *Example 2*. Cognitive behaviour therapy (CBT) is based on a theory developed originally by Aaron Beck that cognitions play an important role in the cause of depression, and that changing erroneous cognitions leads to improvement. Bruce Wampold (Wampold, 2013) and colleagues reviewed several types of data to show that although CBT therapy is effective, its effectiveness cannot be explained by cognitions having the causal role as originally suggested. The findings reported by Wampold and Wampold's analysis have been confirmed by independent authors.

In both cases there is evidence that throws doubt against accepted and dominant paradigms. The serotoninergic hypothesis is the basis for a multi-million-pound drugs industry and CBT provides the accepted rationale for the funding of talking therapies. This is not the place to provide evidence for or against the various positions – which are robustly supported by both sides. Students may wish to do this independently. The argument presented here is simply that the issue of evidence and falsification of scientific theories is by no means a simple logical process. Science involves humans. Humans are messy.

Mistakes, fraud, and scientific misconduct

A central argument of this section is that scientists are human and have the features of other humans. What is the motivation of scientists? To a naïve observer, the motivation of scientists might be to push back the boundaries of knowledge: a pure, noble, and selfless motivation to improve knowledge and the lot of mankind. I am sure there are scientists who are motivated in this way. However, other motivations can come into play. Scientists can be motivated to demonstrate that their theory or hypothesis is correct. Scientists can be motivated by personal glory, and the status and regard achieved by scientific discovery. Some are also motivated by money, though if one were motivated by money a different career would seem a sensible alternative.

Mistakes can be made – it is human to err. Fraud is different. Fraud involves an intentional flouting of the underlying principles of scientific enquiry, namely, that of honesty. One of the best-known cases of fraud in the history of psychology is that associated with the eminent British psychologist, Cyril Burt. Burt published data supporting the idea that there was a substantial heredity component to intelligence. In a study of 53 monozygotic twins reared apart, Burt reported a correlation of 0.77 between the intelligence scores of twins (Burt, 1966). These results were interpreted to support the view that intelligence was largely inherited. Shortly after Burt's death in 1971, Kamin (1974) and then others (e.g., Hearnshaw, 1979) published critiques, arguing that the data had been made up and that the research assistants Burt had cited as co-authors did not exist.

Others came to the defence of Burt, the 'missing' research assistants were found, and it was pointed out that data supporting similar correlations to those reported by Burt were replicated by independent researchers (Rushton, 2002). In 1980 the British Psychological Society condemned Burt as a fraud, but in 1992 revised this judgement, writing:

> Council considers that it is now inappropriate for the Society as such to seek to express a fresh opinion about whether or not the allegations directed at Burt are true. Moreover, in the light of greater experience, the British Psychological Society no longer has a corporate view on the truth of allegations concerning Burt.

To his defenders, Burt was a good scientist who did not fake his data. Others take a different view.

Burt is not the only famous psychologist subsequently accused of creating fraudulent data. Hans Eysenck was a famous psychologist, best known for his work on personality – he developed the Eysenck Personality Inventory. Eysenck argued that personality was a major cause of fatal diseases such as cancer and that the link between smoking and cancer was not because smoking caused cancer, but because both correlated with a cancer-prone personality. Eysenck collaborated with another researcher, Grossarth-Maticek, and together they published cohort data showing an extraordinarily high association between the cancer-prone personality and cancer, and published experimental data showing that psychological therapy, either delivered through a therapist or through bibliotherapy, had a substantial effect of reducing cancers in those with a cancer-prone personality. That this research was funded by the tobacco industry was an early indicator that it might be flawed and at worst fraudulent. Criticisms and analysis of this case have recently been made public (Marks, 2019; Pelosi, 2019). The story has further to go.

Burt and Eysenck were senior scientists. For junior scientists, personal ambition can be a motivator for fraudulent activity (Steen, 2011). There is increasing competitiveness in science between researchers competing for scarce jobs and scarce research grants. University appointment policies and tenure are often linked to publications. In a profession where time is often scarce, there can be a temptation to short circuit the arduous business of collecting data and to make it up (Aulakh, 2016). There is a societal component to fraud created by a competitive research environment: Fraud is not entirely explained by characteristics of some 'rogue' scientists. Although fraud is not common, it occurs with sufficient regularity for it to be something to be taken seriously.

How frequent is fraud in scientific practice today? The term used nowadays is *scientific misconduct* which is defined as (a) any aspect of falsification of data or any other aspects of the study and (b) plagiarism – copying without citation. Gross (2016) provides a useful review of the several studies that have been conducted into scientific misconduct, which includes many based on anonymous reporting by scientists. In this review, Gross reports one study of 99 universities where 44% of students and 50% of staff were aware of scientific misconduct. In a meta-analysis of 18 studies, 2% of scientists had admitted that they themselves had falsified data and 14% had observed others doing it. The frequency of scientific misconduct varies between disciplines: It is most common in cell biology and oncology, least common in politics and sociology, with psychology falling somewhere in between (Gross, 2016).

Exposing others' scientific misconduct carries risks. In one study of whistle blowers, 60% of whistle blowers found that their actions had negative consequences (Gross, 2016). When scientific misconduct is discovered, it has very negative effects on the careers of perpetrators as well as innocent collaborators (Hussinger & Pellens, 2019).

When journal editors become aware of scientific misconduct, they publish a retraction of the original article. However, retractions can also be published because the authors themselves note problems with the way they have reported the study, and the authors themselves initiate the retraction. In a study of 2,047 retractions published in biomedical articles, only 21.3% were due to error, whereas 67.4% were due to scientific misconduct (expected or proved), of which 43.4% were due to duplicate publication (where the author submits the same paper to two journals and both accept), and 9.8% due to plagiarism (copying from someone else's paper), the remaining 11.3% being unknown or miscellaneous causes (Fang, Steen & Casadavell, 2012).

Even if findings are *not* the result of scientific misconduct or error, it does not necessarily follow that they are true. If a probability of < 0.05 is used as the criterion for significance, then 1 in 20 studies that are really non-significant will appear to be significant. Journals are more likely to accept papers with significant results compared to non-significant results, particularly if they are novel results that are interesting in some way. The publication bias towards significant findings means that there is a bias towards Type 1 error.

Type 1 versus Type 2 error

Type 1 error means that something is assumed to be significant when it isn't. Type 2 error means that something was thought not significant when really it is.

The possibility of Type 1 error in publications has led to something known as 'the crisis of replication.' Many studies are conducted – many more than are published. There have been several instances where an initially interesting finding fails to replicate. The interesting finding is often published in a high status journal, because high status journals tend to accept only the most scientifically interesting papers. The crisis of replication occurs across all sciences but particularly those that use statistical testing. This problem – the result of a combination of genuine chance events and publication bias – has become recognised in recent years, and the issue of replication is accepted as an important part of the scientific process (Zwaan, Etz, Lucas, & Donnellan, 2018).

The existence of fraud and the replication crisis could lead to the conclusion that science is fundamentally a flawed process. On the contrary, the fact that these problems are aired in print shows that problems are being attended to, problems that naturally follow from research conducted by messy humans. In some areas of science where there are commercial interests, such as clinical trials of new drugs, the regulatory requirements of conduct and reporting make any kind of fraud very difficult, and the sponsors of such studies are keenly aware of the very negative consequences should there ever be evidence of wrongdoing. Science is not perfect, but just as theories become improved over time, the process of conducting science is also improving. Many journals now require scientists to make their original data available for scrutiny. Conflict of interest statements are routinely required in medical journals.

The rest of this book

One theme runs through the remaining chapters of this book. It is that different groups of psychologists have different assumptions about psychology. These assumptions have changed over time, but differences remain in modern psychology. There are differences about psychology's status as a science, what psychologists should be studying and the role and type of theory that is used to explain psychological phenomena. Understanding the very different underlying assumptions that have been featured in the history of psychology and remain today is a good way of understanding the discipline of psychology as a whole.

Essay questions

1 What is the logic of induction and deduction and how are they used in scientific enquiry?
2 What is a paradigm and what is a paradigm shift? Illustrate your answer with examples with particular reference to the attitudes of those involved.
3 Focussing on just one of these two individuals, did Burt or Eysenck commit scientific misconduct?

2

How did psychology become a science and what kind of science did it become?

When asked, most people today would say that psychology is a science, and, by implication, a science like any other natural science. Psychology certainly fulfils the logical criterion of science, that of falsifiability, described in the last chapter. However, in the distant past psychology was not viewed as a science like any other, and even in the recent past it was viewed with some suspicion. When I was considering which degree to study in 1967, I was advised to study a 'proper science' like physiology rather than psychology – advice I ignored. Going back 150 years, psychology was not considered a science at all. Why was this and how did these changes come about? Not all psychologists think that psychology should be a science like any other natural science, and these other approaches will be described in Chapter 9.

When psychology was definitely not a science

The French philosopher Descartes had a problem. In 17th-century France, the Roman Catholic Church asserted its authority over all knowledge, including knowledge that would now be considered the realm of science. Descartes wanted a diplomatic way of freeing science from the shackles of religion without upsetting the religious authorities. He came up with the following solution. There are two kinds of substance in the world. A mind substance – which the Church could have jurisdiction over, and a body substance – which was the remit of scientists. This solution helped establish science as being independent of religion, but it had several negative consequences. One, and only one, of these negative consequences was that it left the study of the mind as being outside that of real of science. Psychology translates from Greek as 'the study of the soul.' Psyche is the Ancient Greek goddess of the soul who married Eros, the god of love. The link between the soul, psychology, and religion is implicit in Descartes' mind-body philosophy, what is now called Cartesian dualism. Psyche is part of the irrational world of myth and religion.

Over time, the influence of the church decreased, but from the middle of the 19th century onwards there was a replacement: the religion of spiritualism. The essence of spiritualism is that people have a universal soul. Manifestations of souls of dead people in this world take the form of paranormal phenomena. The concept of a universal soul, like the concept of God, is unfalsifiable. Even after religion had lost its influence, psychology was seen as something separate from science and was associated with the paranormal. During the middle of the 19th century until after the First World War there was a widespread interest in contacting people who had died – people who were from 'the other world.' It was considered normal to try to contact relatives either through mediums or through other techniques at home such as the ouija board (pronounced weedy or weedjy board). Although some of the early psychologists believed in paranormal phenomena and thought they could be investigated, the association

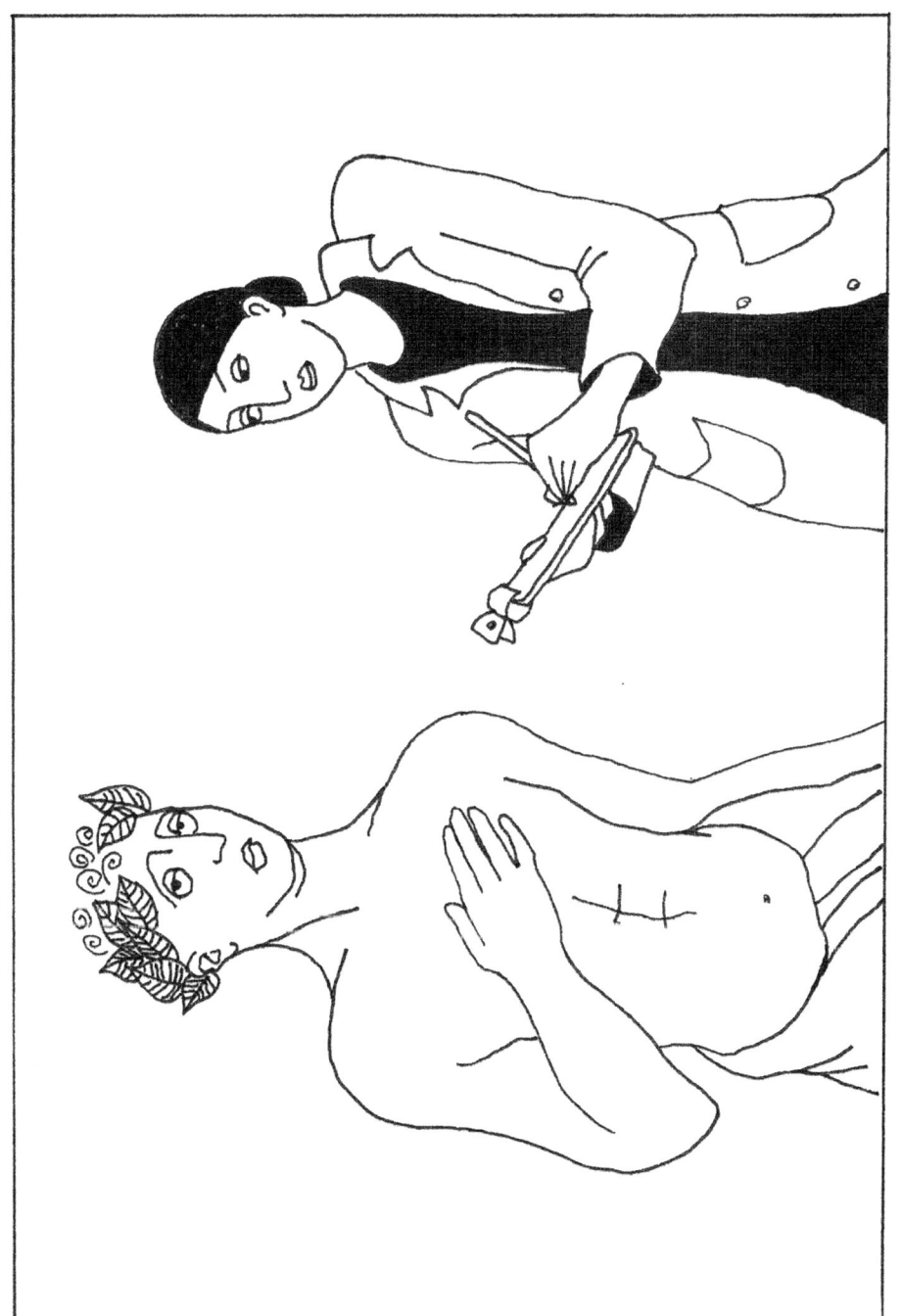

Psyche studying Eros.

with the paranormal was associated, at least in the mind of the general public, with non-science rather than science.

Contacting the dead

The ouija board is interesting in that it illustrates a psychological phenomenon. What happens is that the letters of the alphabet are arranged in a circle on a table and an upside down wine glass is placed in the middle. A group of people sit round the table, each placing one finger on the base of glass. Someone calls out "is there a spirit who wants to talk to someone here?" or some such statement. The glass then starts moving mysteriously from letter to letter, spelling out words and messages for the group of people. Everyone honestly believes that they are not pushing the glass. In fact, people do push the glass. They are simply unaware of what they are doing, and they spell out what they would like the spirit to say to them. Other psychical phenomena of the time can also be explained by psychological mechanisms known today.

The society for psychical research was formed in Cambridge, England, in 1882 to investigate claims of the paranormal. The British Psychological Society was formed in London in 1901.

Psychical versus psychological

There is a cartoon from the magazine *Punch* in the early 1900s entitled "Dinner Dance of the British Psychological Society." The cartoon shows men and women dancing with invisible partners. The confusion between psychical and psychological persisted for many years.

Very early beginnings

One of the points made in the previous chapter is that science is cumulative. Research builds on previous research. Some textbooks provide a definite time and place for the start of scientific psychology – such as the founding of the first psychological laboratory by Wilhelm Wundt in 1879 in Leipzig – but it is never quite that simple in practice. Wundt was influenced by others including but not limited to earlier researchers at Leipzig.

The first psychology laboratory, given the name 'new psychology' by Wundt to distinguish it from the old, came about from an integration of three strands of thinking – it is too much to call them research programmes. These are (a) developments from sensory physiology that provided a scientific approach to the study of sensation, (b) contributions from the philosophy of mind that showed that higher mental processes could be studied, and (c) medical findings that higher or cognitive processes were linked in some way to the brain.

Sensory physiology, sensory psychophysiology, and psychophysics

Ernst Weber (1795–1878) studied anatomy at university and completed his thesis on the anatomy and physiology of sensory nerves at the university of Leipzig. As their name suggests, the sensory nerves are associated with psychological sensations, such as touch. It was therefore a small leap for Weber to study how stimulation of a sensory nerve gave rise to sensations and to study sensations in their own right. During the 19th century, scientific advance was associated with advances in measurement. Measurement was key. Hence, when Weber studied sensations, his first reaction was to measure them. He called his new field of research sensory psychophysiology.

Weber (Weber, 1834) developed a method for assessing touch sensitivity in terms of the ability to discriminate the two-point threshold – i.e., to be able to detect whether the skin is being touched by one or two points.

Weber's method for assessing touch sensitivity

Weber's two-point threshold demonstration is easy to do yourself with the help of a friend. Weber used a draughtsman's compass that had two pointed ends, but it can be done just as well with a couple of pencils. Ask your friend to look away and touch them on the skin with the pencil ends about two centimetres apart, and ask your friend what it feels like. Your friend will notice being touched by two pencils. Now place the ends about 0.02 of a centimetre away: Your friend will now feel just one pencil. Increase and decrease the distance until you arrive at the two-point threshold – the point at which your friend just notices that there are two pencils rather than one. You can repeat this exercise on different parts of the body, and you will find that sensitivity varies over the body. For example, the back is much less sensitive than the hand.

Weber systematically measured the sensitivity of the skin across the whole of the body, using an adjustable compass, which was given the rather dignified name of an aesthesiometer (Weber, 1834/1978). He made a number of interesting observations, for example, that we are less sensitive if the two compass points are placed in the direction of the limb rather than across it. Having started with the sensation of touch, Weber then went on to study the two-point threshold in other sensory modalities, including weights, lengths of lines, and pitches.

In studying the sensory modality of weight Weber asked a person to compare the weight of two objects (he got people to do this sequentially using the same hand) and tell him if they seemed the same or one was heavier than the other. The just noticeable difference (JND) was the smallest difference in weight between the two objects that led to a person saying they were different.

Weber found that, irrespective of the sensory modality tested, there was a relationship between a 'just noticeable difference' (or JND) between two stimuli and the magnitude of the stimuli. Imagine a kilo bag of sugar, and another bag that is 1.5 kilos. It is easy to tell the bags of sugar are different from their heaviness (note they *weigh* different amounts and the *sensation* is also different). Now imagine a 50 kilo sack of sugar, and another sack 50.5 kilos in weight. It is now impossible to tell the sacks apart – they appear equally heavy. Weber noticed that the ratio of the JND to the stimulus intensity was approximately constant, irrespective of the stimulus intensity. So, for example, if the JND is 0.2 kg when the stimulus intensity is 1 kg (0.2/1 = 0.2) then the JND for a stimulus intensity of 50 kg is likely to be 1 kg (1/50 = 0.2).

Weber studied the JNDs in other sensory modalities and found that the ratio of JND to stimulus intensity was always approximately constant, though the ratio differed between sensory modalities. Although the constants were different all sensory modalities could be described by an equation

JND/stimulus intensity = Constant

This equation was described by others as 'Weber's law.'

Weber's family

Weber came from an academic family. His younger brother was a famous professor of physics. Measurement was a family business!

Gustav Theodor Fechner (1801–1887) was a student at Leipzig where he learned about and was influenced by Weber. Fechner continued the work done by Weber, promoted it more widely, and developed it. Whereas Weber called this newly developing science 'sensory psychophysiology,' Fechner called it 'psychophysics,' which is the name that it is known by today (Fechner, 1860/1996).

Fechner developed new methods for assessing thresholds first developed by Weber. Weber had simply asked people to say whether two objects were the same or not. Fechner developed two other methods.

Method 1: The person is presented with pairs of objects, such as a pair of lines, and asked which one is longer. The person is told that they must say which line is longer – they cannot say they are the same. If the lines are noticeably longer, the person will always get it right. As the lines become more similar, the person will tend to make errors. Fechner defined a just noticeable difference (JND) using this method as the level of difference just greater than that which produced a random result.

Notice that the advantage of this method is that it avoids a problem, later noted in psychophysics, of people having different criteria for difference, which is a problem with Weber's method. If people are asked to state whether something is different or not, some people will be more prone to say yes only when the difference is very clear. Others will say yes, even if there is only a slight suggestion of difference. The criterion of difference is something that is not fixed. The result is that 'false alarms' and 'missed hits' vary systemically between people (this may be covered in more detail in your course under the heading of signal detection theory). Fechner's method simply relies on perception. His method has been given a variety of names over the years – Fechner called it the method of correct and incorrect instances.

Method 2: This method required the person to adjust a stimulus so that it appeared to be the same as another. When a person does this, there is always a small error, either greater or smaller. Fechner took the average of these two errors as a measure of JND. Again, this method has been given different names over the years, Fechner calling it the method of average error, others calling it the method of adjustment.

A second development by Fechner was to show that Weber's law followed a logarithmic function, and could be expressed as

$$S = k \log R,$$

Where S is the psychological sensation, which is equal to a constant (k) times the logarithm of the physical stimulus intensity (R) (Fechner, 1860/1966). This equation is called Fechner's law – and it is recognised as a slight extension of the earlier Weber's law.

In addition to developing the science of psychophysics, Fechner developed the experimental study of aesthetics (1865, 1871). For at least a thousand years, there was an observation that a particular ratio had pleasing or divine properties. For example, consider the following three rectangles.

Which do you find most beautiful? Make a decision before going on to read the next sentence. The underlying hypothesis of 'the golden ratio' or 'golden section' is that rectangles where the ratio of the short to long side is 1 to 1.62

are considered most beautiful. Did you find the middle square above the most beautiful?

Fechner developed methods used in psychophysics by asking people to compare two rectangles and say which they thought more beautiful. His results confirmed that the golden ratio is indeed 1 to 1.62. Later researchers, however, showed that Fechner's results were anomalous and that preference for a particular ratio depends on the method used (Höge, 1997). Despite later criticism, Fechner is looked on as the father of experimental aesthetics.

Fechner and health

Illness struck Fechner in middle life, brought on by excessive work. He became deeply depressed. His recovery came suddenly in October 1834, and he embarked on writing books reflecting a deep spiritual conviction, suggesting that consciousness pervaded the whole world. His book titled *The Little Book of Life after Death* was published in 1835 under a pseudonym, the book being translated into English with an introduction by William James some 70 years later (Fechner, 1904/2005).

There is one final point which is important to note in relation to Weber's law and Fechner's law. Both of these laws make quantitative predictions. That is, they present a theory where the prediction is not qualitative, but quantitative. The theories do not only assert that a JND increases with the magnitude of the stimulus. The theories predict precisely how much the JND should increase. Weber and Fechner did not use statistical testing. (They did not have to attend stats classes as students!) It is only later that statistics were used in psychology to test qualitative predictions (see Chapter 1). Why did Weber and Fechner propose quantitative theories? The answer is they were simply copying what was done in physics at the time. Weber's brother was a physicist. The theories of physics in the 19th century were based on mathematical equations that provided quantitative prediction. Weber and Fechner created theories just as physicists were doing at the time.

British associationist philosophy

Although the scientific study of sensation is clearly part of the discipline of psychology, psychology as a discipline is far wider. Where does higher level consciousness, such as thoughts (or what are now called cognitions) come into the story? The story of 'thoughts' starts much earlier with the work of associationist philosophers.

David Hartley (1705–1757) was born in Yorkshire, England, and trained in medicine at Cambridge. Although he is now best known as a philosopher, he worked on philosophy in his spare time. His 'day job' was that of a practising physician. Although medicine was still at an early stage, Hartley would have been well aware of the study of anatomy and pathology and the findings that the body functioned as a kind of mechanical system (see Chapter 1). Hartley was one of the earliest people to suggest that the brain and nervous system were connected to thought. In earlier years, the brain had been dismissed as at best some kind of cooling device as the soul or mind was assumed to reside in the heart, not the brain.

Hartley believed that the brain, spinal cord, and nerves contained particles that vibrated. He suggested that moderate vibration caused pleasure and large vibration pain. Hartley's assumption that the brain contained vibrating particles arose from his observation of positive after-images. Hartley had noticed that if he looked fixedly at a candle, and then closed his eyes, the image of the candle remained. He assumed that this was because the vibrating particles continued to vibrate for a short while after the cessation of a stimulus (Hartley, 1749). Although Hartley's theory is wrong, it adopts the correct metatheory that mental events are the consequence of physical events. Theories can be wrong, even though the metatheory is correct.

Hartley also believed, like others before him, that the mind of the newborn baby was blank and ideas came from experience. Much of his writing is about 'the association of ideas.' He believed that ideas became associated with other ideas to form new ideas. The result is that the ideas a person has are not just the result of the experiences the person has, but from how the thoughts combine. This emphasis on combination of ideas is given the label 'associationist philosophy.'

A blank sheet

The idea that the mind of the newborn baby is a blank sheet – or tabula rasa – was first suggested by the philosopher John Locke (1631–1704). The alternative view is that certain ideas – such as fear of spiders – are 'programmed' into the body. Thus, the tabula rasa hypothesis is relevant to the hereditary-environment controversy (see Chapter 7). Those supporting a tabula rasa interpretation place emphasis on the environment, not heredity.

The idea that thoughts combine to form new thoughts was not accepted by all philosophers. James Mill (1773–1836), best known at the time as a historian, suggested an alternative in his book, *Analysis of the Phenomena of the Human Mind*, in 1829. Mill suggested that the mind was a kind of machine and ideas came into that machine and were fixed in that machine. Note that whereas

Hartley was using a biological model to inform his understanding, Mill used mechanism.

There were therefore two positions being presented by associationist philosophers. Hartley's view that thoughts combined to form novel thoughts was called the 'coalescence' hypothesis. Mill's view that thoughts always remained separate was called the 'brick wall hypothesis.'

James Mill's son John Stuart Mill (1806–1873) (named after James Mill's benefactor, Sir John Stuart) agreed with his father's brick wall hypothesis, but changed his mind, largely because of evidence from chemistry. The science of chemistry showed that, when combined, chemical substances could produce entirely new chemical substances. Copper and zinc are both soft metals, neither as strong as bronze, which is formed when zinc and copper are combined.

Testing the coalescence versus brick wall hypothesis

Lemonade is made from two substances: sugar that tastes sweet, and lemons that taste sour. Is the sweetness of sugar and the sourness of lemon still discernible in lemonade, or is lemonade an entirely new taste? Ask yourself this question and try to come up with an answer. When I ask this question to groups of students, about a third report that the lemon and sugar are still discernible. These students are reporting an experience consistent with the brick wall hypothesis. The remaining two thirds report that lemonade is an experience that is entirely different from lemon and sugar, and the experience of these students is consistent with the coalescence hypothesis. This simple demonstration shows that 'reality' depends on the person doing the reporting. Perhaps both perspectives are, in a sense, correct.

The coalescence and brick wall hypotheses reappear in several different forms in the history of psychology. The gestalt movement is based on assumptions of coalescence. Behaviourism is based on the atomistic assumption of the brick wall hypothesis. Like many opposed views, the truth is neither exclusively one nor exclusively the other.

The findings from neuroscience

The story so far goes as follows. Weber and Fechner had measured sensations. The associationist philosophers had discussed thoughts, ideas, or cognitions. The final building block comes from evidence that the brain is associated with the higher mental content, and not only with sensations via sensory nerves.

Modern medicine developed from earlier discoveries in anatomy in the 17th and 18th centuries. Physicians compared the bodies of people who had died from disease and those who died naturally and found that there were differences. These differences – extended into tissue differences and then cellular differences in the 19th century – were used to define disease. Each disease had a different abnormality or pathophysiology. It was therefore natural for doctors to also look for differences in the brains between patients and those who died of natural causes.

Pierre Broca (1824–1880), who was chief of surgery at a hospital near Paris, had a 51-year-old patient who could understand everything said to him, but could never speak beyond saying "*tan, tan*" or when frustrated "*Sacré nom de Dieu*" (Sacred name of God). When the patient died, Broca carried out an autopsy and found an area missing (a lesion) in the frontal lobe – a part of the brain subsequently called Broca's area – which is responsible for language (Sagan, 1979).

About ten years after Broca's discovery, the German neurologist Carl Wernicke (1848–1904) reported a patient fluent but with meaningless speech. Wernicke found, on autopsy, damage to the top part of the left temporal lobe, the part of the brain that connects speech with meaning. Broca and Wernicke had both demonstrated *localisation of function*, i.e., the idea that different parts of the brain do different things. These findings provided detail to the increasingly accepted view that the brain was responsible for thought. If mental life is caused by the brain, and the brain can be studied through natural science, then it follows that mental life can also be studied through the methods of natural science.

There is one other case that is so famous that it appears in many introductory psychology texts. Wundt also referred to this case in one of his early textbooks, and that is the case of Phineas Gage. The case is shown in the box here for those who have not come across it.

The strange case of Phineas Gage

Phineas Gage worked at as quarryman in the USA where he was responsible for setting explosives in holes that were drilled into the rock face. One day, as he was pushing the explosive into the hole with an iron rod, the explosive exploded prematurely, driving the rod out of the hole like a bullet out of a gun. The rod entered Gage's cheek and came out above his right temple. To everyone's amazement, Gage got off the ground and looked around to see if he could see where the rod had got to. Phineas Gage was taken to hospital where the rod was removed and he made a complete physical recovery. However, his personality was changed. He was no longer the hard-working quarryman he was before. He was irritable, and could not settle to making any decisions. His friends said that he "was no longer Gage." Gage's inability to settle to any decision is now known to be consistent with damage to the prefrontal lobe of the brain. The ending of the story is not a happy one. Gage spent some time appearing as a curiosity in a travelling circus, but never settled to any form of work.

Later beginnings

Many textbooks on the history of psychology, as well as sources on the internet, state that Wilhelm Wundt (1832–1920) was the founding father of modern psychology. Why is that? After all, Weber had been conducting psychological experiments many years earlier and Wundt was a student of Herman Ludwig von Helmholtz (1821–1894) who, like Weber, conducted studies in the physiology of sensation. Furthermore, as will become clear later, the discipline of scientific psychology envisaged by Wundt is very different from that of today. There are two explanations.

> Explanation 1. Wundt deserves his reputation. Whereas others had conducted experiments that would now fall within the remit of psychology, Wundt defined the *discipline* of psychology – except that he called it the 'new psychology' to distinguish it from the old psychology of paranormal phenomena. Also, Wundt was an excellent lecturer and communicator and promoted psychology as a discipline. He trained many psychology students who went to set up psychology laboratories in many other countries. He played a pivotal role in developing psychology and his reputation is deserved.
>
> Explanation 2. Wundt's reputation is the result of a much later interpretation of events. Events happen. Historians interpret those events, and later historians rewrite history. Wundt's fame is the result of historical interpretation by later psychologists studying their discipline who are looking for a neat starting point. In reality, Wundt was just one of several people who helped found psychology.

Wundt and his contemporaries

How was Wundt perceived towards the end of his life? The following comes from the 13th edition of the Enyclopaedia Britannica, which was published in 1926 but written before Wundt's death in 1920. This entry was also written before the first textbook on the history of psychology published by E. Boring in 1929 (Boring, 1929). The entry starts by stating that that Wundt is a "physiologist and philosopher." It notes that "his earlier works deal chiefly with physiology, though often in close connection with psychology." Although the entry states that he "founded an Institute for Experimental Psychology, the precursor for many other institutes" the entry focusses on Wundt's contribution to logic and ethics and the relationship between ethics and psychology. "According to Wundt, the straight road to ethics lies through ethnic psychology, whose special business it is to consider the history of custom and ethical ideas from a psychological standpoint" (Encyclopaedia Britannica, 1926, vol. 28, p. 855).

Students should decide for themselves whether Wundt should be considered the father of psychology at the end of this chapter.

Wundt and the first psychology laboratory

Wilhelm Wundt (1832–1920) trained as a medical doctor, receiving his MD in 1855 from the university of Heidelberg where he then worked at the medical clinic. From 1857–1864 he was appointed as a lecturer, being appointed to a more senior type of lecturer in 1864 to 1874, lecturing in medicine and physiology. During his time at Heidelberg, Wundt assisted and worked with Helmholtz.

Helmholtz

Herman Ludwig von Helmholtz (1821–1894), like Weber before him, studied sensory psychophysiology. One of his achievements was to measure the speed of conduction of nerve impulses, both for motor nerves and for sensory nerves. Helmholtz made significant contributions to the field of vision, developing an early theory of colour perception. He believed that illusions occur when visual conditions are not normal, but that these illusions can provide insight into the normal functioning of the eye, an idea adopted by much later researchers in the field of perception(Gregory, 2007). Helmholtz developed some interesting optical instruments such as optometers, ophthalmometers, and ophthalmoscopes that are used by scientists today to investigate the function of the eye (Pearce, 2009; Wade, 1994; Wade & Finger, 2001).

Wundt developed an interest in the link between physiology and sensory perception while at Heidelberg (Bringmann, 1975). He published a short monograph on sense perception in 1862 (Wundt, 1862), publishing his book *Principles of Physiological Psychology* in 1874 (Wundt, 1874/1996). It should be noted that although this book includes the term *psychology* in the title, most of it is about the physiology of sensory nerves, but with a section at the end devoted to conation – i.e., to higher mental thought. Wundt showed how the experimental method used in the study of physiology could be applied to psychology.

Although Wundt was developing a career in medicine and physiology linked to psychology, he was also interested in philosophy. His skill and understanding of philosophy developed independently of his employment in Heidelberg.

In 1874, Wundt accepted the post of professor in inductive philosophy at the University of Zurich (note the term *induction* – see Chapter 1). He remained at Zurich for only one year, because in 1875 he accepted the post of Professor of Philosophy at Leipzig. As a professor of philosophy, Wundt published an important work on *Logic* (Wundt, 1880–1883) followed in 1886 by a work on

Ethics (Wundt, 1886). At Leipzig, Wundt was at the same university as Weber and Fechner, and was able to put his plan for a discipline of scientific psychology into practice.

We know about Wundt as a person from the writings of others. Elwood Worcester attended Wundt's lectures in Leipzig and provided this description in his own autobiography (Worcester, 1932). He describes Wundt as follows:

> Clad in a conventional black frock-coat and black trousers, he would steal into his great lecture hall, attended by his *famulus*, as if he wished to avoid observation. As soon as his familiar figure appeared, applause in the form of shuffling feet on the part of his hundreds of students would greet him. . . . Utterly unmoved, as if he had not heard us, Wundt would glide to his place on the dais, assume his accustomed position, fix his eyes on vacancy and begin his discourse. There could not be a better scientific lecturer. Without a scrap of writing, he would speak for three-quarters of an hour so clearly, concisely, and to the point, that, in listening to him, one would imagine one were reading a well-written book in which the paragraphs, the important text of the page, the small print, and the footnotes were plainly indicated. Wundt told no stories, gave few illustrations, scorned any attempt at popularity. His only thought was to deal with the topic of the day as thoroughly and exhaustively as the time permitted. . . . With all this, he was followed almost breathlessly, sometimes by eight hundred students, and, if the lecture had been unusually amazing, they would burst into spontaneous applause. As unconscious as at the beginning, Wundt would glide from the hall, and another great and unforgettable experience of life had ended.
>
> (p. 90)

Another of Wundt's students, Bernhard Berliner, wrote in a letter (Boor & Hamill, 1978):

> He spoke without notes in the most beautiful German language. The most fascinating part of his philosophy lectures was on the oldest Greek philosophers for whom he seemed to have a special love.
>
> (p. 191)

So, Wundt was an excellent lecturer, and he was an excellent lecturer not only in psychology but also philosophy.

Wundt's view of psychology
Wundt believed that there should be two different kinds of psychology. First there would be experimental psychology (Wundt, 1862, 1874/1969) that would be studied using scientific methods. Second, there would be Völkerpsychologie

or folk psychology that studied culture, rituals, religion, and so on, and which did not use scientific methods – i.e., the experiment.

The meaning of the word *experiment*

In the 19th century, the term *experiment* was used slightly differently from its use today. An experiment simply meant any active manipulation of a variable by a scientist and the observation of that manipulation on some other variable. The terms *independent variable* and *dependent variable* appear only in the 1930s (Winston, 2004) at the same time that the idea of control conditions appear in medicine.

Note that Wundt's belief that there should be two different kinds of psychology is a metatheoretical assumption (see Chapter 1). No evidence is presented and there can be none. Wundt is suggesting that there are two entirely different paradigms of psychology. In one paradigm, there is active manipulation of a variable by an experimenter. The psychologist makes something happen and observes the result. In the other paradigm, the psychologist simply observes what happens and thinks about what is seen. The former is defined as experimental psychology. The latter is not.

Wundt promoted the discipline of scientific (i.e., experimental) psychology at the University of Leipzig. One thing he insisted upon was that study of the paranormal was outside the field of his new psychology, because the paranormal was associated with non-science. The paranormal was not studied in his institute for experimental psychology. He started a journal with the title (translated from the original German) of *Psychological Research*, because there was an existing journal with the title *Journal of Psychology*, that was devoted to parapsychology. Wundt also defined psychology as a pure rather than applied science for reasons that will become clear in the next chapter.

Wundt's experimental psychology

Wundt believed that only one part of conscious experience could be studied experimentally: that of *immediate experience*. Immediate experience means the immediate reaction of something *independent of prior knowledge or interpretation*. Mediate experience refers to the reaction mediated by knowledge and understanding. Most of our experience is mediate knowledge, as is the knowledge of other natural sciences like physics and chemistry. By limiting the study of experimental psychology to immediate experience, Wundt focussed on the perception of objects – just as he had done when working earlier as Fechner's assistant. This focus also meant that psychology was different from other natural sciences in that there was access to immediate experience, not just mediate experience as in the case of natural sciences (Bringmann & Tweney, 1980). As the historian Van Rappard (2004, p. 146) has pointed out:

> The natural sciences study the objects of experience abstracting from the subject and, since their perspective is mediated by this abstraction they are called mediate. The significance of psychology may be seen in the fact that that it nullifies this abstraction and thus studies experience in its non-mediated reality.
>
> (Van Rappard, 2004, p. 146)

Psychology was therefore 'special.' According to Wundt, the higher mental processes (i.e., mediate experiences) were not amenable to experimental investigation, but they could be studied non-experimentally, and so non-scientifically, as Völkerpsychologie or folk psychology (Farr, 1983). Additionally, Wundt believed that psychological events had a form of causality all of their own, which he referred to as *psychic causality*. Psychic causality exists in parallel with but cannot be explained by physical causality. This idea is referred to as Wundt's principle of psychophysical parallelism.

Immediate experience

A good way of characterising the difference between mediate and immediate experience is by examining the technique used by artists to paint representational paintings. Suppose an artist wants to paint a yellow brick just as it would look like in a photograph. The artist has to look at the brick not as a brick but as a series of yellow rectangular shapes of slightly different colours. The artist then creates the impression of a brick by drawing exactly what the eye sees. The artist does not say "I am drawing the feeling of brickness" – at least not for representational art. The artist just has to draw the immediate experience of the colours and shapes without any interpretation of what those colours and shapes mean. However, artists often do not just try to represent things as they appear visually. They also want to draw the feeling of 'brickness' – something about the way a brick feels rather just looks – and they do this either with abstract art or art that differs from the photograph in some way. It is the difference between the photograph and what the artist draws that captures the mediated experience of the brick, rather than immediate experience that is found in the photography.

Some authors have suggested that Wundt's psychology represents a *dualist* interpretation of the mind-body problem, that is, there is a mind substance and a body substance. This view is not correct. Wundt's interpretation was monist, i.e., one physical substance that manifests in terms of two different kinds of causality (Van Rappard, Sanders, & Swart, 1980). Wundt's approach to the mind-body problem is consistent with more recent mind-body theories, such as methodological complementarity (see Chapter 6). Methodological complementarity derives from the suggestion of an atomic physicist, Niels Bohr, that reality can only be fully described by several mutually incompatible forms of description. The underlying reality is physical, but to describe that reality fully it is necessary to have psychological description (see Chapter 6).

Wundt used a form of introspection to investigate immediate experience, but his introspection was very different from that normally associated with that word. Wundt did not use the word introspection; instead he used the term *inner perception* (*innere Wahrnehmung*). Inner perception means focussing on the experience of sensation itself – not any interpretation of that sensation. The ability to engage in inner perception was a skill only achieved after lengthy training, because there is a natural tendency to report mediate experience rather than immediate experience. For example, if a table is presented as a stimulus, there is a natural tendency to report seeing a table. However, if immediate experience is reported, then the stimulus should be reported as a flat plane under which are four cylindrical objects (assuming the legs are round) of a certain colour.

Wundt developed scientific rules for his form of introspection, all based on the procedure of presenting a stimulus to an observer. These were the following:

First, the observer needs to be properly trained. It is interesting to note that in Wundt's laboratory there was no demarcation between participant and experimenter. His students experimented on themselves!

Second, the observer knows when the stimulus is about to be presented. The observer mustn't be taken by surprise.

Third, the observer must be in a state of 'strained attention.' The observer must be waiting and ready for the stimulus, so the stimulus and not some memory of the stimulus is reported.

Fourth, the stimulus must be repeated several times, so that the description of the stimulus can be ascertained with certainty.

The final condition introduces the importance of the experimental method: the stimulus must be varied in some way and the effect of this variation on immediate experience noted.

Observer, subject, participant

Wundt used the term *the observer* to describe the person who nowadays would be called the participant. However, for much of psychology's history, the term *subject* was used instead of participant. Subject implies someone who is entirely passive – which is seen as demeaning of the person taking part in the experiment. Hence, the change from *subject* to *participant* occurred at least 20 years ago.

It will be immediately apparent that this form of introspection is very different from simply examining the contents of consciousness. It is also worth mentioning that William James (see Chapter 3) considered Wundt's internal perception an exceptionally boring thing to do. However, this method of introspection had one important characteristic: By insisting on rules and rigorous training, it appeared to be a scientific activity. When psychology was in its infancy, 'being scientific' was considered a very positive attribute.

Goals of psychology

Wundt used his form of introspection to achieve three goals of psychology. First, to analyse the contents of consciousness into their basic elements; second, to discover how these elements are connected; and, third, to determine the laws that underlie the connections between elements (Boring, 1929). Wundt's approach to psychology was consistent with the 19th-century view that science should be data driven. This purely inductive approach to hypothesis generation does not generate explanatory theories. For Wundt, scientific psychology was a matter of observing and cataloguing the contents of the mind. Wundt promoted the idea of psychology as a science in a world where psychology and science were viewed differently from what they are today.

The elements of consciousness: sensations and feelings

Wundt distinguished two elements of consciousness: sensations and feelings. Every sensation is connected to a particular sensory modality – touch, hearing, sight, smell, taste. That is, sensations are modality specific. Sensations are also 'out there' in the sense that they refer to some particular event that is occurring in the observer's environment.

Feelings, on the other hand, are not associated with any particular sensory modality. Feelings are not 'out there.' Although an external event may trigger a feeling, the feeling is not uniquely associated with that external event. Wundt developed a three-dimensional theory of feeling. The dimensions were pleasurable – unpleasureable, exciting – depressing, relaxing – straining.

Association and apperception

Wundt suggested that the contents of consciousness were associated in two ways. Associations occur where there is a passive association of one element with another. Apperceptions occur where there is an active association. The difference between association and apperception is that in the case of apperception there is a feeling of intention. There is feeling of trying to find the connection rather than the connection just occurring. Apperception requires attention, association does not. This emphasis on intention and attention lead Wundt to describe his system as *voluntarism*, because it reflected a voluntary act made by the observer.

Voluntarism reflects the fact that immediate experience reflects an active process of intention (Danziger, 2001). In common sense terms, you can control your thoughts. The idea of controlling one's own thoughts is relevant to more recent ideas in psychology, ranging from cognitive behaviour therapy (where the client learns to avoid negative thoughts) to mindfulness meditation (where people learn to focus on the present). The behaviourists (see Chapter 4) rejected the idea of voluntarism along with the introspection, leading to a negative attitude towards Wundt amongst psychologists in the first part of the 20th century (Blumenthal, 1975).

How to experience associations and apperceptions

First, ask someone to call out a word and then say the first word that comes into your head. The caller should use one of the following words: table, up, or black. Likely associations are respectively table-chair, up-down, black-white. These associations will spring spontaneously into your mind. You do not have to try to do anything. Second, ask someone to call out any number, and then say the number which is three more than the number called. Any number can be called. For example, if 12 is called, you must say 15. If you do this you will notice that you have to make an attentional effort to find the number – it isn't automatic. You are now apperceiving, rather than associating.

Wundt suggested that when the elements of consciousness are associated or apperceived, there is sometimes a *creative synthesis*. Wundt's creative synthesis is similar in some respects to the earlier coalescence hypothesis and the later gestalt movement in psychology (see Chapter 10) though in other respects his psychology was consistent with the brick wall hypothesis.

Völkerpsychologie

One mistake often made in describing Wundt was that his interest was limited to the rather narrow confines of what he called experimental psychology, namely, the study of low level perceptual processes. This mistake arose from using Tichtener's account of Wundt. Edward Tichtener (1867–1927) was a student of Wundt who moved to America, and did not agree with Völkerpsychologie; he therefore didn't report this aspect of Wundt's work. Some of the earlier histories of psychology relied on Tichtener's account of Wundt. In fact, Wundt had wide-ranging interests in other aspects of psychology, but he believed that higher mental processes could not be studied experimentally – i.e., from his perspective, scientifically. Evidence for his interest in this 'other' psychology is provided by work carried out in the last two decades of his life, when he wrote the ten-volume *Völkerpsychologie* (Wundt, 1904) The content of these volumes illustrates the topics Wundt studied. They consisted of two volumes on language, two on myth or religion, two on society, and one each on art, culture and law. Wundt's Völkerpsychologie would now be recognised as more similar to anthropology or ethnography than to psychology.

Wundt believed that, when trying to understand the subject matter of Völkerpsychologie, the most basic unit of thought could not be expressed by a word or linguistic term but was a "general impression"(*Gesamtvorstelling*). That is, this subject matter could not be explored with the scientific method because it required an element of intuitive insight (Sabat, 1979). It was the intuitive insight that Wundt rejected as unscientific (Greenwood, 2003). Later psychologists, including those using qualitative methods (Chapter 8) and humanistic psychologists (Chapter 9) showed how it is indeed possible to study intuitive insight scientifically. Although Wundt is often described as the founding father of experimental psychology, in his autobiography, published in 1920, Wundt wrote that Völkerpsychologie was the most satisfying part of his academic life (Wong, 2009).

The impact of Wundt's experimental psychology institute
Wundt starting giving lectures in experimental psychology in 1879, four years after arriving in Leipzig. He encouraged his students to carry out experiments, and initially four rooms were given over to this purpose, the space allocated gradually expanding so that by 1897 there were 14 rooms. Wundt's students attended his lectures and he then encouraged them to carry out their own research in the rooms made available. His students worked in pairs, one working as 'the observer' who did the introspection and one the experimenter. All his students were first trained in the method of introspection described previously, as this skill was required for any study of introspection, though not all experiments required introspection.

Wundt taught many, many students both as undergraduates and postgraduates for PhDs. Many of his PhD students went on to create psychology laboratories in cities in their own countries. Misiak and Sexton (1966) report 16 students who started psychology departments in the USA; 10 in Germany; 2 each in the UK, France, Italy, Poland, and Switzerland; and 1 each in Belgium, Greece, and

Russia. Most universities now have psychology departments, though the psychology taught today is very different from that taught 100 years ago. The staff are also different. Then psychology was dominated by men. Now psychology is predominantly a female discipline – look around you during the next lecture. Psyche was a female Greek goddess, so perhaps we shouldn't be surprised.

Psychology as a science: looking forward

The status of psychology as a science has been lurking in the background throughout the history of psychology. Behaviourism and neuroscience are explicitly scientific (Chapters 4 and 5), but also humanistic psychologists and those adopting qualitative methods (Chapters 8 and 9) have made it clear that their kind of psychology is scientific, not the unscientific Völkerpsychologie suggested by Wundt. Non-scientific psychology does exist in the form of hermeneutical psychology (Chapter 9) but this is a small minority and in any case very different from Völkerpsychologie.

Summary

In the 19th century, the term *psychology* was not associated with science. Psychology, the study of the soul, was associated with the paranormal. Measurement was a feature of 19th-century science. During the middle of that century, sensation was measured in a variety of ways and called sensory psychophysiology or psychophysics. Advances in medicine and earlier work in philosophy was combined by Wundt with the emerging psychophysics to create what he called the new psychology. Wundt's goal was to make the new psychology a respectable science, and he therefore restricted psychology in ways that were consistent with views of science at the time, rejecting the study of higher mental processes as unscientific. Wundt wrote books on what he considered non-scientific, folk psychology whose subject matter is consistent with the broader remit of some of psychology today but is now treated scientifically. Students from around the world studied psychology with Wundt in Germany, though many rejected Wundt's view of psychology and went on to study higher mental processes and behaviour. Wundt made psychology a respectable subject for scientists to study by being aware of what would be perceived as scientific or not in Europe at the time. He was an excellent and much respected lecturer, but psychology today is very different from what he proposed.

Should Wundt be considered the father of psychology? All the reports given by Wundt's students are of a very kind and generous human being. It is nice to have people like that as the father of a discipline. But might that be a reinterpretation of history imposed by people looking for a good story?

Essay questions

1 How did 19th-century science influence the way Wundt defined his new psychology?
2 Discuss arguments for and against the statement that Wundt was the founding father of psychology.
3 What is the difference between association and apperception? Illustrate your answer with examples that are relevant to modern psychology.

3

How did psychology become an applied science and what is the relationship between applied and non-applied psychology today?

Let us begin with terminology: pure science versus applied science; basic science versus applied science, fundamental science versus applied science. These words have different connotations. Pure science is noble and good. If applied is the opposite of pure, then applied must be dirty and bad. Basic science implies that this is something that must be done first – something that is done before applied science. Fundamental science implies the research deals with more general or important issues than the (potentially dirty) applied science. Pure, basic, and fundamental. All three words reflect different attitudes of those who want to make this distinction.

Why 'pure' is better

When Wundt founded an experimental psychology laboratory in Leipzig, he insisted that his new psychology would be a pure science, not an applied science. Why was this? To understand Wundt's reasoning, it is necessary to know a little about social history in Europe.

Before the industrial revolution, there were two classes of people in Europe. The landed gentry and aristocracy who did no work and everyone else who worked and provided for those who did not work. What did the gentry and aristocracy spend their leisure time doing? They did a number of different things, none of which involved growing food, building houses, or serving others, but they were happily involved in 'non-applied' activities, often with some intellectual content. The upper classes did pure; the lower classes did applied. The result of this social arrangement was that applied was seen as inferior. Applied research and applied activity were seen as less noble than activity that had no material benefit. Of course, this is pure snobbery and prejudice, and students today may be surprised at this attitude. Nevertheless, it was a widespread attitude and one which the author was well aware of both as a student and a young lecturer. Academic snobbery is just another form of snobbery. Universities compete for status (there are league tables), and the status of courses within universities are not equal.

The universities were set up as places of learning, originally, the learning of the classics – i.e., the plays, history, and philosophy of the ancient Romans and Greeks. The classics remained an important part of university life in the 19th century and beyond. Almost all subjects that had practical applications and that required some kind of practical skills were taught in technical institutes or technical colleges, not in universities. In the UK, the Science and Art Department of the Board of Trade was founded in 1853 to promote applied learning, and the Technical Instruction act of 1884 enabled local authorities to raise funds to support technical education. Although medicine and engineering were taught in universities in the 19th century, the latter had a very low status in England and hardly featured in 19th-century university life (Albu, 1980). The history of universities is one where gradually more and more applied topics have been moved from colleges, schools and technical institutes to within the university system. Art colleges, colleges of agriculture, nursing schools, physiotherapy schools etc. are now departments or schools within universities. Physiotherapy became an all graduate entry profession in the UK in 1992, and nursing training became degree level in 2000.

Wundt insisted that psychology should be a pure rather than an applied topic because, by doing so, it would form part of the higher status university life, rather than the lower status technical college life. If Wundt had suggested that psychology should be studied in order to solve problems, his psychology would not have fitted the ethos needed for a university science.

Applied results from Wundt's pure research

Although Wundt defined scientific psychology as pure rather than applied, the findings of his laboratory had applications. Research into reaction time (called at the time 'mental chronometry') attracted the interest of astronomers. Stars appear to move across the field of a stationary telescope due to the rotation of the earth. Astronomers wanted to measure the speed of movement by recording the time interval need for the star to move between two parallel wires placed in the field of vision, by pressing a button when the star traversed the first wire and then again for the second. They found that different astronomers pressed at different times. The study by psychologists in Leipzig provided insight into why this occurred. People have different reaction times (Williams, 1912). Although Wundt intended psychology to be a 'pure' rather than 'applied science,' a use was soon found for it!

William James and the beginning of psychology in America

The social structure of America was different from that of Europe. Whereas European wealth was based on hereditary entitlement, American wealth – and therefore social class – was based on practical – i.e., applied – success of varying kinds. The idea that 'pure' was better than 'applied' was therefore not part of American thinking. Hence the development of applied psychology starts in the USA, and the story of psychology development in the USA is connected strongly to the application of psychology to real life problems.

Wilhelm Wundt can be described as the father of psychology in terms of promoting psychology as an institution, and has a prominent position in the history of European psychology. William James (1842–1910) can be described as the father of psychology in America. James helped psychology become an applied science.

The first undergraduate course with the title *Psychology* was taught at Harvard University in 1872 as part of a philosophy degree (Coon, 2000) – note, this was five years before Wundt started teaching psychology at Leipzig. However, that early psychology course at Harvard was not scientific psychology. James had the same problem as Wundt in trying to make psychology a scientific discipline, but his approach to the problem was different. In America, science solved problems. Psychology was a science because it too could solve problems.

William James came from a wealthy liberal, intellectual, and artistic family who travelled widely. James was educated at schools in Europe and in the USA. His younger brother became a famous novelist (Henry James). The young James was skilled in drawing and painting and, when young, decided to be an artist. For unknown reasons (possibly parental pressure) he gave up this career. Instead, he enrolled in a course in science and then studied medicine, graduating with an MD in 1869. Throughout his schooling James suffered from bouts of depression, gastric problems, and what was described at the time as neurasthenia – now known as ME/CFS or chronic fatigue syndrome. He considered suicide on many occasions. After being awarded his MD, he lived at home due to illness for three years, taking up a lecturing post in 1872 at Harvard (Myers, 2001).

James was an excellent university teacher; he enjoyed the process of helping a student develop, and his interest in psychology developed based on his own personal experience and the experience of teaching others (Croce, 1999). James' liberal education included philosophy. He was appointed assistant professor in philosophy in 1880 at Harvard University, and full professor in philosophy in 1885. By 1889 he had changed his title to professor of psychology, changing it back to professor of philosophy again in 1897. The 1926 Encyclopaedia Britannica describes James as a philosopher, though later interpretation is that he remained a psychologist throughout his career (Taylor, 1996). James' personal life almost certainly influenced his view of psychology. He suffered illness even when he was well established as an academic and published a paper in 1895 with the title "Is life worth living?" (James, 1895).

Throughout his life James was plagued with self-doubt (see James, 1895) and felt that his ability to write was poor. In fact, an internet search of 'quotes of William James' will show how many well-written and sensible suggestions he makes. James' best known work is his *The Principles of Psychology*, published in 1890. This book summarises much of what was known of psychology at the time. However, James noted that people he talked to were particularly interested in how psychology could be applied to problems in life, and he wrote a much shorter book focussing on application that was published in 1899. This book is based on lectures he gave to teachers, and has the title *Talks to Teachers on Psychology*. Much of the early practical application of psychology in America was on education and James was a pioneer in this regard.

James and Wundt

James was aware of Wundt's work in Germany. One of the first students to attend Wundt's lectures in 1879 was Stanley Hall. Hall had just completed his PhD at Harvard supervised by James and did postdoctoral training at Leipzig. Both Hall and James respected Wundt but had fundamental differences with his approach to psychology. Apart from the difference of practical application, James believed that Wundt's attempt to identify the components of consciousness was flawed, as consciousness flowed as a stream. Whereas Wundt largely supported the 'brick wall hypothesis,' James supported 'the coalescence hypothesis.'

William James and the function of psychology

William James' psychology was influenced by two earlier developments in philosophy and in science. One was Charles Darwin's book *The Origin of Species*, published in 1859. Darwin showed how the physical structures of animals were adapted to their use. For example, birds evolved bills suited to eat food in their environment. The second source of influence was that of the philosopher and mathematician Charles Peirce (1839–1914), who, like James, was educated at Harvard and was a friend of James. Peirce promoted a form of philosophy called pragmatism. Pragmatism is based on the belief that for any living organism to survive, it must develop habitual behaviour that would enable it to satisfy its needs. Both Darwin and Peirce emphasised the importance that physiology and behaviour must be useful – it must be adaptive in some way.

James took these ideas of Darwin and Peirce to suggest that the mind has use and can be observed in use.

> Our sensations are here to attract us or deter us, our memories to warn or encourage us, our feelings to impel, and our thoughts to restrain our behaviour, so that on the whole we may prosper and our days be long in the land.
>
> (James, 1899/1922, p. 24)

(Note the biblical ring to this quote – James' father was an eccentric theologian.)

James believed that consciousness has a function. Whereas Wundt studied the structure of the mind for its own sake, James believed that the mind had a function in that it controlled behaviour. This idea – that the mind had a function – was to be developed by other American psychologists, and formed a distinction between Wundt's type of psychology (given the label of structuralism) and that of American psychology (given the label of functionalism). Structuralism and functionalism were two competing paradigms for the direction of psychology at the end of the 19th century and early 20th century. Both placed introspection as the defining method of psychology, but used introspection for different reasons – i.e., had different assumptions about how introspection should be used. Two psychologists at the University of Chicago were responsible for developing James' idea that the mind had function. They were John Dewey (1859–1952) and James Angell (1869–1949). Angell was elected president of the American Psychological Association in 1906, and in his presidential address coined the term *functionalism* to distinguish the approach of many psychologists from the structuralist approach advocated by students of Wundt.

Educational psychology: the contribution of James

James made several contributions to education. James provided advice to teachers about how they should teach. Here is a summary of his advice.

James distinguished 'native reactions' from 'habits.' Native reactions are instinctive responses to particular situations, and James makes a list of these including curiosity, fear, imitation, and ambition. Some responses are therefore simple 'native reactions' to a particular situation. Habits, on the other hand, are acquired responses, which, once formed, occur without conscious intention. Much of James' advice to teachers is how to form good habits in children, which is done by exploiting the child's natural tendency to behave in certain ways, i.e., by building 'habits' from 'native reactions.'

> You may take a horse to water, but you cannot make him drink; and so you may take a child to the schoolroom, but you cannot make him learn the new things you wish to impart, except by soliciting him in the first instance by something which natively makes him react.
> (James, 1899/1922, p. 39)

James provides some practical suggestions about how to go about this. Children have a 'native reaction' to movement and change. So the teacher should move about and introduce novelty into the lesson. James states that voluntary attention is of short duration, so the teacher should engage with the pupil by introducing new ideas that are of interest.

What ideas are of interest to the child? James believed that learning was based on the association of new ideas with ideas that are already established. Therefore, learning is most effective if the new material can be linked with the old. This idea of learning by association has been part of the earlier theory of the German educationalist Johann Herbart (1776–1841), which was acknowledged by James – note that Herbart does not feature in the early German psychology as education was separate from psychology.

> When we wish to fix a new thing in either our own mind or a pupil's, our conscious effort should not be so much to *impress* and *retain* as to *connect* it with something else already there.
> (James, 1899/1922, p. 143, emphasis in original)

James argues against 'cramming' as a way of teaching children. New ideas are most effectively retained if they are associated with many rather than few ideas. Therefore the most effective learning is that which is done gradually and where numerous connections are made with the new material. This principle is now accepted in modern educational theory and has been developed in several ways, for example, problem-based learning.

Quoting experimental work by Herman Ebbinghaus (1850–1909), James shows that forgetting occurs more rapidly at first, but the rate of forgetting decreases with time. James used words such as 'recency' and 'immediate memory,' both of which will be familiar to modern students of cognitive psychology. James showed that although a pupil may not be able to recall something, the memory trace was not completely absent as memorisation would be faster the second time. Recognition can occur even if recall does not – which is why examinations (James points out) may not be the most effective form of assessment.

Finally, James provided advice about the will. If a child wants to do something that the adult disapproves of, then rather than inhibit the 'native reaction' of the child, the adult should find a substitution for that native reaction. This substitute should be something else that the child is interested in. Modern child rearing advice is similar – distraction is a very effective technique for managing young children as parents soon find out.

From where did James get the advice he gives to teachers? Part of it is based on his theory of habit, which he developed from the observation of people. Some is based on a theory of memory, partially supported by research carried out by others. What James does not do is test whether his recommendations actually work. James' recommendation that teachers should move around when teaching was not based on any evidence and is not supported by any subsequent research – even though teachers' non-verbal behaviour is important (Gorham, 1988). James did not test his theory on children. His recommendations are based on theoretical speculation, albeit sensible theoretical speculation. His recommendations are based on deduction from theory but without the subsequent testing that is required in scientific research.

William James and Stanley Hall: Was this applied psychology?
William James was a teacher and educator rather than administrator. It was his ex-pupil, Stanley Hall (1844–1924) who set up the first psychology laboratory in the USA in 1883 at John Hopkins University, moving to Clark University at

the time it was founded in 1889. While still at John Hopkins University, Hall founded the *American Journal of Psychology* in 1887 and after moving to Clark University founded the American Psychological Association in 1892.

James and Hall

William James came from a wealthy liberal family, Hall from a wealthy conservative family. Despite James being Hall's mentor, the relationship between the two men was not good – Hall formed the American Psychological Association in 1892 when William James was out of town (Taylor, 1995)! William James was very close to his author brother Henry, and one of Henry's novels is really worth reading. The novel is called *The Aspen Papers* and describes an academic who is ruthlessly pursuing his academic goals while at the same time oblivious to the destruction he is causing to the lives of others around him. A clever aspect of the novel is that it is told in the first person from the point of view of the academic, who feels completely justified in doing what he is doing because his academic goals take precedence over everything else. My guess is that Henry knew about academic competitiveness from his brother and wrote a novel about it. All academics should read this novel and be warned!

Hall wrote a textbook on adolescence in1904 that influenced educational policy. Hall argued that adolescence was characterised by heightened emotions and vigour, something that is self-evidently true, but nevertheless worth saying. Hall recommended sex-segregated schooling (Hall, 1906) in part due to his own personal experience and guilt-ridden feelings concerning sex (Graebner, 2006). Most modern educationalists do not support sex-segregated schooling, though arguments for and against remain.

What is clear from reading the works of William James or Stanley Hall is that these authors did not make a distinction between applied and non-applied psychology. James refers to the nature of consciousness in the same book that he makes recommendations for teachers. Hall points out that adolescents have a heightened interest in sex, and recommends segregation, but also points out that they have a heightened interest in spirituality without making any specific recommendations. Their recommendations were based on theory confirmed to some extent by experience. Neither attempted to test their theories with children in educational settings. Modern research on educational psychology is completely different in the sense that recommendations are based on evidence gathered from pupils. Is the work of James and Hall 'applied psychology'? Their psychology certainly had application, but it would not have counted as applied according the writing of one of James' colleagues, Hugo Münsterberg.

Münsterberg and forensic psychology

Hugo Münsterberg (1863–1916) was German but criticised Wundt's idea that psychology should be a pure rather than applied science. Although Münsterberg had set up a psychology department in the University of Freiberg, his negativity towards Wundt's ideas led to difficulties and, at the invitation of William James, Münsterberg took up a post in Harvard in 1897. This invitation stemmed from the fact that James was not personally interested in running a laboratory and he felt that Münsterberg was the man for the job – because Münsterberg was a critic of Wundt. Münsterberg has been described as the father of applied psychology because he took a particular interest in the meaning and promotion of applied psychology.

Münsterberg is best known for his book *On the Witness Stand*, which was published in 1908 but is based on essays written earlier. This book was a bestseller in its day and was reprinted as recently as 1976. In the introduction to this book, Münsterberg provides a clear distinction between experimental psychology and applied psychology. The difference is one of the intent of the researchers. This is what he wrote:

> If experimental psychology is to enter into its period of practical service, it cannot be a question of simply using the ready-made results for ends which were not in view during the experiments. What is needed is to adjust research to the practical problems themselves and thus, for instance, when education is in question, to start psychological experiments directly from educational problems. Applied Psychology will then become an independent experimental science which stands related to the ordinary experimental psychology as engineering to physics.
>
> (Münsterberg, 1908, pp. 8–9)

So the difference between what Münsterberg calls experimental psychology and applied psychology is whether the researcher is trying to solve applied problems, or is interested in psychological problems that may or may not have an application. Münsterberg defines applied research in terms of intention, and his comparison between engineering and physics shows how he perceives the difference. The difference is not so much pure and applied but basic and applied. Although physics comes into many explanations of engineering, there will also be explanations that are found in engineering but not physics. The applied science solves problems that are not solved by the basic science, even though some applied problems are solved by the basic science.

Münsterberg's lasting contribution to the field of applied psychology was in the field of forensic psychology. Münsterberg carried out experiments that showed that witnesses were not reliable. The experiments took place during his lectures. Münsterberg would arrange for a scene to be enacted – for example, two students having a heated argument. Then he asked the other students, who were naïve to this enactment, to write down what they had witnessed.

Münsterberg showed that many of the descriptions were factually inaccurate. Similar experiments were carried out by other researchers in other universities leading to the same conclusion.

Münsterberg carried out other experiments with students. In one type of experiment he showed students a picture and asked them to memorise the content. Then he provided a list of questions that the students were asked to answer. Some of the questions referred to objects that were in the picture. Some of the questions referred to objects that were not present. Münsterberg found that many students provided answers to the 'not present' objects, and therefore made up content of the picture. He concluded that people were 'suggestible' and he also showed that children were more suggestible that adults. The implications of this to modern research on false memory should be clear (Principe & Schindewolf, 2012). Not only did Münsterberg demonstrate suggestibility, but he also was able to show that prejudice could affect memory.

> All our prejudices and all our convictions work as such suggestions.
> (Münsterberg, 1908, p. 190)

As part of his work on suggestibility, Münsterberg studied false confessions where someone says that they have committed a crime that they have not committed. He provided examples of this happening in the American criminal justice system and shows how people, when placed under pressure, can imagine and therefore report what they have not done.

Münsterberg experimented with an early form of lie detection test based on an association task. In this task, a person is asked to say the first word that comes into their head when presented with a word. The rationale for this test was that dangerous words (i.e., those associated with guilt) have longer reaction times.

> A word which stirs emotional memories will show an association-time twice or three times as long as a commonplace idea.
> (Münsterberg, 1908, p. 86)

As part of his study into detecting lies, Münsterberg showed that safe words tended to produce the same association when repeated, dangerous words produced associations that tended to change.

Münsterberg concluded his studies with principles that remain true in forensic psychology today:

1   It is important to obtain eyewitness testimony as soon as possible after the event as forgetting increases with time.
2   Leading questions should not be asked because doing so induces false memories.
3   Witnesses can genuinely believe they saw something, and swear that what they say is true, and yet their memory is false.

Münsterberg was at first a popular figure in American psychology and contributed to a number of different areas in applied psychology, including (though not to any great significance) psychotherapy and industrial psychology. However, over time he became a very unpopular figure, and in part this was due to his personal style. Münsterberg never fully integrated into American society and was always hoping for a post back in Germany. William James was irritated by his vain and self-aggrandising personal style. The idea of Herr Doctor Professor was not welcome in a society that was democratic. Coupled with Münsterberg's defence of German intentions just prior to the First World War, Münsterberg became the object of ridicule, receiving letters addressed to Dr Monsterbug and Baron Monchausen – named after the fictional character Baron Munchausen, who told exaggerated stories of his ability (Landy, 1992). Münsterberg's papers were hardly ever cited after his death.

Witmer and the first clinical psychology clinics

In the 19th century, mental illness was treated by medical doctors who specialised in psychiatry. Although both Wundt and James had medical training – and although James had experience of mental distress – neither contributed to the study or the understanding of mental illness.

Lightner Witmer (1867–1956) trained under Wundt in Leipzig and on returning to the USA in 1882 took up a position in the University of Pennsylvania where he taught psychology, the kind of psychology taught by Wundt. Witmer also joined the American Psychological Association (APA) as a charter member when the APA was formed in 1892. In 1894, his university put on courses for schoolteachers and Witmer became involved in teacher education. One teacher described a boy who had difficulty learning to spell – what would now be called dyslexic. Witmer met the child and tried to help him. Soon after that, Witmer offered a course on how to work with students who were "mentally defective, blind, or criminally disturbed," and formed the world's first psychological clinic at his university in 1896. Witmer coined the term *clinical psychology* to name this new profession which he set about promoting, publishing an article entitled "Practical work in psychology" in the journal *Pediatrics*, also in 1896 (Witmer, 1896). In 1908 Witmer set up a residential school for the care and treatment of children with intellectual or behavioural problems.

Although the diversity of Witmer's clinical cases increased, there was always an emphasis on education in his clinical psychology (Witmer, 1907). Witmer emphasised measurement, in particular physical and neurological traits. Witmer first believed that heredity was important for mental illness, but later came to the conclusion that the environment was more important. Although many people in the 19th and early 20th century believed that mental illness had a biological and hereditary cause, an alternative approach, called 'moral treatment,' had been developed and promoted by people from a religious or non-medical background. William Tuke (1732–1822) was a Quaker and philanthropist who founded the York Retreat in England (Tuke, 1813/1964) for 'insane' people, as he believed that contact and influence by a moral person would be helpful. Similarity, in the USA, Dorothea Dix (1802–1887) campaigned for better treatment of the mentally ill (Dix, 1843–1852/1971) in contrast to the asylums where they were often incarcerated.

If mental illness is purely genetic, then there is little that can be done about it, other than lock up the poor wretches out of harm's way. However, if mental illness is the result of an unsatisfactory environment, then improving the environment of patients may help them get better. Whereas the environmentalist approach had been associated with morality and religion, Witmer promoted it in a way that brought the environmentalist approach within the scientific sphere. Instead of moral treatment where the emphasis was contact with a morally superior person, Witmer proposed that mental illness was caused by a poor environment and that the mentally ill could recover their health if exposed to a better environment. This environmental and educational focus for the mentally ill was consistent with the broader educational focus that was feature of late 19th-century and early 20th-century psychology. The related idea that mentally ill people had learned things incorrectly was to resurface in the later behaviourist approach to mental illness.

Witmer's clinic was headed by a psychologist, was staffed primarily by psychologists, and was a starting point for psychologists rather than medically trained staff managing mental illness. Other and later clinics in the USA also had a focus on mentally ill people. William Krohn started a laboratory for the study of the insane in 1897 in Illinois, and in the early part of the 20th century several hospitals in the USA introduced the practice of a psychological examination of patients on admission. Psychologists worked alongside psychiatrists in a way that was later to be characteristic of clinical psychology in general. These early psychologists provided ways of measuring mental illness, and although there was no specific psychological treatment (Reisman, 1991), the introduction of measurement was the beginning of a scientific analysis of mental illness provided first by psychologists. Note: Witmer was not influenced by Freud – Freud visited the USA in 1909, though Freud had published much earlier – see Chapter 5.

Scott and the beginnings of industrial psychology

Walter Dill Scott (1869–1955) obtained his PhD with Wundt, but like many others rejected Wundt's insistence that psychology should not be an applied science. Scott was appointed Professor of Applied Psychology at Carnegie University, and combined his academic with practical contributions to industry. In 1919 he set up his own corporation which helped develop industrial psychology.

Scott made two contributions to industrial psychology, the first being that he was one of the pioneers of advertising (Scott, 1911). Scott believed that "consumers are not rational beings and can be easily influenced" and so set about finding ways of influencing consumers. Part of this was through advertisements that provide a direct suggestion to purchase a product. For example, he developed a successful advertisement that had a picture of Pears Soap, and under which was written in large letters "Use Pears Soap." He also introduced advertisements aimed at women that had an emotional component as he felt that feelings of sympathy were more likely to be responded to by women. Finally, he introduced the idea of return coupons. Consumers were able to return a coupon for a small free sample. Scott argued that this required positive action on the part of the consumer, and so was likely to generate a positive purchase at a future date. The idea of return coupons became particularly popular in the 1960s – Green Shield stamps were introduced in 1958, and unused ones are now collectors' items.

The second contribution Scott made to industrial psychology was in the field of personnel testing. Scott was interested in finding ways of distinguishing good from bad employees, and developed his own way of researching this question. He asked businessmen to rate their employees in terms of their usefulness, and then gave the employees questionnaire-based tests. The tests were similar to intelligence tests, except that they were administered in groups. Scott found that some of the items in his tests distinguished the good from bad employees (as rated by the employers), and then employed these items for his tests of personnel selection. Like James, Scott used psychological theory to make recommendations without testing them, but like Witmer, he developed methods of assessment. Psychological assessment was to become a major factor in the development of psychology as a science in the early 20th century.

Binet and psychological testing

Alfred Binet (1857–1911) was born in Nice, France, the son of wealthy parents. He was independently wealthy. He was appointed to the important but unpaid post of director to the Laboratory of Physiological Psychology at the School of Advanced Studies in 1894.

In the late 19th century, the French government introduced a law that all children should be provided with (at least a limited amount of) education by the state – i.e., the beginning of universal state education. However, a problem soon emerged that some children had such low intelligence that they were unable to benefit from the standard education in schools. In 1904 a government commission was set up to investigate the education of these pupils. Binet was appointed a member of that commission, partly because he had started working in 1899 with a physician, Théodore Simon (1873–1961), on measuring people who were called mentally retarded.

The first test produced by Binet and Simon was produced in 1905 with revisions in 1908 and 1911, the year Binet died (Binet, 1903, 1909/1975). Binet introduced about 30 different tests to measure mental faculties, and these included a kind of testing of higher mental facilities that are now recognised as standard in intelligence tests. His tests enabled him to compare the 'mental faculties' of different pupils. Binet assumed that there were many different mental faculties, and that it was possible to be high on one and low on another. So Binet was not measuring intelligence as a single concept. The concept of general intelligence or *g* was introduced some 20 years later by Charles Spearman (Spearman, 1927). Binet believed that his tests could not "make us know the totality of an intelligence." Instead, Binet's aim was to measure the many mental faculties that he thought were important to guide the selection of pupils through an educational system. Spearman used the finding that the scores on the different mental faculties correlate (he used the method of factor analysis) to infer there was an underlying construct of general intelligence that affected all mental faculties. Spearman's idea of general intelligence was used later to allocate children to different schools in the UK – in contrast to Binet's assumption that differences in specific intelligence were important for allocating students to different classes within schools.

When the author was young, intelligence tests were used to allocate pupils to three classes of school in the UK: grammar school, technical school, and secondary modern – this tripartite system was introduced in the education act of 1944. The arguments for the early allocation of pupils to different types of school was later condemned as discriminatory as well as being having significant disadvantages in terms of the underlying assumption that intelligence remains constant as children grow older. Comprehensive schools (i.e., schools that were non-selective) were introduced in 1965 by the Labour government. Some grammar schools still exist and have both supporters and detractors. The several factors that inform this debate are beyond the scope of this book but may be interesting for students.

The politics of applied versus non-applied research

In Europe in earlier times, pure research – i.e., research carried out for its own intrinsic value – had higher status that applied research – i.e., research carried out for commercial gain or for other practical reasons. That attitude still remains amongst some people, primarily by those doing the pure research. However, attitudes are changing, and for some applied research has higher status. Differences of opinion between those supporting applied versus non-applied research have a long history.

The author of *Gulliver's Travels*, Jonathan Swift, was a satirist. His book, published in 1726, describes several different lands, each of which is a satire on some aspect of his society. One of the chapters, about the 'flying island

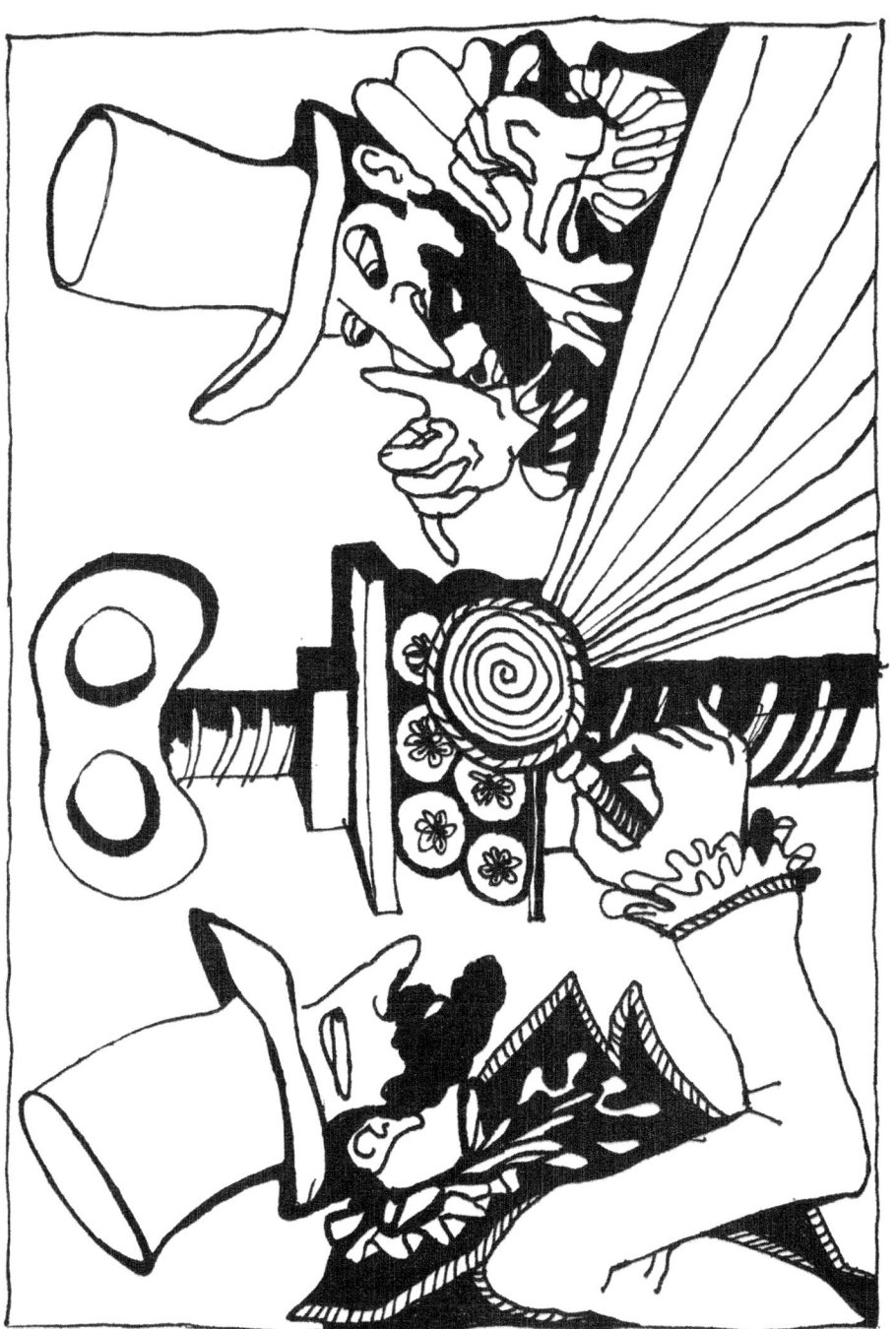

Pure science: extracting sunbeams from cucumbers.

of Laputa' is a satire on the Royal Society – i.e., a society of scientists. The inhabitants of Laputa are a nasty bunch. They have mastered levitation and have created a flying island that they use to extract taxes from ordinary people by hovering over towns and throwing rocks down if they are not given food and drink. Other than that, they spend their time in useless pursuits, such as extracting sunbeams from cucumbers and making marble soft so it can be used in pillows. Swift wrote that there are no women in Laputa because they are too sensible to live there. Swift spoke Spanish. His choice of name for this land was not accidental. *La puta* means 'whore' in Spanish.

Although university authorities in the 19th century might consider Latin and Greek the pinnacle of academic achievement, the need for applied education at a higher level was clear to politicians. The 19th century saw the formation of the first polytechnics in the UK. These provided education in applied topics, but were few in number. The polytechnics awarded diplomas but they did not have degree conferring status. In 1964 the labour government created several new polytechnics to meet what was described by Prime Minister Harald Wilson, as "the white hot heat of the technological revolution." The intention was to shake up the educational system with brand new, shiny polytechnics that would forge ahead with applied topics. At the same time the Labour government formed the Council for National Academic Awards (CNAA), a body that enabled the existing and newly created polytechnics to award degrees validated by the CNAA. Only applied courses (including psychology) were taught in these new polytechnics but with recognition of the need for a broader, more liberal education within the curriculum. However, the polytechnics were seen as having lower status than universities, possibly because they lacked degree awarding status. The polys, as they were known, never achieved that high status which was their original intent. The polytechnics were given degree awarding status and hence converted to universities in 1992. Although the 'new universities' as they were now called had an emphasis on technological subjects, the 'upgrading' of the old polytechnics to new universities also meant that their original aim was abandoned. The universities, not the government, had won.

This is how the government eventually won. Universities receive money to carry out research, money that is allocated to universities without any strings attached to the type of research carried out (i.e., money in addition to money allocated to teaching). The money comes from a block of money from the treasury and the government had to find a way of allocating this money in a way that would be perceived as fair, as some universities did more research than others. The solution was the 'Research Assessment Exercise' (RAE), which was invented and carried out every five years starting in 1986. The RAE was in practice a type of competition between universities for research money, and the assessment was based on the quality of research – as defined by the universities, and represented, primarily, in the form of published journal articles. University authorities are (quite reasonably) interested in their funding, so academics were encouraged to engage in high status research – high status as defined by their university colleagues – and publish in high status journals. After this competition had been running for several years, the government came up with a novel idea: Why not specify that as part of the competition, universities have to explain what impact their research has outside the academic field? The RAE was replaced by the Research Excellence Framework (REF) in 2014. The REF broadened the criteria for assessing research. Not only did the competing universities have to specify their research outputs in the form of journal articles, but they also were required to specify how their research had made a beneficial impact on society at large.

The government got what it wanted. The universities were used to the idea of competition for research funding, but now they had to compete for funding on the basis of impact. When the REF was proposed, many academics were highly critical. I remember one head of department saying that impact would never catch on because there was so much criticism from other department heads. On the contrary, the next REF, conducted in 2020 has a higher weighting applied to the impact of research. University authorities (quite reasonably) are interested in funding. The result is that applied research – or at least the impact of research – has suddenly achieved a status it did not have previously in the UK university system.

Research versus teaching

One of the consequence of the RAE and REF was that staff were encouraged to do research. However, if time is spent doing research it is possible for less time to be spent teaching. Recently the government felt that teaching quality was sometimes being sacrificed for research, simply because universities were rewarded for the quality of research, not the quality of teaching. The government had found that competitions between universities work. The teaching excellence framework (TEF) is the new kid on the block. At the time of writing, the first TEF that was carried out did not affect university funding. Watch this space!

What is applied research impact and how is it achieved?

What is research impact? The guidance provided by the 2020 REF committee identifies two criteria, reach and significance. Reach equates to the number of people who are affected by the change in practice. Significance equates to the degree of change on those affected. An estimate of research impact is therefore assessed by some (intuitive) combination of the number of people affected and the degree to which they are affected by the change in practice. The guidelines make one more and very important requirement for impact: It must be based on research. There must be a research paper or papers that provide a justification or rationale for the change in practice.

According to these guidelines, neither William James nor Stanley Hall created impact. It is certainly true that they influenced practice, and did so to a large degree. However, the change in practice was not based on research, but on observation-based theory. They developed theories on the basis of observation of people around them, but did not test those theories with independent data. By contrast Münsterberg did carry out experiments, and his recommendations for practice were supported by the evidence of his experiments. Other psychologists (Witmer, Scott, Binet) developed methods of assessment that were used where the method of assessment was based on research methodology. If the criteria of impact are used, then applied psychology requires underpinning by research.

What kind of research leads to impact? Chapter 1 provided an account of two types of research and research programme. In one, theory is developed inductively by collecting data relevant to a particular problem. This type of research is data-led. In the other, speculative theory is tested using deduction to provide tests of the theory. This type of research is theory-led. Data-led versus theory-led is a continuum rather than a binary classification, though for simplicity it is treated as such.

If research is data-led, then impact must come from research in an applied field. Research in clinical psychology, health psychology, educational psychology, occupational psychology, counselling psychology, and forensic psychology need to be conducted with, respectively, people with mental illness, people with somatic illness, children or students, workers, people with problems of varying kinds, and perpetrators or staff involved in crime. Applied research in these different areas of application is well established with journals specific to each different type of application.

By contrast, if research is theory-led, then impact can come from a variety of sources. One of the arguments for those carrying out or supporting pure or non-applied research is that their research may have practical applications in the future. The history of science provides examples of how research that had no apparent use at first turned out to have use in the long run. When quantum mechanics was first envisaged, none of the theoretical physicists thought that their invention would be used in mobile phones almost a century later. However, although mobile phones use quantum technology, other research was needed to translate the original theory and fundamental research into something practical. This 'other' research, research that develops an application from non-applied research, is called 'translational research.' So, although the argument that 'pure' research can lead in due to course to applications, those applications require the addition of another type of research, translational research. What happens in the laboratory may not happen in real life. Translational research is needed to confirm that the predictions deriving from non-applied research do actually occur in real life.

Some psychological research is carried out using undergraduates as participants. It may be that some psychological phenomena observed in undergraduates generalise to other populations, just as it may be that some phenomena observed with rats generalise to people (see Chapter 4). However, translational research is needed to confirm that theory and data obtained from undergraduate students apply in other settings. Some applied journals will not publish research that is carried out only on undergraduates. These journals have a policy that they will publish studies only if the participants belong to the target group of the applied journal.

Münsterberg defined applied psychology in terms of intention, the intention of trying to solve a practical problem. It is possible to distinguish three types of research intention in psychology. The aim of non-applied, also called pure, basic or fundamental research, is to understand psychological phenomena for the intrinsic goal of advancing knowledge. There is no intention that the research will lead to any extrinsic benefit. The aim of applied research is to find a solution to a practical problem. Although intrinsic knowledge may result from this research, the aim is extrinsic rather than intrinsic. The aim of translational research is to use research findings developed by those motivated by the intrinsic knowledge and provide evidence of extrinsic benefit. Most psychological research falls into the first two categories: research carried out with the intention of solving a practical problem and research carried out with the intention of furthering knowledge.

Theory and application

Kurt Lewin's famous dictum is "there is nothing so practical as a good theory" (Lewin, 1943a, p. 118). A good theory is practical. In Chapter 1, an account was provided of Lakatos' analysis that theory-led research programmes (progressive problem shift) were more effective than data-led research programmes (degenerating problem shift). The conclusion from Lakatos' analysis is that theory-led research is better both for solving practical problems as well as scientific advances.

Both applied and non-applied research have value. As a science develops and becomes more theoretical, the distinction becomes less important because there is nothing so practical as a good theory. However, the distinction remains important from a political perspective. If research is mostly funded, as it is in the UK, by tax payers' money, then tax payers expect their scientists to do something more useful than extract sunbeams from cucumbers.

Summary

Wundt presented psychology as a pure, non-applied subject in order to gain intellectual acceptance in European society where applied subjects were valued less. Psychologists developed psychology as an applied discipline in America. William James and Stanley Hall developed theories based on observation and used these theories to make recommendations in education, but did not attempt to test their theories or the validity of their recommendations. Münsterberg made an explicit distinction between applied and non-applied psychology research, defining the former in terms of the intention of the researchers. Münsterberg carried out experiments in applied settings and his recommendations for forensic psychology were based on evidence, not only on theory. Other applied psychologists also made empirical contributions to their fields. Witmer developed the first clinical psychology clinics in America, focussing on measurement and improved environmental conditions for the mentally ill. Scott pioneered organisational psychology, developing tests for personnel selection and advertisements based on psychological principles. In France, Binet developed the first intelligence tests, intelligence tests that exist with little modification today.

The UK government has increased the status of applied research by introducing impact as a criterion for competitive university funding. Impact is achieved most often when researchers have the intention of solving a practical problem. However, impact can result from non-applied research with the addition of translational research.

Essay questions

1 How did Münsterberg define applied psychology and what was his contribution?
2 William James provided advice to teachers about education. Evaluate that advice in terms of modern theory and practice.
3 Imagine that you are in charge of all psychology research funding in the UK. There is not enough money to fund all the good quality research applications which divide into two main groups, those that are primarily applied and those that are not. What proportion of that funding would you allocate to applied psychology versus non-applied psychology research topics? Justify the reason for your decision and describe how you would assess impact.

4

Why did behaviourism occur, what forms did it take, and why and how was it replaced by cognitive psychology as the dominant paradigm in psychology?

This is a long chapter, the longest in this book. It covers a number of inter-related concepts: Why introspection was rejected as a method by psychologists, the assumptions and different forms of behaviourism, why cognitive psychology replaced behaviourism as the dominant paradigm, and how cognitive psychology differs from or is related to behaviourism.

From 1920 to 1950 most psychologists working in university departments would have considered themselves behaviourists. Research psychologists wore white coats and they worked in laboratories with cages of white rats. Psychology was the psychology of the white rat. Behaviourism did more than anything else to convert public opinion to the view that psychology was a science. When a member of the general public evaluates whether something is a science, they seldom use Popper's criterion of falsifiability. If something looked like science – and scientists wear white coats – then it must be a science. Even by the 1960s, when the height of behaviourism was well and truly gone, rat psychology was still an important part of the student curriculum. When the author was an under-graduate in Bristol (1968–1971), the top floor of the three storey psychology department (a converted Georgian house) was devoted entirely to animals – and students were expected to get used to handling rats. I still remember the smell of rat urine on sawdust that greeted you when entering the front door – entering a pet shop brings back the memory of long ago.

Paradigms in psychology are based on assumptions, untested metatheoretical assumptions. Behaviourism was one of those paradigms. It is based on a set of assumptions, the primary one being that human behaviour has the same causes as that of rat behaviour. However, the assumptions of behaviourism changed slightly as time went on, so although it is perfectly possible to write about 'behaviourism' as a single 'thing,' this chapter tells the story of a series of ideas that developed between the beginning of the 20th century till about 1950. This chapter tells the story from the time before behaviourism started until after it was no longer the dominant paradigm.

Behaviourism started as an explicit rejection of an earlier paradigm of psychology. That earlier paradigm was psychology based on introspection. Wilhem Wundt and his students defined psychology as the study of the structure of the mind. William James and his students defined psychology as the study of the function of the mind, including what the mind could tell us about behaviour. The problem was that introspection, as practised in several laboratories across the world, did not easily provide the answers that scientific psychologists (calling themselves experimental psychologists) were looking for. Behaviourism arose as an explicit rejection of introspection. That rejection was based on evidence not prejudice.

There were two kinds of problem that arose using introspection as a method of experimental psychology. One was that introspection as a method failed to explain certain types of psychological problem. The second was that laboratories were coming to different conclusions using introspection and one of the characteristics of a science is that the findings must be replicable. These two problems are described before the description of behaviourism itself.

The failure of introspection

What introspection failed to explain

Wundt believed that the higher mental processes could not be studied through experimental psychology. One of his students, Oswald Külpe (1862–1915), disagreed, and when he set up his own laboratory in Würzburg, he and others started using introspection to study higher mental processes.

One of the first studies of the Würzburg school was reported by Karl Marbe (1869–1953) in 1901 (Marbe, 1901). Marbe was interested in the way people form judgements of weight. Marbe asked people to lift two weights, one after the other, and then say which was heavier. The task is simple enough. Marbe expected people to be aware of some kind of residual mental sensation of the first weight that could then be used to compare with the second weight. However, Marbe did not find this. He found that people could not really explain how they could judge one weight heavier than the other. They just did it.

The finding that people cannot introspect judgements is important because it suggests that introspection is not a useful tool in finding out how the mind works. In fact, later cognitive psychologists studying reasoning have come to a similar conclusion – the reasons we report for our actions are not necessarily the reasons that actually direct our behaviour (Kahneman, 2011).

Other research conducted at Würzburg confirmed Marbe's finding that introspection did not always provide an answer when trying to understand higher mental processes. H. J. Watt (1879–1925) investigated the way people name objects. Watt found that people produce the name of an object without conscious thought. It as though the name just appears in consciousness from nowhere (Watt, 1913).

Narziss Ach (1871–1946) studied something that at the time was known as 'the will' but which is now known as motivation. Ach was interested in what happens in consciousness when people engage in intentional behaviour. Common sense tells us that before we engage in an action, we 'intend' doing that action. That common sense interpretation certainly does happen. For example, if you hold your arm out and think to yourself 'I intend to raise my arm' you will be aware of the intention before raising your arm. However Ach found that sometimes goal-directed behaviour occurred without the need for prior thought, and he called this a *determining tendency* (Ach, 1910a, 1910b).

Has the following ever happened to you? You intend to go to one place – for example, to the shops – but you find you have gone somewhere else – for example you have gone home. Most people have had an experience of this kind. It is an example of a determining tendency. A determining tendency is a tendency to achieve a particular goal but where there is no conscious awareness of the intention when the action is carried out.

Ach presented people with two numbers written on a piece of paper, and asked them to say the first number that came into their head. Before showing the numbers, he presented them with one of four words: add, subtract, multiply, or divide. The word presented before the task had an effect on the associated number without conscious awareness. For example, when Ach presented the numbers 6 and 2, if he had said 'add,' the associated number was invariably 8, whereas if he said 'divide' the associated number would be 3. People's behaviour was determined independently of introspection. Exactly the same phenomenon is sometimes used by magicians when they perform magic tricks of mind reading.

Introspection produced different results in different laboratories

The imageless thought controversy was a controversy over whether it was possible to have thought without images. On one side of the argument were the German psychologist Buhler and the American psychologist Woodworth. They demonstrated in their laboratory that it was possible to have thought without any images – i.e., imageless thought. On the other side of the argument was Wundt in Germany and his student Titchener in America. They showed that images always accompanied thought.

Part of the argument concerned the methods used for introspection. Bühler and Woodworth argued that Wundt and Titchener's introspectors were insufficiently skilled to detect imageless thought – despite the extensive training in introspection that Titchner (Titchener, 1912) insisted upon for his students (Schwitzgebel, 2004). Wundt and Titchener retorted that Bühler and Woodworth's reports of imageless thought were created by suggestion, and were illusory. The controversy was never resolved. The problem is that if different laboratories produce different results using the same method, then it is difficult to see how that method could be described as scientific. The problems with introspection were fertile ground for a new type of psychology, one that rejected introspection altogether.

Precursors to behaviourism

Before the term *behaviourism* was coined, psychologists had started to do animal experiments. One of these psychologists was Edward Thorndike (1874–1949). For reasons that are not entirely clear, Thorndike wanted to study animal behaviour for his PhD at Harvard University – where William James was a professor. The only problem was that psychologists didn't study animals, and biologists didn't study behaviour. In the end Thorndike carried out his experiments in William James' basement – James was a generous person.

Although Thorndike is remembered for his animal research (1899, 1905), he only spent a few years on it, as he soon "followed the path of least resistance" as he put it and turned to research in educational psychology (Thorndike, 1921, 1932). Educational psychology at the time was an important and respected field of psychology (see Chapter 3).

As part of his research, Thorndike set out to discover how kittens or young cats could open a 'puzzle box' (Burnham, 1972). There were various types of puzzle boxes, each requiring a different solution to how it was opened. For example, Thorndike would place a hungry cat in the box with food outside and then time how long the cat took to open the puzzle box. What he found was that over repeated exposure to this situation, the length of time to escape decreased. That the animals appeared to learn gradually led to Thorndike formulating his famous laws.

Thorndike suggested two laws, the law of effect and the law of exercise. Thorndike defined the law of effect as follows:

> Of several responses made to the same situation, those which are accompanied or closely followed by satisfaction to the animal will, other things being equal, be more firmly connected with the situation, so that, when it recurs, they will be more likely to recur; those which are accompanied or closely followed by discomfort to the animal will, other things being equal, have their connections with that satiation weakened, so that, when it recurs, they will be less likely to recur.
>
> (Thorndike, 1911, p. 244)

He defined the law of exercise as follows:

> Any response to a situation will, other things being equal, be more strongly connected with the situation in proportion to the number of times it has been connected with that situation and to the average vigor and duration of the connections.
>
> (Thorndike, 1911, p. 244)

When students read these laws nowadays, common reactions are incomprehension and boredom. In fact, what they are saying is very simple. The law of effect means that animals do more of the things they enjoy and less of the things they find unpleasant. This is hardly a novel idea. However, what was novel was the quasi-scientific way in which this simple idea was expressed. Calling it 'the law of effect' meant psychology had its own laws, just as Newton had invented the laws of physics. Well, almost! The law of exercise is an equally unsurprising idea. The basic idea had already been expressed by William James in his analysis of habit. Put simply, the law of exercise says that animals tend to repeat behaviours that they have done before. Nevertheless, Thorndike's laws are important in that he expressed ideas that are self-evident in humans if one focusses on consciousness, but may not be self-evident in animals. At the same time, these laws must be contenders for the first prize for 'The psychology of the bleedin' obvious.'

Student rat revising.

Problem with Thorndike's laws

Are Thorndike's laws always correct? The answer is no. Although the term *law* sounds impressive, ancient Greek legend has it that whenever someone becomes too cocky, the gods find a way to take them down – the gods punish hubris (hubris = pride)! If a rat is placed in a T maze and always is reinforced for turning right, then according to Thorndike's laws, the rat should always turn right. In fact, it doesn't. At some point after turning right on several occasions, it turns left. This is called spontaneous alternation and is explained in the following way. Whenever an action is carried out, it generates 'reactive inhibition' to that action. Reactive inhibition accumulates and dissipates with time (Zeaman & House, 1951). When you start feeling bored with your revision, think on this: You are a big rat without a tail and your boredom is caused by reactive inhibition. The answer is simple. Don't revise for long periods of time. Have a break, and do something else.

Thorndike's law of effect has one other feature that is worth noting. Thorndike used the term *satisfaction* but without clearly defining what *satisfaction* is. In fact, Thorndike's approach to satisfaction was circular. If the probably of an action increases, this indicates that the action was satisfying; satisfaction is therefore defined in terms of its effect. However, the idea of 'satisfaction' does imply some form of motivation, and this motivational aspect was developed by later behaviourists.

The beginning of behaviourism: Watson and methodological behaviourism

John Broadus Watson (1878–1958) came from a family background that was rather different from other early American psychologists. His father was neither wealthy nor a minister of the church; he was a confirmed atheist who did little to help his family. Watson's mother, who kept the family together, was deeply religious and made Watson promise that he would become a Baptist minister – Watson's second name came from John Broadus, a well-known 'hell-fire' Baptist minister. This was not to be, as Watson decided to work in psychology, applying to the University of Chicago to do graduate work when his mother died. Watson's PhD and his subsequent work at Chicago involved rats – his dissertation (Watson, 1903) was published in 1903 with the title: *Animal education: the psychical development of the white rat*. Watson enjoyed studying rats (Cohen, 1979).

Watson began to realise that the methods he used to study animals could be applied to humans. In other words, it was not necessary to use the method of introspection in order to be a psychologist. This rejection of introspection was not based only on his dislike of the technique. As shown earlier in this chapter, there were problems with the introspective method. Watson's solution to the problems of introspection was simple: Don't use it. He viewed introspection as an unreliable and esoteric form of analysis that should have no place in a scientific psychology. Instead, Watson suggested that psychology should use the methods developed in animal psychology where introspection is not possible (Buckley, 1989). This type of behaviourism is called *methodological behaviourism* because its rationale is based on its method. Methodological behaviourism is based on the assumption that objective observation is a better method for understanding psychology than introspection.

Watson was happy at the University of Chicago, but he was employed at a low grade of pay. In 1908 he was offered and accepted the post of professor and director of the psychological laboratory at Johns Hopkins University. It was at Johns Hopkins that Watson made his mark (Watson, 1916, 1919a, 1919b).

The founding of behaviourism is often dated as 1913, the date that Watson published an article titled "Psychology as the Behaviorist Views It" in the journal, *Psychological Review*. The opening paragraph neatly sums up Watson's position:

> Psychology as the behaviorist views it is a purely objective experimental branch of natural science. Its theoretical goal is the prediction and control of behavior. Introspection forms no essential part of its methods, nor is the scientific value of its data dependent upon the readiness with which they lend themselves to interpretation in terms of consciousness.
>
> (Watson, 1913, p. 158)

Watson's behaviourist psychology changed the goal of psychology. Whereas Wundt and structuralists interpreted psychology as the study of the mind, and James and the functionalists interpreted psychology of the study of how the mind influenced behaviour, Watson rejected the mind completely. Watson introduced a psychology that was without the mind and which was dedicated to understanding and controlling behaviour (O'Donnell, 1987).

In 1914 Watson published a book *Behavior: An Introduction to Comparative Psychology*, which applied behaviourist principles of learning to animal behaviour. One of the developing assumptions of behaviourism was that it was possible to understand humans by understanding animals: There is no fundamental difference between animals and humans.

Humans are like other animals

The assumption that there is no 'dividing line' between animals and humans is an assumption that is shared with all the different versions of behaviourism. It is a defining feature of the paradigm – or paradigms – that make up behaviourism.

Watson's ideas developed over time, but central to his theory was the idea of the stimulus-response bond. The stimulus-response bond was responsible for habits. Habits developed over the lifetime were responsible for much of behaviour. The idea of a stimulus-response bond has clear links with Thorndike's law of effect and James' concept of habit. However, Watson also linked his use of the term *habit* with the phenomenon of conditioning that had been discovered by Ivan Pavlov (1849–1936) in Russia. In his well-known studies of dogs, Pavlov showed that it was possible to form associations between stimuli – between an unconditioned stimulus (e.g., food) and a conditioned stimulus (e.g., a bell). Watson thought that habits could be conditioned by environmental circumstances, as these circumstances and consequent habits led either to a well-adjusted person or a neurotic person. His strong belief in the environmental determination of behaviour is summed up in his claim, made in 1924.

> Give me a dozen healthy infants, well-formed, and my own specified world to bring them up in and I'll guarantee to take any one at random and train him to become any type of specialist I might select – a doctor, lawyer, artist, merchant-chief and, yes, even into beggarman and thief, regardless of his talents, penchants, tendencies, abilities, vocations and race of his ancestors.
>
> (Watson, 1924/1970, p. 10)

Why did Watson think this possible? Although he did not use this modern terminology, Watson thought that animals and humans were adaptive systems. That is, it would be possible to mould people into different types of specialist because they would adapt to the environmental characteristics of those specialists.

Watson gained psychiatric experience by working at the Hopkins' Phipps psychiatric clinic and it was there that he began to apply his ideas of conditioning to the development of neuroses. Watson demonstrated a conditioned fear response in a young child. Watson's study on the conditioning of fear was carried out with Rosalie Rayner and published in 1920 (Watson & Rayner, 1920) – the study would not obtain ethical approval these days, and it is referred to as the study of Little Albert. Watson selected a 'solid and unemotional' child for his experiment, Little Albert, who was about nine months old. Little Albert was afraid only of a sudden loud noise, which is a normal fear response for children. Two months later Little Albert started training. Training involved placing a white rat in front of Little Albert, who showed no fear of the rat. Then, when Little Albert reached out to touch the rat, as soon as he touched the rat, the experimenters made a loud noise by striking a steel bar with a hammer. Little Albert jumped at the loud noise. This was then repeated. A week later, there were five more presentations of the rat and noise at which point Little Albert was clearly afraid of the rat and would cry and crawl away. Five days later, when the rat was presented and without the loud noise, Little Albert was still afraid of the rat. Watson believed that this showed that neurotic responses in patients were also caused by conditioning.

Who was Little Albert?

Detective work has led to two competing hypotheses, one that he was a sick child with hydrocephalus called Douglas Merrit (Beck, Levinson, & Irons, 2009) the other that he was a healthy child called Albert Barger (Digdon, Powell, & Harris, 2014). The difference is not trivial in that, if the former, then Watson's description of Little Albert as healthy would have been untrue, and finding a falsehood in his study would add to other questions about the true reporting of this study.

The reporting of the Little Albert story has become elaborated over time like a game of Chinese whispers (British English) or game of telephone (American English). In fact, the conditioning effect was weak, and on subsequent occasions Watson had to 'freshen up' (Watson & Rayner, 1920, p. 9) the original response by repeating the loud noise. Watson and Rayner were able to show that the fear did generalise – for example to a white rabbit, dog, fur coat, cotton wool, and a Father Christmas. In later accounts of the experiment, fear was reported as generalising to other objects not mentioned in the original paper. Watson (1928/1972) mentions a rug, and inventions in textbooks include a furry glove and even a teddy bear (Harris, 1979). Harris (1979) suggests that these additions were probably invented to make the story more acceptable and believable to students and other readers.

Watson and Rayner not only collaborated on research together, but they also became lovers. Watson's marriage had not been good for several years, and Watson found in Rayner the romance that he was lacking at home. In1920 he divorced he wife and married Rayner. This action scandalised the authorities at Johns Hopkins University, particularly as Rayner came from a family who had given large sums of money to the University. Watson was dismissed from his post. From then on Watson never obtained a good academic job, but for a short time he continued to publish on his work on child rearing (Watson 1928/1972).

Invented history

Those interested in Watson's personal life might like to note that Watson was, in 1919, voted the most attractive male professor by female students (Benjamin, Whitaker, Ramsey & Zeve, 2007). There is an interesting postscript to Watson's story. It was suggested that the real reason he was sacked was not because of his affair with Rosalie Rayner, but because he was conducting experiments investigating the physiological effects of sexual intercourse – using himself and Rosalie as subjects. This story, however, has been shown to be nothing more than that – just a story (Benjamin et al., 2007), but the fact that the story is told shows how history is elaborated to fulfil the perceptions of the teller – perhaps more so for Watson than for others.

Out of academia, Watson developed a very successful career as a businessman working in the field of advertising (Buckley, 1982). His strategy was to apply behaviourist principles to advertising, in particular by using advertisements to elicit emotions in the population. For example, Watson created advertisements for Johnson and Johnson's baby powder that stressed the dangers of infection for babies and the 'purity' and 'cleanliness' of baby powder. In addition, Watson used basic conditioning principles to associate celebrities with a product. Queen Marie of Romania was shown endorsing Pond's cold cream. Similar techniques are used today.

With the arrival of two sons, Watson and Rayner applied behaviourist principles to their upbringing. Watson's book *Psychological Care of the Infant and Child*, published in 1928, became a bestseller. Watson's approach to child rearing was based on the assumption that children were simply mini-adults. Just as there was no fundamental difference in terms of conditioning principles between a rat and human, so there was no difference between adults and children. Watson believed that children should be encouraged to be independent and the demonstration of emotion by parents would lead them to be overly protective. He wrote in his 1928 book

> Mothers just don't know, when they kiss their children and pick them up and rock them, caress them and jiggle them upon their knee, that they are slowly building up a human being totally unable to cope with the world it must later live in.
>
> (Watson, 1928/1972, p. 44)

This harsh form of childrearing is now considered to be entirely wrong. It is worth noting that both of Watson's children experienced depression in later life, and one committed suicide. Whether this was due to the style of childrearing they received or influenced by the early death of their mother when she was 35 is unknown.

In summary, Watson introduced a new type of psychology that entirely rejected the idea of the introspection as a method. Some of his ideas still have currency today, such as the idea of a conditioned fear response, but others, such as his beliefs about childrearing, are now rejected. His legacy is controversial. Some considering him second in influence only to Freud whereas others see him as just a footnote in the development of modern psychology (Weyant, 1968).

Skinner and radical behaviourism

Watson's methodological behaviourism was based on his rejection of the introspective method. Skinner's radical behaviourism (Schneider & Morris, 1987) was based on an idea from the philosophy of science: Theoretical terms are redundant.

Explanatory fictions

The content of scientific explanations is made from two different types of term: observation terms and theoretical terms. Observation terms refer to things that can be seen (e.g., tables, chairs, dials, levers). Theoretical terms refer to things that cannot be seen (e.g., electrons, atoms). The purpose of scientific explanation (or one purpose of scientific explanation) is to predict cause and effect relationships between observation terms. After all, it is the observation terms that really matter in terms of everyday life. No one will worry if an electron is misplaced, but they do if their car won't start. For many explanations, theoretical terms *intervene* between the observation terms:

Observation terms → Theoretical terms → Observation terms

The following example comes from chemistry:

Add pink metal filings to copper plus
colourless liquid → sulphuric acid becomes copper sulphate → blue coloured
liquid

In most explanations involving theoretical terms, the theoretical terms provide a rationale for the causal link between the observation terms. This link can be stated in the general form:

A (observation) causes B (observation) because of C (a rationale based on a theoretical level of description).

Exactly the same rationale of:

Observation terms → Theoretical terms → Observation terms

occurs in psychology, only the labels are different.

The first observation term is called a *stimulus* – S. The second observation term is called a *response* – R. And the theoretical term is called an *organism variable* – O.

So, in psychology, explanations have the form:

Stimulus → Organism variable → Response

Or

$S \to O \to R$

(Note: do not confuse 'organism variable' with 'observation term.')

The crucial question is this: What is the organism variable? As far as the early functionalists were concerned, the organism or O variable was introspection. So, for example, a theory might be

Lion → Fear → Running away

However, the O variable does not necessarily have to be introspection. It could equally well be a physiological variable, for example

Lion → Cortical activation → Running away

The distinguishing factor of the organism variable is that it is some kind of theoretical term – i.e., it is not directly observable.

This idea of observation terms with intervening theoretical terms has been widespread in science and psychology. However, there are those who object to the use of theoretical terms. The objection is based on a simple argument called the paradox of theorising. This paradox was described by Hempel in 1958, and it goes somewhat like this:

1   The purpose of theoretical terms is to form links between observation terms.
2   A successful theoretical term is one that links observation terms.
3   Once theoretical terms have formed those links, then these terms are redundant as the links can be made between the observation terms independently of those theoretical terms.

In terms of psychological theory, the argument goes like this:

1 An organism variable links stimulus to response.
2 Once the organism variable linking stimulus and response is known, then the organism variable becomes redundant because the stimulus and response can be connected directly.

That is, if a theory starts with the form

$$S \rightarrow O \rightarrow R$$

Then, once the connections between stimulus, organism, and response are known, this relationship can be simplified to

$$S \rightarrow R$$

In other words, if the organism variable does what it is supposed to do, then it can be ignored.

Skinner argued that psychology should restrict itself to S-R links and ignore psychological theoretical terms *irrespective of their nature*. Thus, Skinner rejected physiological explanations just as he rejected mentalistic explanations in psychology.

Skinner's argument for a strict S-R psychology included a damning criticism of the way organism terms are used in psychology, a criticism that theoretical terms in psychology were 'explanatory fictions.'

To illustrate the case of an explanatory fiction, let us return to the example given previously:

Lion → Fear → Running away

Let us suppose that John sees a lion, becomes afraid, and so runs away. How do we know that John is afraid? Because he runs away. If John approached and stroked the lion, we wouldn't suppose that John was afraid. John's fear is *inferred* from his behaviour, the same behaviour which the fear is being used to *explain*.

To give a slightly more banal example, let us suppose that we observe John smiling. We infer from this that John is happy. Because John is happy, therefore he smiles. But we only know that he is happy because he smiles.

Skinner points out that the organism variable in psychology is an explanatory fiction. It masquerades as an explanation. It cons us into thinking that an explanation is provided, when all it does is redescribe the behaviour. While Skinner's argument has merits, a later section in this chapter will explain what it takes to make an organism variable *not* an explanatory fiction.

Skinner's contribution

Burrhus Frederic Skinner, or B.F. Skinner (1904–1990) originally planned to be an author, but after reading works by Watson and Pavlov he enrolled in a graduate programme of psychology at Harvard in 1928 (Catania, 1992). His career as a behaviourist psychologist lasted six decades and included not only academic books and papers, but also many non-technical books written for the general population, so that his original aim of being an author was in fact realised (Bjork, 1993). Skinner's book *The Behavior of Organisms* (1938) was his major work. Although focussing on the behaviour of the white rat, Skinner believed that humans were organisms just as the rat was. By organism he meant a unified system of stimulus-response connections (Catania, 1992). Skinner investigated the rat's behaviour with an invention of his that is now known as *the Skinner box*. The Skinner box consists of a box in which the rat is placed with a lever on which the rat can press. The rat's lever presses are the response – and various stimuli, such as food or electric shock, can be applied by the researcher.

Skinner's main academic contribution to behaviourism was that he established the idea of operant conditioning in contrast to respondent conditioning – respondent conditioning was the form of conditioning studied by Pavlov. Operant conditioning involved the shaping of behaviour through reinforcement, and this idea is directly linked to Thorndike's law of effect. That is, organisms tend to do more of an action that is reinforced (i.e., creates satisfaction) and less of one that does not. Behaviour is controlled by its consequences. The astute student may query whether the idea of satisfaction is an explanatory fiction. Skinner avoided this problem by simply identifying those conditions that were reinforcing – i.e., led to an increase of a particular behaviour. However, in contrast to Thorndike, Skinner believed that reinforcement was better able to shape behaviour than punishment and so advocated the use of encouragement rather than punishment for modifying human behaviour.

The two main assumptions of behaviourism

One assumption is that human behaviour can be predicted from observations made on animals. The second assumption is that behaviour is controlled by its consequences.

Skinner's contributions were not only in the academic sphere (e.g., Skinner, 1935, 1957, 1984a), he also made contributions in three other ways. First, he wrote a number of books and articles that provided a blueprint for a 'better way of life' based on behaviourist principles (Skinner, 1938, 1953, 1974). His novel *Walden Two* published in 1948 describes a happy society based on principles of positive reinforcement (Skinner, 1948). A similar idea forms the basis of a book by Aldous Huxley, called *Brave New World*, except that Huxley's title is satirical as he wanted to expose the emptiness of a happy life controlled by others (Huxley, 1932). Skinner's book *Beyond Freedom and Dignity* (Skinner, 1971) suggests that these two emotions, freedom and dignity, are both illusions and happiness is increased by avoiding these often sought goals. This book was on the *New York Times* bestseller list for 26 weeks. It is worth noting that in his personal life Skinner was an unassuming man who kept his many honorary degrees in a box in his basement, and whenever he allowed himself to be interviewed it was not to promote himself but to promote behaviourism. He believed strongly that the application of behaviourist principles could increase human happiness (Skinner, 1976; Wiener, 1996). People who knew him have told the author what a charming man he was.

As a second practical contribution Skinner invented something called the 'baby tender' and later renamed the 'aircrib.' The baby tender consisted of a box with sound absorbing walls and a large picture window. Heated, filtered, and moistened air was pumped into the box, which had a tightly stretched canvas floor, which was made from a long strip of canvas that could be cranked so that a fresh section could be easily put in place. The baby tender followed Skinner's principle of providing children with a pleasing environment, and he used it for his first child, a girl called Deborah – apparently this device was designed because his wife did not like looking after children. Deborah spent her first two and a half years in the air crib and grew up to be a happy and successful adult – whether this was despite of or because of the baby tender is impossible to say. Skinner tried to sell his baby tenders – which were renamed as aircribs commercially. Although about a thousand aircribs were sold, with satisfied owners, the idea never really took off (Benjamin & Nielsen-Gammon, 1999).

As a third applied contribution, Skinner applied behavioural principles to education. After noticing that some children in a class completed work early and so waited, looking bored, whereas others were rushed, Skinner reasoned that the pace of learning should be adjusted to each individual student's rate of working. In addition, he reasoned that learning should involve immediate feedback about whether a solution to a problem was correct, rather than the child having to wait till the end of the lesson or some time on a future occasion. Skinner applied these two principles (individualised rate of working and immediate feedback) to developing teaching machines. Although IBM and other American companies expressed interest in marketing these machines, negotiations came to nothing and in the end this educational innovation never materialised. A final invention of Skinner's that has received little attention is that of the 'summator.' In essence, the summator was a kind of auditory ink-blot. It consisted of barely audible sounds that Skinner assumed would be associated with verbal content that had meaning to the person. Hence, by describing what the sounds 'were saying' the person provided a description of their latent behaviour. This idea was taken up initially by physicians (it was renamed the tautophone), but again, never really caught on (Rutherford, 2003).

Skinner was a multi-faceted person. His contribution included a philosophical perspective on psychological theory, the application of psychological theory in the form of operant conditioning and several applications of behavioural principles to real life situations. That these applications were not particularly successful were a great disappointment to Skinner. Why they were not successful is a matter of speculation and a useful topic for discussion. Despite his earlier popularity, by the 1960s popular opinion was moving away from a mechanistic view of people as mindless machines to one that was more in line with the liberalism of the time – where flower power and free love were the new idiom (see Chapter 9). Skinner's interpretation of psychology was criticised in the popular press (Rutherford, 2000). Nevertheless, he has had an immense influence on psychology with the central belief that people are the product of their environments. At the age of 86 he was still working on the final correction on a paper entitled "Can Psychology Be a Science of Mind?" the evening before he died (Fowler, 1990).

Neobehaviourism: Hull and Tolman

Methodological behaviourism and radical behaviourism both rejected the use of theoretical terms or organism variables. Nevertheless, despite the paradox of theorising and despite the problem of explanatory fictions, organism variables have a value. It is this value, the value of theoretical terms, that was responsible for the development of a type of behaviourism called neobehaviourism.

Imagine a rat placed in a maze. In this experimental situation, the stimulus is the maze and the response is how the rat runs in the maze. If naïve rats are placed in the maize – naïve in the sense that they have not had experience with mazes before – then they will engage in a variety of exploratory responses. The stimulus-response link can be represented as this:

Stimulus of maze → exploratory responses

Now, imagine what happens if non-naïve rats, rats who have learned where the goal box is, are used instead. The non-naïve rat will run straight to the goal box where a reward of food is waiting. The prior history of the rat makes a difference. Equally, if a rat is hungry because it has not been fed, this rat will behave differently to one that is satiated because it has just been fed. Again, prior history makes a difference. It seems that any explanation of the behaviour of a rat must take into account prior history.

The radical behaviourist solution to the effect of history on present behaviour was to incorporate the historical stimuli into the explanation of stimulus and response. The stimulus-response links of the non-naïve rats on the occasions before the test period become part of the explanation.

The radical behaviourist solution retains the original objective of avoiding organism variables. However, the problem with this solution is that it is very cumbersome. A rat may have a long history of maze running, and so to describe the rat's behaviour it is necessary to describe a long list of prior stimuli and responses. Thus, although radical behaviourist solution 'works' it is not particularly practical: It is inconvenient. It was this particular problem of inconvenience that faced the neobehaviourists.

The neobehaviourist solution was simple: Allow in certain organism variables, but only those that had passed a test. The test the organism variable had to satisfy was that it was *operationally defined*. So, there are some 'good' organism variables you can use and some 'bad' ones you can't. An operationally defined organism variable is one that is defined in terms of its *operations*. Defining something in terms of operations means defining it in terms of observation terms – i.e., defining the organism variable in terms of what it does in terms of observable effects or what observable events cause it. Thus, operational definition means that the organism variable is defined in terms of objective observation. The particular solution of operational definition differed between the different neobehaviourists, and two different ones will be considered here: the theories of Hull and of Tolman.

Hull's quantitative theory of animal behaviour

Clark Leonard Hull (1884–1952) is remembered as a behaviourist, but his earlier works had a wider focus, including a book *Aptitude Testing* published in 1928 and one on *Hypnosis and Suggestibility* published in 1933. These works appeared at the same time he was publishing on learning theory (Hull, 1929, 1930, 1945, 1951). Hull is best known for his book *Principles of Behavior* published in 1943, and his final book *A Behavior System*, which was published the year he died (Hull, 1952).

A distinctive feature of Hull's approach to psychology is that he proposed a quantitative theory, one that involved mathematical formulae. Hull's theory of behaviour 'grew' over time.

There are three organism variables in Hull's theory, each of which is *operationally defined*. The first is called *net reaction potential* and is given the expression

$$_sE_R$$

$_sE_R$ or net reaction potential is the potential to engage in a particular behaviour. The reaction potential is not exactly the same as the behaviour, as the rat may be prevented from engaging in the behaviour, but it can be treated as more or less equivalent with behaviour. Thus, $_sE_R$ is defined operationally in terms of behaviour:

$_sE_R$ is approximately equal to behaviour.

Mathematical psychology

Hull was one of the first psychologists to introduce quantitative theory into psychology in a way that mimics the quantitative theories of physics and chemistry (but see also Weber's fraction and Fechner's law, Chapter 2). Although a fraction of psychological theories are quantitative, the *Journal of Mathematical Psychology* was first published in 1964 and continues publishing articles to this day. Although some papers relate to reinforcement, others describe human behaviour. For example, Luce's choice axiom (Luce, 1977) provides quantitative predictions about choice. If, for example, the proportion of people choosing chicken over beef in a restaurant is X/Y, then, if pork is added to the menu, although the absolute number of people choosing chicken and beef reduces, the proportion, X/Y, remains the same. The theory is tested not with statistical hypothesis testing but by a quantitative estimate of the extent to which that proportion, X/Y, remains the same under different conditions of choice.

The second of Hull's organism variables is called drive, and given the expression

$$D$$

D or drive is operationally defined in terms of the number of hours the rat has been without food. Hull thought that there was one central drive, D, that motivated all behaviour, and that when D was high the rat was more likely to engage in behaviour, any behaviour.

The third of Hull's organism variables is called habit, and given the expression

$$H$$

H or habit is operationally defined in terms of the number of occasions the rat has performed that behaviour in the past.

Using these three organism variables, Hull then proposed the following theory

$$_sE_R = D \times H$$

Or net reaction potential equals drive times habit.

What this theory suggests is that rats are motivated to behave as a function of the level of drive (otherwise they just sit doing nothing), but the direction of behaviour (i.e., what they actually do) is determined by habit. That is, drive energises behaviour and habit directs behaviour.

Notice that Hull's three organism variables are operationally defined in terms of external observable variables. Drive is not some internal physiological state, and habit is not a pathway in the brain. These concepts are *entirely* described in terms of objective external conditions. Notice that this form of description of organism variables is not very different from Skinner's proposal that there should be no organism variables at all. Because drive is *only* the number of hours without food, it would be possible to dispense with the concept of drive and rely only on the number of hours without food. That is, it would be possible to include the historical stimuli (number of hours without food) with the present stimulus of the maze in order to explain the rat's behaviour. Hull's organism variables are simply a convenient summary of the external, objective stimulus. He does not make the error criticised by Skinner of creating an explanatory fiction by supposing that there is an internal state, called drive, that 'makes' the rat run. Drives are simply convenient summaries of the external objective data.

In a typical behaviourist experiment conducted by Hull, a rat would be placed at the beginning of a maze. There was food at the goal box at the end of the maze. The behaviour of the rat would be observed. It was found that the rat ran faster if it was deprived of food, and it would be more likely to go to the correct goal box if it had received food there in the past. However, over time Hull found that other variables would affect the rat's behaviour. For example, the attractiveness of the reward would make a difference, as well as the amount of effort needed by the rat to achieve the goal. These additional variables could not be explained by his initial theory of

$$_sE_R = D \times H$$

As a consequence of this, Hull introduced new concepts. New concepts began creeping into the theory. Initially there was the concept of incentive, given the letter K, and then the amount of work, given the letter W. Then other organism variables had to be added so that the equation ended up looking very complex indeed. This gradual increase in organism variables was the inevitable consequence of how the theory developed. At first Hull was interested in a relatively limited laboratory setup. Over time, that setup became more complex, with the consequence that he had to make the theory more complex. This additional complexity results because of the very nature of Hull's theory. Hull assumed that behaviour could be explained atomistically. That is, the various determinants of $_sE_R$ are simply added up together, and the whole is *not* more than the sum of its parts. The eventual outcome of this kind of theorising is that one ends up with an incredibly complex theory.

The reason a theory is useful is that it helps people make sense of the world in which we live by simplifying the complexity that people observe around them. However, as Hull's theory grew it became less good at simplifying and making sense. The more comprehensive the theory became – and Hull wanted to explain all behaviour – the more unwieldy it became. As a theory for explaining a limited number of events in a restricted setup, the theory was very successful. But as a theory of all behaviour, Hull's approach failed to be successful.

There is a reason for focussing on Hull's theory. The historian Imre Lakatos observed that research programmes that are driven by data are less successful than those driven by theory (see Chapter 1). Lakatos used the term 'degenerating problem shift' to describe research where theory lags behind data. Lakatos did not refer to Hull's theory as an example of a degenerating problem shift, but it is an excellent example of what happens. Theoretical terms were introduced to explain behaviours of the rat that were observed and could not be explained by the existing theoretical terms. To be successful, a theory needs to be able to simplify behaviour, not just redescribe each behaviour using a different theoretical concept. Despite its influence in its day, nowadays Hull's mathematical theory is largely forgotten (Mills, 1978).

Tolman's purposive behaviourism

Edward Chace Tolman (1886–1959) was influenced by the work of Gestalt psychologists, particularly Kurt Koffka and Kurt Lewin, and spent time working with Koffka. However, Tolman was also influenced by animal psychologists, and it is in this field that he made his name (Tolman, 1922, 1932, 1948, 1959). Nevertheless the Gestalt influence is evident throughout his work. This Gestalt influence makes Tolman a transition figure between behaviourism and cognitive psychology.

One important difference between Hull and Tolman was that Tolman believed that behaviour should be treated as a molar event – hence the term *molar behaviourism* is sometimes used to describe Tolman's approach. Hull treated the rat's behaviour as a sequence of *actions*. For example, the rat would take two steps forward, then three to the left, then another four forwards and so on until the goal is reached. Each step is an action. The central argument of Hull and other behaviourists was that it is the *action* that is reinforced by the goal in the goal box. By contrast, Tolman refers to *acts* meaning that it is 'the arriving at the goal box' which is the act. Thus, Tolman describes behaviour in terms of a *larger* unit than that used by Hull (acts versus actions). However, there is an additional implication of the idea of an act. It is that an act is defined in terms of a goal or purpose. Tolman's behaviourism is referred to as purposive behaviourism.

Hull and Tolman had different views about the nature of learning. According to Hull's theory, learning was associative and incremental. That is, habits were gradually strengthened by repeated actions. By contrast, Tolman believed that learning could be 'all-or-nothing' where there was a rapid change in behaviour. In all-or-nothing learning, the animal either knows or it does not know – there is no point in between. Tolman had worked with Koffka, and Koffka had worked with Köhler who had demonstrated that apes could learn through insight learning (see Chapter 10). So, Tolman was maintaining the tradition started by the Gestalt psychologists (see Chapter 10) whose theories focussed on wholes rather than on parts. By contrast, Hull was maintaining the tradition started by Wundt of associationism. In Hull's case, association is a gradual process. The all-or-nothing versus associative or gradual learning controversy was a major point of discussion at that time (Bruce, 1998).

The difference between Hull and Tolman about incremental versus all or nothing learning lasted for many years. Each side found that 'their' rats performed in the way their theory predicted. When placed in a maze Tolman's rats looked around, and (according to Tolman) formed a cognitive map of their environment, and once they had formed that cognitive map, then they always went straight to the goal. Note the *term cognitive map* – Tolman's theory anticipates cognitive psychology. By contrast, Hull's learned gradually, making progressively fewer and fewer errors. Just as the debate was becoming irrelevant (with the advent of cognitive psychology) a possible reason for these different results emerged. Hull and Tolman were using different strains of rats. Hull's rats had been selectively bred to be unemotional. Tolman's rats were more closely related to the emotional rats that are found in the wild. Tolman's rats were more afraid, and more hesitant and so went to the goal box only when they had learned where they were (Jones, 2003).

The author's rat, Sheila

Rats are bred to be genetically consistent, but they actually do not behave in exactly the same way. As a student, the author was allocated a rat. She was a female, and he called her Sheila. Sheila was not like the other rats. She was neurotic and didn't want to be handled. The author understood how Sheila felt and gradually got her used to a hand being placed close by. The technician who was in charge of the students looked in and told the author he was far too slow, and put in his hand to pick up Sheila. Sheila bit the technician. The author is ashamed to admit that he felt a degree of smug satisfaction at this turn of events.

Like Hull, Tolman introduced organism variables, and these organism variables included expectancy, purposes, cognitions, hypotheses, and appetite. To illustrate what is meant by expectancy, Tolman suggested that when a response is rewarded, then rats develop an expectancy that the response is going to lead to another response. Although this idea of expectancy may appear to be mentalistic, in fact Tolman was careful to avoid treating organism variables in that way. At least he was careful to make sure his concepts were operationally defined, which he termed *intervening variables*. However, in a final paper appearing in the year of his death (Tolman, 1959), Tolman reconsidered his own position and suggested that his concepts should be treated as hypothetical constructs rather than intervening variables – following a distinction that had been made some ten years earlier, see the next section. Tolman used concepts that were later used by cognitive psychologist. In retrospect, it is possible to see that Tolman was conflicted between the dominant paradigm and assumptions of behaviourism and the very different assumptions and paradigm of gestalt psychologists with whom he had worked when young.

Hypothetical constructs and intervening variables

Behaviourists allowed only certain sorts of organism variable into their theories, namely those that were operationally defined. The implication is that there are other organism variables, those that are not operationally defined, and which by implication the behaviourists disapproved of. However, it was not until 1948 that this distinction was made formal and this was done in a paper by MacCorquodale and Meehl published in *Psychological Review*. Their paper was titled "On a Distinction Between Hypothetical Constructs and Intervening Variables." MacCorquodale and Meehl proposed two things: First that two distinctly different kinds of organism variable were being used in psychology, and second there should be a linguistic convention for describing these different kinds of organism variable.

MacCorquodale and Meehl's (1948) central argument is that if one accepts the operational definition of a term, then one also has to accept that the term does not refer to an entity that has independent existence beyond its definition. This is not an easy concept for students to grasp, so the easiest way to explain it is to take an example. The example is the concept of intelligence. Intelligence can either be treated as an intervening variable or as a hypothetical construct.

Consider two statements:

1 Intelligence is what intelligence tests measure. (*Here intelligence is treated as an intervening variable.*)
2 Intelligence tests measure intelligence. (*Here intelligence is treated as a hypothetical construct.*)

Statement 1 is an example of an operational definition, because intelligence is defined in terms of its operations, namely, the way it is measured. That is, intelligence is *defined* by the intelligence test. Intelligence is nothing more than the information provided by the intelligence test – it does not exist independently of the intelligence test.

Statement 2 provides a description, not a definition, of how intelligence is measured. It is measured by an intelligence test. But if intelligence is measured by an intelligence test, then intelligence must exist independently of the intelligence test.

The key point made by MacCorquodale and Meehl is that if there is nothing more to an organism variable than its procedures for measurement, then the organism variable should be treated as an intervening variable – i.e., a shorthand summary of that measurement procedure. However, if the organism variable has properties beyond that of measurement *because the organism variable is hypothesised to exist*, then the organism should be called a hypothetical construct. The crucial issue is the hypothesis that something exists independently of its measurement procedures. Hypothetical constructs are organism variables that are hypothesised to exist independently of measurement. They are there whether or not you measure them. Intervening variables are only there if you measure them. They exist only because of the measurement procedures.

Hypothetical constructs are assumed to exist as entities. The technical term is that hypothetical constructs have *ontological status* – there is something 'there.' What exactly it is that is there can be disputed, but the assumption is that there is *something* there. By contrast, intervening variables do not require the assumption of an entity and they do not have ontological status – there is nothing there other than the measurement procedure.

There are two additional features that distinguish hypothetical constructs and intervening variables. First, the description of an intervening variable is precise in that it is defined exactly by its operations. There is nothing more to add than the operational description. Hypothetical constructs are not precisely defined by describing what they do. Hypothetical constructs have 'surplus meaning.' Surplus meaning refers to ways of describing the hypothetical construct without referring to what it does. So, for example, if we were to say that there is a motive, a hypothetical construct, called *achievement motivation* which motivates people to achieve, the implication is that achievement motivation does things other than motivate people to achieve – for example, it may make them more prone to write stories about achievement. The surplus of the hypothetical construct acts as a heuristic that guides future research, and in particular is a source of inspiration for developing new empirical predictions (Hyland, 1981, 1985)

There is yet one more difference between hypothetical constructs and intervening variables. The measurement of the intervening variable is precise; in the case of the hypothetical construct it is only approximate. If it is said that intelligence is what intelligence tests measure, then the measure of intelligence tests provides an exact account of a person's level of intelligence, because that is exactly what intelligence is. There is no measurement error. However, if it is said that intelligence tests measure intelligence, then it is assumed that intelligence exists independently of the test, and the test will never be able to provide a perfect description of that independently existing entity of intelligence.

Why was the paradigm of behaviourism rejected and what is its legacy today?

History is written by the winners. Behaviourism lost its status as a dominant paradigm, cognitive psychology won. Several authors have suggested that Chomsky's criticism of Skinner's explanation of language was the catalyst for change (Virués-Ortega, 2006).

Skinner and Chomsky

Skinner published his book *Verbal Behavior* in 1957, in which he suggested that human language could be understood using the same behavioural principles that governed animal behaviour. The book is largely theoretical. Skinner's book on verbal behaviour (Skinner, 1957) was criticised by Noam Chomsky (1959). Chomsky believed that language developed due to an innate language acquisition device, and so could not be explained simply in terms of associative learning. Although Chomsky's criticisms were themselves widely criticised on the basis that he failed to properly understand learning theory, nevertheless his criticism is widely believed to have heralded the demise of behaviourism (Virués-Ortega, 2006).

The controversy between Skinner and Chomsky was over the explanation for the development of language. Skinner took an environmentalist position that all that was needed were principles of reinforcement and the right circumstances. Chomsky argued that there is a genetic difference between humans and animals, humans having a 'language acquisition device' that enabled the formation of language. Skinner's view was not as simplistic as it is often made out to be (Skinner, 1984a, 1984b), and he did provide a way of explaining language using behaviourist principles. The problem is that just because a theory can explain something does not make that theory true (see Chapter 1). The difficulty Skinner's theory faced was not why humans had language but why other animals, when given all the advantages of language development that humans have (e.g., dogs reared in domestic household), do not develop language. The theory explains some but not all parts of the phenomenon of language.

Given the dominance of behaviourism, given the ubiquity of psychology labs full of rats, is it really likely that the empire of behaviourism was demolished by one theoretical controversy? There are two other good reasons for the demise of behaviourism, one cultural and the other related to types of explanation.

Cultural factors in the rise of cognitive psychology

Behaviourism developed at a particular time in western history. It coincided with the introduction of production lines in factories. In production lines of the 1930s, most workers made simple repetitive movements. Factory workers needed little cognitive input when working. If one is interested in simple repetitive movements, then the assumptions of behaviourist theories make sense. A modern and more familiar example of a simple repetitive movement is that needed when gambling with a slot machine. Research using rats shows that a variable reinforcement schedule produces the most amount of work without reinforcement. So, if a gambling machine is set up to pay out on a random basis, then this is more likely to produce compulsive gambling than one with a fixed reinforcement schedule. Gambling machines are based on reinforcement principles. Reinforcement does work. Furthermore, as the behaviourists found with rats, reinforcement is a better way of controlling behaviour than punishment for humans.

Computers were being developed in the 1950s and 1960s. Computers process information, information that cannot be represented in the form of stimulus-response bonds. A computer stores information that can then be combined with the input to make an output, an output that corresponds to a solution of some problem. The development of computers coincided with the development of cognitive psychology. The technological developments led to a new kind of question that was asked: How do people process information? How do they remember things? The principles of association – the bedrock of behaviourist theory – could not explain information processing. Cognitive psychology differed from behaviourism in that it explained a type of behaviour that behaviourism did not explain.

Behaviourism and cognitive psychology

Behaviourism and cognitive psychology differ in two ways. One is the type of question which is being asked. The other is the type of answer that is being provided. The Skinner-Chomsky debate was a rare case where both were explaining the same phenomenon. The rise of cognitive psychology was not that it was a universally better way of explaining things – it was a new type of question.

Donald Broadbent's book *Perception and Communication* (Broadbent, 1958) was an early influential work in cognitive psychology. Note that this book was written before the Skinner-Chomsky debate about language. The titles of its chapters will be recognised as relevant to a modern psychology course in cognitive psychology – e.g., Chapter 2, 'Selective listening to speech'; Chapter 9, 'Immediate memory and the shifting of attention'; and Chapter 10, 'The selective nature of learning.' Broadbent makes explicit reference to computers in this book showing how ideas developing to understand information processing in computers can be applied to humans. Cognitive psychology, the paradigm to replace behaviourism, arose not because behaviourism was shown to be wrong, but because it addressed a type of question that was relevant to the information age.

Memory versus learning

As an undergraduate I remember being puzzled by two courses with similar names. The course labelled 'learning' taught us about animal learning, and the effect of different reinforcement schedules. The course labelled 'memory' taught us about the difference between long-term and short-term memory in humans. What I did not realise at the time was that one course provided an answer to the question 'how is information retained?' The other answered the question 'how does an animal adapt to its environment?'

Types of explanation

A second reason for the demise of behaviourism was mentioned previously in the evaluation of Hull's theory. The behaviourists did not try to understand underlying mechanisms. By limiting theoretical terms to those that were operationally defined, research took the form of observation followed by explanation. Research was data-led rather than theory-led. Lakatos (see Chapter 1) provides a description of research where theory lags behind data. He described these as having a degenerating problem shift, in contrast to the progressive problem shift where theory precedes data. Cognitive psychology arose from an attempt to try to understand the mechanisms that were responsible for information processing. They speculated about mechanisms.

The idea for a new type of mechanism or a new type of explanation for cognitive science predates Broadbent's (1958) publication by 15 years. Kenneth Craik (1943) provided an elegant argument, which goes like this: The brain controls behaviour, but it is difficult to understand what is happening in the brain. The brain is able to manipulate structures in the outside world through its effect on behaviour. Because events in the brain parallel those external structures, it should be possible to use the structures themselves as the elements of a theory without having to understand the minute details of what is happening in the brain. It is this idea that Broadbent adopts in his book *Perception and Learning* but citing Craik (1948) only in relation to Craik's description of a self-correcting or control system.

Control systems

The idea of a control system is a good example of the application of a mechanical concept to psychology. The feedback loop, the basis of a common thermostat, has been used in several different ways, including motor control (Todorov &

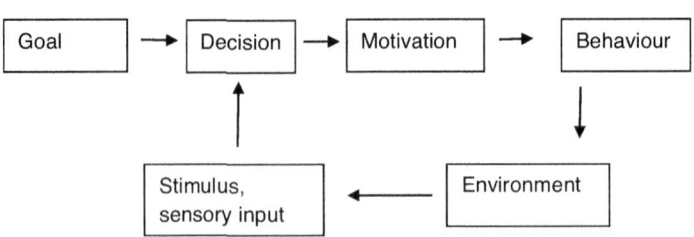

FIGURE 4.1 This figure shows how psychological concepts can be 'modelled' onto the form of a control system.

Jordan, 2002); social, personality, and health psychology (Carver & Scheier, 1982, 1990); and depression (Hyland, 1987). The set point in the thermostat corresponds to a person's goal. The thermometer in the thermostat corresponds to the sensory input. The central heating boiler corresponds to behaviour, and the room temperature to the environment (see Figure 4.1).

Unlike behaviourists, the new cognitive psychologists were comfortable with terms that were not operationally defined, and which MacCorquodale and Meehl (1948) would have been classified as hypothetical constructs but were later referred to as 'person variables' (Hyland, 1985). The hypothesis of, for example, working memory, is based on the assumption that people really do have working memories. Working memory is a structure that has ontological status and is an idea that is derived from computers. The acceptance of person variables soon spread to the rest of psychology. Personality theorists assume that personality constructs really do exist. The term *personality construct* derives from the word *hypothetical construct*. One of the authors in the Mac-Corquodale and Meehl (1948) paper provided an early definition of construct validity (Cronbach & Meehl, 1955). The theoretical terms that come after the behaviourist era are not just a description of data; they provide an explanation in terms of a hypothesised mechanism.

The introduction of the new hypothetical constructs used by cognitive psychologists coincided with the introduction of a new term, *psychological model*. The term *psychological model* is rare before 1950. What does the term *psychological model* mean?

A model car has four wheels like a proper car. The relationship between the four wheels is the same, as is the relationship of the wheels to the rest of the car. Almost everything in the model car looks the same as a proper car, except that the model car is smaller. The relationship between the parts remains the same but the parts themselves are different.

The word *model* is used as a synonym for theory, when the theory is 'modelled' on something else, such as a physical structure. The cognitive theory has the same *form* as the physical technology (i.e., the same relationship between the parts), but different *content* (i.e., the parts are actually different). The word *psychological model* therefore refers to the similarity in form between the psychological theory and something else. In the case of the control theory examples, the psychological theories have the same form as a thermostatic control system, but the content of the theories is different because they refer to the control of psychological phenomena rather than temperature control. The hallmark of cognitive psychology and the new theories that replaced behaviourism was that they used technology as a heuristic for understanding human behaviour (i.e., for modelling theories) and, specifically, information processing (Miller, Galanter & Pribram, 1960).

Behavourism and cognitive psychology

Although behaviourist psychologists investigated topics that were largely outside the remit of modern cognitive psychology, some of their findings were developed subsequently using the theoretical terms of cognitive psychology. For example, the original work on learned helplessness theory was conducted with animals (Seligman & Maier, 1967; Seligman, 1968). Subsequent research with humans showed that learned helplessness altered attributions which then had negative consequences (Abramson, Seligman, & Teasdale, 1978).

Cognitive psychology developed in order to explain how people process information, which was something reinforcement theories were unable to adequately explain. In doing so, cognitive psychology shifted attention away from a notable achievement of behaviourism. Since the work of Thorndike, behaviourists have been able to show that behaviour is controlled by its consequences, so that in their natural habit animals become better adapted to their environment. This idea of adaptation underpins the concepts of reinforcement and habit and can be traced back to the ideas of Darwin (see Chapter 3). An information processing device such as a computer does not behave. The computer does not alter its external environment. Computers do not learn from the consequences of their decisions. They do not adapt to the behaviour of their user – at least, not until very recently (artificial intelligence is discussed in Chapter 10).

Cognitive psychology experiments

Most undergraduates will have been a participant in a cognitive psychology experiment. The student comes into the lab, takes part in a study of learning, reasoning, perception, or whatever cognitive processes are under study, and provides responses, typically on a computer. At the end of the study, the student leaves the lab and gets on with life. There is no long-term change. If you were a rat and reinforced in a T maze for turning left, from then on you would prefer to take left-hand turns. Your behaviour would have been changed.

Although cognitive psychology has not provided a focus on how people adapt to their environments, the theoretical approach initially developed by cognitive psychologists provided the impetus of doing just that, under the heading of deep learning that forms part of artificial intelligence (see Chapter 10). The mechanical analogy can be used as a way of understanding adaptation, but it took the invention of robots for a technology to develop that was capable of behavioural adaptation.

Final thoughts

Behaviourism was an important stage in the development of psychology. It lost its position of dominance because it was no longer seen to be relevant to questions that were being asked as psychology developed. It was a research programme that ran out of steam. Behaviourism was never 'proved wrong' – only shown to be irrelevant to some important questions in psychology, but it developed ideas that are relevant today, and may be relevant for the future. To conclude, here is a quotation from Tolman. Students should interpret it as they wish.

> Rats live in cages; they do not go on binges the night before one has planned an experiment; they do not kill each other off in wars; they do not invent engines of destruction, and, if they did, they would not be so inept about controlling such engines; they do not go in for either class conflicts or race conflicts; they avoid politics, economics, and papers on psychology. They are marvelous, pure, and delightful. And, as soon as I possibly can, I am going to climb back again out on that good old philogenetic limb and sit there, this time right side up and unashamed, wiggling my whiskers at all the silly, yet at the same time far too complicated, specimens of homo sapiens whom I shall see strutting and fighting and messing things up, down there on the ground below me.
>
> (Tolman, 1945, p. 166)

Summary

Behaviourism arose because of a failure of the introspective method to explain behaviour. Behaviourists shared the common assumption that animal and human behaviour had the same causes, and so the study of rats could be used to develop explanations of human behaviour. Methodological behaviourism, radical behaviourism, and neobehaviourism are based on different assumptions. These assumptions relate to the type of the theoretical term, if any, used to explain behaviour. Behaviourism was superseded by cognitive psychology because the former failed to adequately account for information processing, an aspect of human behaviour that became increasingly important after the development of computers and because the operational definition of theoretical terms created a degenerating problem shift. Cognitive psychology introduced mechanistic person variables into explanations, using theoretical terms that are described in terms of technology including the technology of computers.

Essay questions

1 Why did Skinner reject theoretical terms? What were the advantages and disadvantages of doing so?
2 Compare and contrast methodological behaviourism, radical behaviourism, and neobehaviourism.
3 Why did cognitive psychology arise, and how and what does it explain?

5

Is psychoanalysis scientific, what are its assumptions, why is therapy effective, and what is the legacy of psychoanalysis today?

To many members of the general public, Freud is the most famous psychologist of all time. Yet, Freud was not a psychologist, and some academic psychologists have a very low opinion of Freud. This chapter examines the concepts that underpin psychoanalysis and describes their origins and relevance today.

Paradigms of medicine

Freud's significance in the history of science is that he initiated a paradigm shift. It was a paradigm shift within the discipline of medicine, not within psychology. Freud trained as a medical doctor: He received no training in psychology. To understand what this paradigm shift was and why it was so significant, it is necessary to know about the medical paradigm that Freud rejected.

The paradigm of modern western medicine is based on the assumption that the body is a kind of biological machine. Like any other machine, the body develops faults, and these faults can be corrected by doctors. The faults are referred to as *pathophysiology*. Diseases are defined by different types of fault, each disease having its own, unique and specific pathophysiology. The theories of medicine are biological theories, each theory showing how different parts of the body can go wrong to create disease.

The paradigm of modern western medicine developed gradually, starting in the 17th century. Early support for the paradigm came from the observation that there were anatomical differences between people who were healthy and those with disease. Later, tissue differences and eventually, with the development of powerful microscopes, cellular differences were discovered between those with and without disease.

Before the 20th century, the main alternative to modern western medicine was Hippocratic medicine. Hippocratic medicine assumes that to be healthy it was necessary to balance the four bodily humours, black bile, yellow bile, phlegm, and blood, and that the same imbalance can create many different diseases. Hippocratic medicine had lost favour by the end of the 19th century when Freud was working. The pathologist Rudolf Virchow (1821–1902) was famous for his declaration that there was no such thing as a non-specific illness (the basis for Hippocratic medicine) only specific illness (the basis of modern western medicine).

Nearly all diseases known today had been identified by the end of the 19th century. However, there was a group of diseases where, despite best endeavours, there was no evidence of pathophysiology. This group of diseases was given the collective name of 'nervous diseases' because it was assumed that they were diseases of the nervous system. Nervous diseases included melancholia (i.e., depression), mania, hysterical paralysis, and lunacy. Only one nervous disease had its pathophysiology identified – the one named after its discoverer, Alois Alzheimer – and that discovery was published in 1906, a short while after Freud had presented his new ideas.

Doing more harm than good

Homeopathy was another contender for a paradigm of medicine in the 19th century. In fact, homeopathy was particularly successful in treating typhoid. The reason was this. Those working in general hospitals noticed that people sweated a lot when they had typhoid. They reasoned that the bodies of people with typhoid had too much water, and so treatment involved depriving the patient of drink. Homeopaths did not deprive patients of water and gave treatments that were ultra-diluted and therefore did no harm (they may even have done good via the placebo effect). Much of medical treatment in the 19th century did more harm than good. This example illustrates an important principle (also relevant to Freud): Just because the paradigm is a good one, it does not follow that the theory is correct.

Freud's new paradigm

Sigmund Freud (1856–1939) studied medicine at the University of Vienna, receiving his MD in 1881. As a student, Freud had worked on the structure of nerves, but would have been aware that no pathophysiology had been discovered for nervous diseases. In 1893 Freud formed a friendship with a Viennese physician, Josef Breuer (1842–1925) who had been treating patients with neuroses with a 'talking cure' and learned how Breuer had treated Anna O. In 1895–1896 Freud was awarded a research grant that enabled him to visit J. M. Charcot (1825–1893) in France who had been treating symptoms of hysteria with hypnosis. Charcot, however, assumed a purely biological cause – his research included detailed photographs of his (largely women) patients, because he felt the physical appearance of the patients held a clue to their illness (De Marneffe, 1991). As a young man, Freud had been exposed to two worlds, one where nervous diseases were treated as a fault with the nerves, and one where non-biological treatments had benefit.

In 1895 Freud completed two works, one based on the existing paradigm and the one for which he was to become famous. In his *Project for Scientific Psychology* (Freud, 1895a) (but published posthumously), Freud predicts that the brain would provide the answer to 'psychical' phenomena – and therefore nervous diseases. This work presents the standard medical paradigm (Lothane, 1998). However, he also published a book with Breuer, a book with the title *Studies in Hysteria* (Breuer was the first author), where several case histories are explored, each being successfully cured by the talking cure, and where Freud presents ideas about a new way of understanding nervous diseases (Freud, 1895b).

The paradigm shift initiated by Freud was simple. Instead of assuming that symptoms were caused by a biological abnormality, the abnormality should be described in terms of psychology. That psychological abnormality, for example, repressed memories, results from events in the patient's life. The abnormality could be corrected by talking about those events. Freud was aware that the two paradigms were competing ways of explaining and treating nervous diseases. Notice that the new psychological paradigm was consistent with the biological paradigm of modern western medicine in defining disease with a specific abnormality associated with symptoms – in contrast to Hippocratic medicine where the imbalance was non-specific. So, although Freud's paradigm was new, it shared something with the old – the idea of a fault.

Hippocratic medicine

According to those working in the Hippocratic tradition of the early 19th century, madness was caused by excessive phlegm. So were respiratory problems. Madness and respiratory problems were treated by the same 'cure,' the vomiting cure, where the patient was made to vomit. If someone was made to vomit every time they exhibited mad behaviour, it is not too surprising that this 'cure' sometimes worked. As for respiratory complaints, there is no possible reason why vomiting could help.

Historians have speculated as to why Freud rejected a biological interpretation of what came to be known as mental illness, and instead adopt a psychological one. They are just speculations, but here are two of them.

The first is that Freud was aware of the very harmful effects of those who were using biological interventions. At least, he would have become aware from his association with Wilhelm Fliess (1858–1928), a nose and throat specialist in Berlin. Fliess attended one of Freud's lectures and struck up a friendship. Fliess believed that all manner of problems were caused by the nose – he even operated on Freud's nose. It wasn't long before Fliess convinced Freud that nervous diseases had their origin in the nose. Freud sent Fliess one of his patients, Anna Eckstein, whom Freud had diagnosed with hysteria. Fliess operated, but within a month Anna was at the point of death due to a botched operation – some gauze was left in her nose. The relationship between Freud and Fliess cooled. Fliess accused Freud of stealing his theories, and Freud asked for all correspondence between them to be destroyed (which wasn't possible as Fliess had sold them). Perhaps, because of this, Freud was aware of the danger of biological treatments for nervous diseases (Zucker & Wiegand, 1988).

A second possible reason that motivated Freud to reject a biological explanation was that the biological explanation was strongly connected with the view that mental illness was hereditary (see Chapter 7). There was then a widespread view in Vienna that Jews were degenerate, and that they suffered from mental illness because of their poor heredity. Hitler did not invent anti-Semitism. Hitler visited Vienna in 1908 and was impressed by the mayor's strongly expressed anti-Semitic views. Freud was Jewish – though non-practicing – and he was aware of anti-Semitism and this negative view of Jewish heredity. Explaining mental illness in terms of events, not heredity, therefore provided a counter-argument to the view that Jews tended towards mental defectiveness.

Freud introduced a new paradigm where mental illness was explained in terms of psychological theory, but he also introduced a theory within that paradigm. It is that theory that is controversial. Later psychologists used the same paradigm of a psychological fault, but with different theories and different types of fault. For example cognitive psychologists explained mental illness in terms of erroneous cognitions. It is possible that even if Freud had not developed his theory and paradigm, later psychologists would have developed their theories of mental illness anyway. It is impossible to tell. An environmental approach to treating mental illness was developed in the USA in the early 20th century independently of Freud (see Chapter 3), but there was no specific treatment other than the idea of an improved environment. The early American clinical psychologists measured but did not treat patients.

Although Freud was not a psychologist, his reputation became such that he was invited to visit the psychologists at Clark University in the USA in 1909. The invitation was given by Stanley Hall, the American who founded the American Psychological Association (see Chapter 3). The invitation included one of Freud's students, Carl Jung, who was also becoming well known. Psychoanalysis soon became part of the content of psychology courses, so it comes as no surprise that Freud was and is perceived as a psychologist by the general public. By the 1920s Freud's and Jung's theories featured in standard text books in psychology, such as Tansley's *The New Psychology* (Tansley, 1920) and McDougall's *Outline of Psychology* (McDougall, 1923).

Freud and the unconscious

In addition to suggesting that mental illness had a psychological cause, Freud also proposed the idea of the unconscious. To what extent was this idea novel? Psychologists working within the Würzburg school had already established that some voluntary action and some kinds of problem solving were carried out without conscious awareness (see Chapter 4). The idea that people were not able to introspect some psychological processes was already established, though it is unlikely that Freud would have been aware of this research. If the term *unconscious* is equated with *non-introspectable* then the concept is uncontroversial and consistent with ideas in current psychology. For example, Kahneman (2011) showed that there are two ways in which people make judgements, one non-introspectable, fast and 'automatic,' called System 1, and one slow and deliberate in the sense that the process can be introspected and reported, called System 2. Non-introspectable intuitive processes are also a feature of connectionist psychology (Greenwald, 1992). The idea of implicit attitudes and the implicit attitude test (IAT) are based on a theory that people have attitudes that are not introspectable, or at least, that they do not report accurately. These later authors did not derive their ideas from Freudian theory, but the parallel with Freud is obvious.

The idea that some mental processes are unconscious or non-introspectable is only part of Freud's concept of the unconscious. Not only did Freud suggest that people had unconscious desires but he also suggested that these desires were in conflict with other desires. One novel feature of Freud's theory of the unconscious was that it was a theory of mental conflict, a conflict that occurs at an unconscious level. The idea of conflict between desires is not specific to Freud. Ethologists subsequent to Freud noted that animals exhibited 'approach-avoidance conflict' when a goal has both positive and negative consequences, and psychological conflicts whether conscious or not also feature in modern psychotherapeutic approaches. The uniqueness of Freud's contribution is not in the existence of the unconscious, nor in the existence of conflict, but it is in the specifics of each of these.

In summary, Freud not only presents the idea of the unconscious, but also the idea of particular mechanisms occurring at an unconscious level. The idea of mechanisms occurring at an unconscious level is not only plausible but supported by evidence. The autonomic nervous system is complex and functions without the help of conscious awareness. However, the unconscious mechanisms used in later theories are very different from the mechanisms proposed by Freud. It is Freud's mechanisms in the unconscious, not the concept of the unconscious or non-introspectability, that are controversial.

Freud, sex, and the seduction hypothesis

It cannot have escaped the notice of even the most inattentive student that Freud's theory has a strong emphasis on sex. Why is this and where did it come from? To understand the sexual element of Freud's theory, it is necessary to know something about Viennese society at the end of the 19th century.

Nineteenth century Vienna was a mix of two societies. The first was the establishment made up of people whose parents, grandparents, and great-grandparents lived in Vienna. The establishment was bourgeois in the sense that it was respectable and comfortable with its respectability. The Hapsburg court was at the top of the establishment and presented itself as very respectable. Sex before marriage was not considered respectable. It was a society of 'high moral fibre.' The second society was made up of immigrants from the East. These immigrants, mainly

Poles and Jews, came to Vienna for the same reasons immigrants travel today: a mix of economic opportunity and escaping from danger. It was more dangerous to be Jewish in the East than in Vienna in the 19th century (in Russia, Jews were massacred through pogroms). Freud was born in Czechoslovakia and his family arrived when Freud was four years old. The immigrants brought with them new energy and creative ideas in art. These immigrants included Gustav Klimt and his student Egon Schiele. Klimt shocked Viennese society by his art, which was modern and sexually explicit in a way that had not been seen before. Schiele also painted pictures that were at the time considered pornographic.

There was therefore a mix of two societies in 19th-century Vienna. One respectable, rule following, and sexually inhibited, and the other rule breaking and sexually liberated. It will immediately strike the student of psychology that there is a parallel between this society and Freud's concepts of the id and super-ego. The conflict between sexual energy and repression was all around him. There is also an interesting development in Freud's concept of the id. The id is a kind of instinct: It makes you want to do things. Freud originally thought there was one desire called the Libido. The Libido is the sexual instinct. Later (after 1921) Freud thought there were two instincts, Eros and Thanatos. Eros is similar to the Libido in that it drives people to sexual activity. Thanatos is the death instinct – it drives people to kill others. Thanatos as a concept arose after the First World War, a war when people killed each other but in greater numbers than before. It would appear that Freud's theories mirrored his experience of society.

Later authors working within the psychoanalytic tradition accepted the idea that there was a 'bad' element to people, but did not assume the over-arching connection with sex. For example, Jung proposed that each person had a 'shadow.' The shadow was bad in the sense that it encouraged bad desires that were not necessarily sexual. Jung proposed that recognition of these desires ('confronting the shadow') is important for well-being.

Where Freud got his concept of the id from is unclear. A similar idea had been proposed shortly before by the philosopher Schopenhauer, though Freud reported that he had not read Schopenhauer. However the idea of 'the bad within all of us' is repeated many times in literature and philosophy. In book 9 of Plato's republic (Plato, 380 BCE approximately) there is a description of desires that occur when people dream.

> When the rest of the soul, the reasoning, gentle and ruling part of it is asleep, then the bestial and savage part . . . begins to leap about, pushes sleep aside, and tries to go and gratify its instincts. . . . It does not shrink from attempting incestual intercourse in its dream, with a mother or with any man or god or beast. It is ready for any deed of blood, and there is no unhallowed food it will not eat.
>
> (Plato, book IX)

The relationship with the Oedipus complex is clear from this quote, and Freud reported that he based his concept of sexuality on Plato's concept of

Eros – though there are clear differences (Sandford, 2006). The idea of the 'bad within' is also a feature of Buddhist philosophy which presents the idea that people have bad desires and that controlling these desires is important to happiness: Desire is the root of sorrow (Rahula, 1959)

In addition to philosophers who recognise that people have a 'dark side,' this idea appears in literature. The short novel *The Strange Case of Dr Jekyll and Mr Hyde* was published by Robert Louis Stevenson in 1886 (Stevenson, 1886) and anticipates Freud's ideas. The story tells of a good man, Dr Jekyll, who, with a mysterious medicine, is transferred into a very bad man, Mr Hyde. The assumption that humans are basically bad assumes a degree of genetic determinism that may not (or may) be entirely justified, but it is clear that the idea of a bad part of the psyche, which is a characteristic of both Freud and Jung, has a long history.

It is easy to dismiss Freud's preoccupation with sex as a reflection on his own life and society, but the evidence suggests that Freud did find references to sex in his sessions with patients. Among the more controversial of these references was that young women would report sexual contact with adults when they were children. Freud interpreted this child-adult sexual contact as damaging to the child, and the idea became referred to as the seduction hypothesis. Freud later changed his mind suggesting that women imagined sexual abuse rather than experiencing it.

Historians have disagreed as to why Freud changed his mind. Masson (1984), in a book entitled *The Assault on Truth: Freud's Suppression of the Seduction Theory*, argues that Freud abandoned the idea because of social pressure from his colleagues who were unwilling to countenance the possibility of sexual exploitation of children. Freud certainly refers to negative reactions in some of his letters. More recently Esterson (2002a, 2002b) argued that child sexual exploitation was recognised at the time but that Freud's colleagues rejected it as a cause of mental illness. According to Esterson, Freud's change of mind reflected Freud's own conviction that his original interpretation was wrong. Whatever the reason, Freud changed his mind on this point, but the association between sexual abuse of children and mental health problems had been established. In the novel written by F. Scott Fitzgerald, *Tender Is the Night*, published in 1934, part of the story concerns a young psychiatrist who treats a young woman who has been sexually molested by her father with resulting mental illness. Thus, although Freud may have retracted his theory, he drew attention to something that eventually became recognised as true and is reflected in the literature on child abuse today.

What was the talking cure?

Freud influenced others through his books and other forms of writing. Like health professionals who write books for the general public today, some of those books included accounts of 'patients I have treated and cured.' It is these case studies that provide insight into how Freud treated his patients.

When Freud referred to his patients, he gave them pseudonyms to protect their identity. Later historians have been able to track down who these people really were and find out more about their history – and whether Freud really cured them. The following are a selection of case studies published at different times in Freud's career.

The case of Anna O

The case of Anna O is one of the best known of Freud's case studies and is the first case where he describes the success of the talking cure. Anna O was treated initially by Breuer and described in Breuer and Freud's 1893 and 1895 publications (Breuer & Freud, 1893/1955, 1895/1955).

Anna O was really Bertha Pappenheim, a young Jewish woman who developed symptoms that included a nervous cough while caring for her seriously ill father. Because of her cough, Bertha was prevented from caring for her father. She first visited Breuer in 1880. Her symptoms progressed, including paralysis and mood fluctuation, deteriorating still further, including anorexia, when her father died in 1881. Breuer introduced Bertha to Freud in 1883, but had stopped treating her in June 1882. Breuer stopped treating Bertha because the amount of time he devoted to Bertha (who was an attractive young women) had come to the notice of his wife. Also, Bertha felt an emotional bond with Breuer. Correspondence between Freud and Breuer's wife shows how Freud first noticed what he later called *transference* and *counter-transference*, something that Freud was to develop in his later work. These terms refer to the observation that patients can transfer their affections to the therapist, and therapist can reciprocate with feelings towards patients, both of which can create considerable problems. The evidence from correspondence shows that Breuer behaved professionally throughout but felt guilty about the situation (Forrester, 1986).

Breuer and Freud wrote in their 'preliminary communication' published in 1893:

> For we found to our great surprise at first, that each individual hysterical symptom immediately and permanently disappeared when we had succeeded in bringing clearly to light the memory of the event by which it was provoked and in arousing the companying affect, and when the patient had described that event in the greatest possible detail and had put the affect into words.
>
> (Breuer and Freud, 1893/1955, pp. 6–7)

Ellenberger (1972) however, suggests that although some symptoms did subside, the overall treatment of Bertha by Breuer was not successful. There are three factors that lead to this conclusion. First, although notes were taken during consultation, the case was written up many years after Breuer and Freud had stopped treating Bertha. Second, Bertha was prescribed morphine and chloral hydrate (probably by Breuer) and she was maintained on these drugs till she recovered. Third, despite starting treatment with Breuer in 1880, she was hospitalised in 1881 – her name appears in the register of patients in a hospital in Vienna. It was only in 1882 when she was in hospital that any attempt was made to wean her off the drugs – which may have been contributing to the worsening of her symptoms in the first place.

De Paula Ramos (2003) says "After a review of Bertha's clinical picture, it is clear that the vast majority of her symptoms . . . are compatible with dependence on a nonbarbiturate sedative and narcotics" (p. 46).

Despite later evidence that Bertha's treatment was not as successful as Breuer had suggested, this early case provided the impetus for Freud to develop his later theories and treatment. It is significant, however, that Breuer notes in this case study that "the element of sexuality was astonishingly undeveloped." The emphasis on sexuality, which forms an important part of Freud's later case studies, is missing in this first case study.

The case of Dora

The case study of Dora (real name Ida Bauer) was published by Freud in 1905 (Freud, 1905/1955). It is in this publication that Freud suggests that dreams represent repressed desires and that hysterical symptoms are the result of repressed desires. Dora – or Ida – fitted the description of a hysterical girl. She was 18 years old, was depressed and had episodes when she lost her voice. By all accounts her family life was chaotic – including a father who was having an affair with the wife of the couple for whom she babysat, and where the husband of the couple propositioned her from the age of 14. Ida first visited Freud in 1898. Freud analysed her dreams and interpreted her problems as being due to repressed desire for her father, and both members of the couple for whom she babysat. Ida rejected this interpretation and ceased analysis. However, her father encouraged her to return in 1900. After further analysis of her dreams, combined with Freud's interpretation, her symptoms reduced and Freud reports that she felt there was some truth in what Freud had said. Others have suggested that this case illustrates that Ida got better when she matured sufficiently to stand up to Freud and the group of dysfunctional characters who made up her life (Decker, 1991). This case is often cited because Freud emphasises a sexual element that at first the patient rejects and then comes to accept.

The case of the wolf man

Freud published the case of the 'wolf man' in 1918 (Freud, 1918/1955). The wolf man was in fact Sergei Pankejeff, a Russian aristocrat. Sergei came to Freud because he was very depressed and constipated. Both Sergei's father and sister had committed suicide due to depression, and, when young, Sergei had a fear of animals. The label 'wolf man' comes from a repeating dream reported by Sergei where he saw six or seven white wolves outside his bedroom window. He was afraid of being eaten by the wolves, screamed, and woke up. Freud's interpretation was that the source of Sergei's problems was his relationship with his father, who Sergei admired because he believed him to be a perfect gentleman. Freud believed that in reality Sergei suffered from castration anxiety, was frightened of his father and interpreted this dream as being caused by Sergei seeing his parents having sexual intercourse – though he later suggested that Sergei might have witnessed copulation between animals that then generalised to his parents. Sergei was not impressed by this interpretation. After all, young children in well-off families did not sleep in the room of their parents but with a nanny. Freud treated Sergei over a period of four years (1910–1914) and claimed to have cured him, but the evidence suggests that Sergei was in and out of treatment throughout his long life – he lived until he was 92 years old (May, 1990).

The case of Little Hans

Little Hans (in fact Herbert Graf) was a four-year-old boy who developed a fear of horses. Freud treated Herbert primarily using the father as an intermediary, and published his analysis in 1909 (Freud, 1909/1955). Freud was convinced that this fear of horses stemmed from hostility towards the father and an unresolved Oedipal conflict. Herbert had pointed out to his mother that horses have 'widdlers' and that his mother did not have one – i.e., he was aware of sexual differences. His mother had previously told Herbert not to play with his widdler – "If you play with your widdler, Dr A will cut if off and then what will you have to widdle with?" This admonition by his mother led to an association of castration anxiety and horses. Freud believed that Herbert associated horses with his father as Herbert told him he particularly didn't like horses with black bits in their mouths – which Freud assumed was a symbolic representation of his father's moustache. According to Freud's interpretation, whenever Herbert saw a horse he was reminded of his hostility towards his father, his love for his mother, and this produced fear of castration. The very long and detailed case history provides lengthy descriptions of conversations with Herbert and his interest in widdlers, and who did or did not have them. Herbert is unlikely to be the first young boy who, when presented with a younger sister, was surprised to find she had no widdler – or as Herbert put it, "it is very small but it would grow."

An entirely different explanation might be that Herbert saw a horse and cart fall down in the street and became afraid simply due to associative learning (compare with Watson's account of Little Albert, Chapter 4, children are afraid of loud noises). Students can make their own mind as to whether the Freudian or behaviourist explanations of Little Hans is more likely.

There is a rather nice postscript to the Little Hans story, as most people reading it would have assumed that Little Hans would grow up to be a big Hans with lots of psychological problems. In fact, in 1922 Herbert Graf visited Freud at the age of 19 and told him that he was Little Hans – Freud having lost contact for at least 10 years. Herbert Graf (or big Hans) was a perfectly happy and well-adjusted young man. So, if a child of yours develops an interest in his widdler, there is nothing to worry about.

Freud concludes his case study with this postscript that was added to the original case study:

> One piece of information given me by little Hans struck me as particularly remarkable; nor do I venture to give any explanation of it. When he read his case history, he told me, the whole of it came to him as something unknown; he did not recognize himself.
>
> (Freud, 1909/1955, p. 148)

Whereas Freud interpreted this as amnesia associated with the case, students might like to come to their own conclusion.

Why does the talking cure work?

Despite doubts over some of Freud's case studies, Freud was undoubtedly successful in treating patients. He was nominated for the Nobel prize 13 times between 1915 and 1938 but was never awarded it (Stolt, 2001). His reputation would not have occurred without success as a therapist. Freud described his psychoanalysis as a form of archaeology. He tried to find out what happened in the past to the patient, primarily using dream analysis but also by examining other forms of description provided by the patient. This type of analysis has three important features. First, Freud provided his patients with a narrative. The narrative explains how patients got ill and how they can get better. Second, Freud provided patients with an opportunity to talk about themselves. Patients talked about themselves to someone who was prepared to listen, someone who was prepared to take a good deal of interest in the life of the patient. Third, Freud provided patients with the expectation that they would get better as Freud was perceived as an expert. These three features are in fact shared with *all* psychotherapies. Whatever the approach taken by psychotherapists, there is always a narrative, there is always a relationship with a clinician, and there is always the expectation of therapeutic benefit. One possible interpretation is that the success of psychoanalysis is not in the truth of the particular narrative given, but the fact that there *is* a narrative, and the narrative is accompanied by a caring health professional who gives the patient the expectation of recovery.

By the 1930s there was a sufficient variety of different types of psychotherapy for Saul Rosenzweig to carry out a review. His review was published in 1936 with the title *Some Implicit Common Factors in Divers Methods of Psychotherapy: "At Last the Dodo Said, 'Everybody Has Won and All Must Have Prizes.'"* Rosenzweig was quoting from the children's story *Alice in Wonderland*, and illustrated an extraordinary finding: All the different psychotherapies were equally effective.

Talking therapy.

The finding that 'all psychotherapies produce equivalent outcomes' has come to be known as the Dodo bird effect. Despite the invention of newer therapies, the results have remained the same: Recent reviews and meta-analyses come to the same conclusion, and the Dodo bird effect remains alive and well today (Wampold, 2013). Irrespective of whether the psychotherapy is psychoanalytic, or cognitive (for example, cognitive behaviour therapy) or humanistic, the results, on average, are similar and possibly identical. All therapies work, and any differences, *on average*, between the effectiveness of different therapies is small. Interestingly, believing in your therapy is one factor that seems to help the outcome – and this is known as the allegiance effect. Therapists need to have 'allegiance' to a therapy to be effective (Wampold, 2013). The common factors explanation of psychotherapy (also known as the contextual model) is that it is the factors that are common to all psychotherapies, not the therapy-specific factors that create therapeutic change.

So what are the common factors of psychotherapy? These have been identified (Frank & Frank, 1991) as

1   An emotionally charged, confiding relationship with a helping person.
2   A setting where the patient believes they are being helped and therefore expects to get better.
3   A rationale, conceptual scheme, or myth that provides a plausible explanation for the patient's symptoms and prescribes a ritual or procedure for resolving them.
4   A ritual or procedure that requires the active participation of both patient and therapist and that is believed by both to be the means of restoring the patient's health.

Frank and Frank (1991) argue that the narrative or conceptual scheme does not have to be true. It just has to be accepted as true by the patients. It is clear from Freud's case studies that Freud provided all of the above. Patients describe their dreams. Freud provides a conceptual scheme for analysing the dreams that is then discussed with the patients. Freud undoubtedly helped patients with his talking cure and at the very least spared them some of the more harmful forms of biological therapy – vomiting therapy, nasal operations, strong psychoactive substances etc. – that came from a biological explanation of nervous diseases. Freud introduced the idea of a 'talking cure' to the world of medicine. Talking therapies are now an accepted part of treatment for people with mental illness, but exactly *why* talking cures help is a matter of considerable debate even today and is beyond the scope of this book.

One of the lasting contributions of that Freud introduced were the concepts of transference and counter-transference (see the case of Anna O). Modern psychotherapists and counsellors are taught to recognise that patients can develop emotional feelings towards their therapists, and that therapists can develop emotional feelings towards their clients. Freud's recognition of this phenomenon – and the need to manage it – provides evidence that he had insight into the therapeutic process and an ability to recognise that which may not always be comfortable to recognise.

Scientific status of Freud's theories

Freud was writing books before Karl Popper proposed the criterion of falsifiability as a criterion for science. When Freud was writing, the assumed scientific model was one of induction. Theories should be induced from data. This point needs to be borne in mind when evaluating the scientific status of Freud's work.

Freud's theories have been criticised in two different ways. One criticism is that the theories are unfalsifiable and therefore unscientific. The other is that the theories are false – i.e., that there is evidence that is inconsistent with the theory and therefore falsifies it. At first sight both criticisms cannot be true. If something is false, then it has been falsified, so it cannot be unfalsifiable. Both criticisms could be true because Freud presents a number of different ideas.

Freud's ideas are based on assumptions. Some of these assumptions are the same, albeit with different theories, as those of modern psychology. There is an assumption that mental illness can be explained with non-biological or psychological concepts, and that events in a person's life can predict mental illness. There is an assumption that psychological processes can occur without conscious awareness. There is an assumption that talking therapies are effective for mental illness. These metatheoretical assumptions are comparatively uncontroversial because they are accepted today, though with other theories. It is the specifics of the theories themselves that create problems in terms of scientific evaluation.

Some of Freud's ideas can be inferred from his case studies where he interprets symptoms in terms of a narrative, a narrative that typically involves sexuality. These interpretations are unfalsifiable. The statement 'some swans are green' is unfalsifiable because there may be green swans on planet Zog (see Chapter 1), and so is the statement 'sex is sometimes an important factor in a patient's symptoms.' Also, Freud asserts that the psychoanalyst has superior insight into the patient's mind, so whatever the psychoanalyst says is true. The psychoanalyst's conclusion is unfalsifiable. If tonight you dream of a pen, it may be that the pen is a phallic symbol. Alternatively, it may that a pen is simply a pen. There is no independent criterion for establishing whether either statement is false. If you call me a grumpy old man, and I tell you that you are projecting your own faults on me, there is no criterion for you to argue that my criticism of you is false. Their unfalsifiability makes Freudian statements of this kind difficult to counter.

Freud's theory is not so much a theory as a narrative that is used to interpret observation. Much of it corresponds to what Royce and Powell (1983) call 'philosophic speculation' (see Chapter 1). There is not much theory in Freud's theory.

Freud's idea of psychic energy is based on the concept of catharsis. Freud suggested that psychic energy accumulated and that this energy required a release in some form or another, and failure to release this energy creates symptoms. Sublimation is an acceptable way of releasing energy. For example, playing football is a way of 'sublimating' the aggressive energy of the id. The prediction from catharsis theory is that people should be less aggressive after playing football. Despite considerable cultural support for the idea of catharsis, experimental research has found the reverse to be the case (Bushman, 2002; Bushman, Baumeister, & Stack, 1999). The theory of catharsis as part of Freud's theory is false, even though talking about traumatic events can be helpful.

History of catharsis

The idea of catharsis stems from the days of Ancient Rome. The rulers of Rome believed that the common people were happy fighting wars and if there were no wars, the people would become restless. The assumption of the Roman Games was that if the common people saw something aggressive happening, then they would be less likely to be restless and aggressive. Seeing Christians thrown to the lions would make the common people more docile and more easily managed by their rulers

---

Much of Freud's theory of personality is unfalsifiable. According to this theory, the oral, anal, and phallic personalities form due to either under- or over-stimulation at each of the stages of the erogenous zones. So, for example, the oral personality (needy, dependent on others, always pleading for help) is the result of either too little or too much oral stimulation below the age of two years, the anal personality from too harsh or too lenient potty training, and the phallic personality from failure to resolve the Oedipus conflict. It should be apparent that determining over- or under-stimulation is more or less impossible. This aspect of the theory is so weak (see Chapter 1) that it amounts to being unfalsifiable. Additionally, Freud's theory of personality suggests that certain personality traits go together. So, for example, tidiness, meanness, and obstinacy are the features of the anal personality – also referred to as the 'anal triad.' If these three traits are found to coincide, then the conclusion drawn is that the person is the anal type, but if they are not found to coincide, then the conclusion is that the person is not the anal type. Whatever is found is consistent with the theory and so this aspect of the theory is also unfalsifiable.

One final empirical argument in support of Freud's ideas is that psychoanalysis is effective, as demonstrated by the continuation of psychoanalysis as a form of therapy today. The counter-argument is that psychoanalysis is effective because the common factors model applies to any psychotherapy. Cognitive behaviour therapy (CBT) is sometimes described as the most tested and validated of all psychotherapies. This is perfectly true. More studies have been conducted showing that CBT is effective than the number of studies showing that other types of psychotherapy are effective. What the data do not show convincingly is that CBT is more effective than any other psychotherapy (Wampold, 2013). The finding that therapy is effective provides only weak corroborating evidence for both psychoanalysis and CBT.

A possible conclusion about the scientific status of Freud's ideas is that some of them are true, some of them are untrue, and some of them are unfalsifiable. Freud did not test his ideas with independent data, but he was writing at a time before the scientific criterion of falsifiability was proposed and accepted. Freud followed the science of the time in making observations and then providing a theory that was consistent with those observations. The need to test that theory, the hallmark of modern science, came later. With the hindsight of history, it is possible to say that Freud was a good scientist in developing speculative theory. His failure was in assuming that theory was correct. It is the ability to speculate, to test, to find lacking and then to start again or modify that makes a good scientist.

Freud, Jung, and their theories of personality

Carl Gustav Jung (1875–1961) studied medicine at the University of Basel, obtained his degree in 1900, and became a lecturer in psychiatry at the same university in 1905. Jung read Freud's book *Interpretation of Dreams* in 1900, and the two men began corresponding in 1906, with Jung meeting Freud for the first time a year later. The two set up an immediate friendship. Together the two men were invited to attend a conference organised at Clark University by Stanley Hall in 1909 – but with the recognition by Hall that Freud was the more eminent of the two (Evans & Koelsch, 1985). During the trip over the Atlantic, the relationship between Freud and Jung began to break down. According to Jung, this was due to Freud's refusal to be analysed by Jung – Jung had been analysed by Freud but Freud felt that the reverse was unacceptable due to his higher status. There were several other reasons for the breakdown between the two men, including personal issues – Jung felt Freud's addiction to smoking was bad and Jung disagreed with Freud's emphasis on sexuality.

The relationship between Jung and Freud was to break down fully in 1912. In a letter to Freud, Jung wrote

> If ever you should rid yourself entirely of your complexes and stop playing the father to your sons, and instead of aiming continually at their weak spots take a good look at your own for a change, then I will mend my ways and at one stroke uproot the vice of being in two minds about you.
>
> (Jung on December 18, 1912)

Freud and Jung both developed theories of personality that were in some ways similar and some ways very different. Both theories were type theories. Both are inventions by their respective authors on the basis of their personal experience, but without independent data. Freud's types were the oral type, the anal type, and the phallic type (see the previous section). Type theories can be contrasted with trait theories. Modern theories of personality are trait theories. In a type theory a person is either the type or not the type – it is a binary classification. For example, a person either has the oral personality or doesn't have the oral personality, but cannot be somewhere in between. In the case of modern personality theories (e.g., the Big Five personality theory), a person varies along a dimension such as extraversion-introversion. Type theories reflect a medical tradition of diagnosis. A person either has a disease or does not have a disease. In fact, for some diseases (e.g., asthma) it is possible to be have 'a little of the disease' whereas others are clearly binary (e.g., Type 1 diabetes), but nevertheless the medical tradition is one that puts people into categories. Where there is a physiological continuum (as in the case of asthma) medical doctors apply a cut-off point to determine whether or not the person has the disease.

Jung's personality types are different from Freud's in that there is no attempt to explain them in terms of developmental stages. Jung distinguishes four types of mental function, *Thought* (i.e., rational judgement, true or false), the opposite of which is *Feeling* (i.e., emotional judgement, nice or nasty), and *Sensation* (i.e., understanding the detail of things), the opposite of which is *Intuition* (i.e., understanding the inner potential of things).

Jung suggested that whatever function occurs in the conscious, the opposite occurs in the unconscious. So the personality type of a person who is dreaming is different from the personality type of a person when awake. In addition to his four psychological functions, Jung proposed two mental attitudes (again, these are types not traits). The mental attitudes were extraversion (i.e., a tendency to respond positively in uncertainty) versus introversion (i.e., a tendency to respond negatively in uncertainty).

Jung's theory has a number of other differences from Freud's. Jung was interested in similarities between different cultures and hypothesised the existence of a 'collective unconscious' which he distinguished from the 'personal unconscious.' The collective unconscious is responsible for symbols that are universal to all people. The idea of a collective unconscious is dismissed by most psychologists today, though a minority claim empirical evidence in support of the concept (e.g., Ivonin et al., 2015; Rosen, Smith, Huston, & Gonzalez, 1991).

Freud's theory of personality is not used in personality assessment today, but Jung's theory of personality is. The Myers-Briggs personality inventory is a widely used personality questionnaire used in industry. Few of those using this questionnaire realise that it is based on the theories of Jung.

The Myers-Briggs personality inventory

The Myers-Briggs personality inventory was developed by Katherine Briggs (1875–1968) and her daughter Isabel Myers (1897–1980). Neither were educated as psychologists and neither had faculty positions. Katherine Briggs' interest in personality developed on meeting her future son-in-law (nickname 'Chief') in 1917, who was so different from other members of her family. She began developing a personality theory of her own but realised, on reading Jung's account of personality types, that his theory was more extensive and better than hers.

Katherine Briggs' work on personality development was extended by her daughter, Isabel (who by now had married her 'Chief'). Isabel Myers, who also wrote two novels, gained experience working in a personnel department of a large bank and became aware of test theory and test development from the perspective of personnel management (see Chapter 3 and the development of occupational psychology). The original Briggs-Myers scale was published in 1942 with the name changed to Myers-Briggs in 1956. The Myers-Briggs Type Inventory (Myers, 1962) is based largely on Jung's ideas of types and extraversion-introversion and four functions, but with a development of Jung's ideas to produce 16 different personality types, with names such as the giver, the provider, the visionary, the supervisor, the idealist, and the mastermind. What is particularly interesting about the scale is the way people have responded to it.

The Myers-Briggs Type Inventory categorises people into types – you are either one thing or another. Psychologists have been almost universally rather negative about the Myers-Briggs scale, both in terms of concept (type versus trait) and theory. For example, McCrae and Costa (1989) conducted factor analysis on the Myers-Briggs questionnaire and showed that this analysis produced a five-factor structure similar to that of the Big Five Theory of personality. Although McCrae concluded that the underlying theory used by Myers and Briggs is wrong, an alternative interpretation is that trait theories of personality and motive theories of personality, such as Jung's and the Myers-Briggs, are fundamentally different, so it is unfair to judge one by the other (Winter, John, Stewart, Klohnen, & Duncan, 1998).

Despite negative reaction by many academic psychologists, the Myers-Briggs Type Indicator, as it is known, is one of the most widely used personality scales in the world – and possibly *the* most widely used as some claim. It is used in personnel management and selection by a wide variety of different well-known companies all over the world. Why is the Myers-Briggs scale so popular?

There are several possible reasons for the popularity of the Myers-Briggs scale. One is that laypeople and users of the scale (who are typically not psychologists by training) find typologies easier to understand. A trait describes how much you are of something. In the case of measures of the Big Five traits, everyone is somewhere on dimensions of neuroticism, extraversion, agreeableness, conscientiousness, and openness. Many people fall in the middle of these dimensions – for example, being a little neurotic or a little extravert, with the result that differences between people and descriptions of people are complex. In the case of the Myers-Briggs, everyone is only one of the 16 types and this produces a much simpler way of understanding differences between people. Types are easier to describe and understand than traits, even though it is implausible that personality differences are binary.

A second possible reason for the popularity of the Myers-Briggs Type Indicator is that all types are positive in nature. With the Big Five, a person can be neurotic, disagreeable, or un-conscientious. In Freudian theory, being described as oral, anal, or phallic is not a compliment. No such negativity exists with the Myers-Briggs, which has been likened by some critics to a Chinese fortune cookie. All 16 types of the Myers-Briggs indicator are positive. Whichever type a person is, the scale provides information that is nice and sufficiently vague to appeal to everyone.

Students should try to decide for themselves why the Myers-Briggs scale has been so popular (details of the scale can be found online). Perhaps you don't need to be right to be successful! Alternatively, the questionnaire may reflect a more useful motivational approach to personality that is lacking in trait theories (Winter et al., 1998). Jung never actively supported Briggs or Myers or their scale, even though Myers wrote to him about it.

Theories of psychoanalysis are seldom taught in psychology degrees today. Students taking psychology degrees will be trained in statistics and perhaps trained in psychophysiological measurement, but not trained in dream analysis. One possible reason why psychoanalysis plays a minor role in psychology education today is that some of it is inconsistent with the accepted view that psychology is a science. The theories of psychoanalysis are at best weak theories, sometimes they are wrong, and the different theories developed by psychoanalysts after Freud can be very different from each other. Compare, for example, the personality theories of Freud and Jung. Could any two theories of personality be more different? Both were simply guesses by each man about personality, but without any attempt to test their theories with data. It is the lack of independent evidence that leads to some psychologists being unsympathetic towards psychoanalysis. We should not be too harsh on Freud and Jung. They were writing at the same time as Hall and James, and although the ideas of the latter are more consistent with modern psychology, none used independent empirical testing of their ideas.

Science proceeds best when there is a combination of brave theoretical speculation and rigorous theory testing. Chapter 4 demonstrated the disadvantage of a paradigm where data collection was rigorous but there was an absence of theoretical speculation. This chapter demonstrates the disadvantage of bold theoretical speculation with the absence of rigorous theory testing.

What is the greatest impact of Freud and Jung today? Is it the continuation of psychoanalysis as a form of therapy, is it the concept of mental illness, is it the talking cure that is now used in one form or another in all psychotherapies, or is it the Myers-Briggs inventory? Students should decide for themselves.

Summary

Sigmund Freud qualified as a doctor of medicine and at first accepted the dominant paradigm that 'nervous diseases' could be explained in terms of the pathology of nerves. He developed an alternative paradigm, hypothesising that 'mental illness,' as it came to be known, could be explained in terms of psychological pathology. This psychological paradigm forms the basis of all modern psychotherapies. Freud treated patients with 'the talking therapy' and reported how this helped patients. Later evidence shows that some of Freud's claims of treatment success were over-optimistic. There are two possible explanations why psychoanalysis is helpful – the theory of psychoanalysis and the common factors model. The possibility that common factors are responsible for therapeutic benefit is a potential criticism of all psychotherapies, including cognitive behaviour therapy. Carl Jung was influenced by Freud but developed a different kind of psychodynamic theory and theory of personality. Jung's theory of personality influenced the development of the Myers-Briggs scale, a scale that is in general use today but criticised by modern personality theorists.

Essay questions

1 How did Freud's personal experience shape the theory he proposed?
2 Is Freudian theory falsifiable?
3 To what extent are concepts used in psychoanalysis shared with later psychologies? Give examples and justify the reasons for your choice.

6

What is the relationship between psychology and physiology, will neuroscience replace psychology, and what is biopsychosocial interactionism?

Wilhelm Wundt trained in physiology and had a medical degree. His early books described the physiology of the sensory nervous system (see Chapter 2). How did Wundt view the relationship between physiology and his new experimental psychology?

Wundt assumed that mental content was the result of the body's physiology, but could not be *described* in terms of physiology. For example, the image of a chair is represented somewhere in the brain, but that biological representation does not describe what a chair actually looked like. Wundt's approach to the mind-body problem is referred to as *psychophysical parallelism*. Mental events occur in parallel with physiological events. Psychophysical parallelism is a philosophy of science based on materialism (also called physicalism), a philosophy that assumes that only the physical world exists. Although mental events occur in parallel with physiological events, the material world is the only 'stuff' that exists. There is no 'mind stuff.' The experience of mind is a consequence of the physical world.

Materialism is not the only philosophy of science. The philosopher Descartes had suggested some years before that mind stuff and body stuff both exist, and that the mind – or soul – exists after the body is dead (see Chapter 2). Although several of the early psychologists were sympathetic to the idea of an independent soul, this hypothesis will not be explored here, though most religions assume some form of independence of the soul or mind from the body. If the soul exists independently of the body (and can exist after death) then theories about the body will not be able to explain the phenomena associated with the soul. Although religious views and dualism are accepted as true by many people, the examination of how psychology relates to physiology in this chapter is limited and based on one simple assumption: Minds do not exist without bodies.

Alternatives to materialism in science

Materialism is the dominant assumption of science, but it is not the only possible assumption. A minority of scientists believe that mind is not secondary to the physical world but has some independent effects, albeit in a non-regular fashion, possibly linked to quantum mechanics. Those supporting this alternative paradigm cite anomalies including reports of near death experiences, children's reports of past lives, and other parapsychological phenomena in support of their theories (Walach, 2020; Walach et al., 2019). Those operating within the dominant materialist paradigm believe anomalies to be artefacts and therefore not real. As ever, scientists interpret the world according to their assumptions. Taking a view that is opposed to the dominant paradigm, particularly one as fundamental as this one, can be unhelpful for academic careers.

Like Wundt, Sigmund Freud had a degree in medicine and was trained in physiology. Freud initially assumed, like everyone else, that nervous diseases, as they were then called, were the result of nerves. Because no abnormality of nerves could be discovered, Freud adopted a psychological *explanation* for nervous diseases (see Chapter 5). The psychological explanation led to a new way of thinking about and describing symptoms. The term and concept of mental illness replaced the earlier term and concept of nervous diseases. The first effective psychoactive drugs were developed in the 1950s, providing clear evidence that nervous diseases/mental illness was indeed due to something wrong with the nerves. One might imagine, therefore, that if mental illness is due to something wrong with nerves – as it must be if one assumes materialism – then mental illness should be treatable through biology and one can forget about talking therapies. This has not happened. Will it happen in the future? These and other questions are explored in this chapter.

A brief history of physiology and psychology

The relationship between psychology and physiology can be approached from several different perspectives, and different words have been used to describe these perspectives. They are psychophysiology, physiological psychology, psychoneuroimmunology, and neuroscience. Terminology has changed over the years and the term *neuroscience* has replaced many of the older terms and is sometimes used as a generic term for any relationship between psychology and physiology.

Psychophysiology: electroencephalography (EEG) and functional magnetic resonance imagery (fMRI)

The aim of psychophysiology is to measure the activity of the brain, and match that activity with psychological events, typically using non-invasive technology. Electroencephalography or EEG measures the minute electrical currents that are generated by the brain and detected by electrodes placed on the scalp. The Scottish physiologist Richard Caton (1842–1926) was the first person to notice that the brain generated spontaneous electrical activity. He discovered this using two electrodes placed on either side of the head of dogs and monkeys and found that the electrical current increased or decreased depending on whether the animal was awake or asleep, and disappeared when the animal died. His work was published in the *British Medical Journal* in 1875 (Caton, 1875). However, the discovery of the EEG is attributed to Hans Berger (1873–1941), a German psychiatrist. Unlike Caton, Berger measured the EEG of humans in 1924, but delayed publication until 1929 when he published the first EEG trace – the trace was taken from his young son (Brazier, 1961). Since then there has been a steady stream of research using the EEG. There are two limitations of this research. The first is that EEG trace is very complex and information often needs to be extracted by complex statistical procedures. The second is that although the position of the electrodes gives some information about the activity of different parts of the brain, because of the way electrical signals travel through the brain, it is not a very accurate measure of the localisation of function (Haas, 2003).

In 1990 a new technique for investigating the brain was published, called functional magnetic resonance imaging or fMRI. This technique enables researchers to measure blood flow through the brain. This is possible because the water molecules in the brain act as very weak magnets. By briefly disturbing the magnetic field in the brain, the water molecules shift, and the energy released as they regain their original position is detected. fMRI can be used to generate pictures of brain activity and can provide accurate localisation of function. fMRI gives a time-based picture of the activity of different parts of the brain.

What do EEG and fMRI tell us? They tell us where things are happening in the brain when certain sorts of mental activity are taking place. Knowing the position of a book in a library catalogue will give some information about the content of a book. For example, if the book is in the poetry section, then it is likely to contain poems. However, the location of a book in a library does not provide information about the detailed contents of the book (it does not tell what poems are in the book or whether they are beautiful). The same can be said about the EEG and fMRI. They provide information about which parts of the brain are active, but they do not provide the fine detail of description, nor do they provide the kind of psychological account that Wundt believed psychology was able to provide.

There are two reasons why psychophysiology is important despite its limitations. The first is that the demonstration that brain and psychological phenomena are correlated has had a substantial impact on the perception of psychology by the general public. The reader will recall from earlier chapters that the history of psychology is one where psychologists have felt the need to present what they are doing as a science. The demonstration that there are correlates between mental events and physiology shows that psychological phenomena are 'real' in the minds of those who believe that the only reality is physical. Of course, students will be aware that there *must* be correlates of physiological events with psychological events. Minds do not occur without bodies. So the impact of what is now referred to as 'neuroscience' on how psychology is perceived by the public may seem surprising, but it would be wrong to underestimate the social impact neuroscience has had on the perception of psychology. Psychologists are sometimes described as 'cognitive neuroscientists' when they do not even take physiological measurements.

The second reason why psychophysiology – or neuroscience – is important is that measurement techniques are improving. As techniques improve, more and more detail is provided about what happens in the brain when thoughts or tasks take place. Knowing where something happens in the brain is like knowing where a book is in a library. However, as the detail gets finer and finer, the position of the book gets more and more accurate so that not only do we know

> ## Physiology makes psychology real
>
> The author was at a conference on placebos where there was a presentation on the neurological changes that take place when a placebo is given. The results showed that when a person took a placebo, there were changes in the brain that mimicked the effects of the active drug. These findings were welcomed by the audience. The research showed that placebos were 'real' because they produced biological effects. But placebos *must* have a biological effect. Minds do not occur without bodies. The author was sitting next to a friend who remarked drily "where else would you expect a placebo to create a physiological effect? In a person's toe?"

that a book is in the poetry section, but which poet it is, and eventually which poem it is. Some believe that eventually, with increasing accuracy of measurement, it should be possible to associate particular thoughts with particular events in the brain so that thoughts and indeed the whole of psychology can be explained by physiology. The contribution of psychophysiology to psychology and whether it is possible in practice or in principle to replace psychology with physiology will be examined later in this chapter.

Physiological psychology: the development of psychoactive drugs

The aim of physiological psychology is *either* to alter the physiology of the brain through chemicals (drugs) or other means and then measure the psychological consequences, *or* to measure chemicals in the brain and relate those chemicals to psychological phenomena. Whereas psychophysiology uses primarily non-invasive measurement, psychophysiology is interventionist. Techniques of altering the brain include electrodes that are inserted in the brain, more recently transcranial magnetic stimulation (TMS) (Walsh & Cowey, 2000) and perhaps most important in terms of impact, the use of drugs.

The mind-altering effects of certain drugs have been known for thousands of years. The effects of alcohol and the opium poppy did not wait for discovery by scientists, and these and other mind-altering substances were used to treat nervous disease from the 19th century onwards. Up to the middle of the 20th century, patients with mental health problems were treated with a variety of chemicals, most of which did more harm than good. This unfortunate situation arose because there was no credible biological explanation for what were then called nervous diseases (see Chapter 5). Chemical treatment was based on spurious theories or chance experimentation.

Around 1950 there was a 'pharmacological revolution' when three chemicals were discovered that were effective as antipsychotics. These chemicals were lithium salts, chlorpromazine, and reserpine. There was still no biological explanation for psychosis, and the antipsychotic effects of these drugs were discovered by accident. For example, chlorpromazine comes from a class of drugs originally developed for the dyeing industry. These dyes were used to stain specimens that were examined under a microscope. Evidence from these specimens seemed to indicate that the stains also had anti-microbial effects, though this was later not confirmed. So chlorpromazine had biological effects, but it was a drug looking for a treatment. Experimentation showed it had antipsychotic effects (López-Muñoz et al., 2005).

Reserpine was another drug that was discovered as part of that pharmacological revolution, and again its discovery occurred without any theoretical rationale as to why it should have antipsychotic effects. The chemical property of reserpine is such that it depletes mono-amines and this was known by chemists at the time. Because the experimental use of reserpine for psychosis also seemed to cause depression – though the depressive effect of reserpine has been questioned (Baumeister, Hawkins, & Uzelac, 2003), a theory was proposed that depression was caused by lack of serotonin and dopamine. This hypothesis, called the serotoninergic theory, led to the first serotonin-enhancing drugs for treating depression in the 1960s. New types of serotonin-enhancing drugs were developed over the years. So, unlike antipsychotics, antidepressants were developed on the basis of a theory of a biological cause of depression (Hillhouse & Porter, 2015).

Serotonin-enhancing antidepressants are widely used today. Is the serotoninergic theory of depression correct? Certainly undergraduate students are often taught that it is correct. However, several authors have questioned this theory, in part because increases in levels of serotonin have a relatively small effect on depression – at least 80% of the effectiveness of antidepressants is due to the placebo effect (Kirsch, Moore, Scoboria, & Nicholls, 2002; Kirsch, 2014). Perhaps if depression were *just* a lack of serotonin, depression would be less of a problem than it is today (see Chapter 1). So, like antipsychotics, antidepressants affect the mind but the underlying theory remains less secure than many believe.

Since the 1950s many different pharmacological agents have been developed that alter the chemistry of the brain and hence alter a person's psychology – including new recreational drugs. What does this demonstrate? It shows that psychological phenomena have a biological basis. This demonstration is hardly new. The biological basis for mental phenomena was assumed by Wundt. Despite continuing problems, the fact that drugs do have effects on mental life opens the possibility that mental illness could one day be treated successfully with drugs and talking therapies would become a thing of the past. Equally, some might argue that the failure to determine the chemical basis of mental illness and find a definitive form of treatment, despite more than a century of looking, might suggest that another type of theory and therapy, i.e., psychology, is needed.

Psychoneuroimmunology

The term *psychoimmunology* was coined by the psychiatrist George Solomon (Shubla, Solomon, & Dosli, 1979), but the term soon changed to *psychoneuro-immunology* – a change that reflects the status given to the term *neuro* but also because the link between the brain and immune system was now included in investigations. Whereas physiological psychology examined the effects of drugs on the brain – and the effect of behaviour on chemicals in the brain – psycho-neuroimmunology examined the relationship between the mind, the brain, and the immune system. Amongst other things, the research shows the effect of stress on the immune system and the effects of the immune system on the psychological state. Research shows, for example, that stress increases inflammation in part through an increase in pro-inflammatory cytokines (Segerstrom & Miller, 2004). Cytokines are the messengers in the immune system that tell other parts of the immune system that there is infection. The inflammatory effects of pro-inflammatory cytokines exacerbate a number of disease processes, (e.g., cancer, heart disease, asthma, multiple sclerosis) with the result that there is now a well-established relationship between stress and disease (Cohen, Janicki-Deverts, & Miller, 2007).

Stress → inflammation → disease

The pro-inflammatory cytokines also have effects on the brain and hence psychological state, causing, amongst other things, fatigue and depression. One might imagine that there should be a one-to-one relationship between particular cytokines and particular mental states, but this has not been found to be the case. It is not possible to say, for example, that depression is caused by one pro-inflammatory cytokine and fatigue with another. What seems to happen is that all pro-inflammatory cytokines increase with fatigue and depression, but in a way that is not consistent across people. As with physiological psychology, there is a relationship between physiology and psychology, but not one that is very precise, and certainly not one that allows a one-to-one linking of psychology with physiology.

Psychoneuroimmunology has played an important role in the story of physiology of psychology, and has had an effect on the way psychology is viewed by those outside the discipline of psychology. It showed that psychology was relevant to the cause and mechanisms of somatic diseases, and not only mental illness. Whereas psychophysiology and physiological psychology focussed on the relation between the brain and psychology, psychoneuroimmunology showed that the immune system was also part of the equation when trying to understand the physiology that underpins psychology. The relevance of psychology to the body therefore increased. Clinical psychology as a sub-discipline dates from the early 20th century. The sub-discipline of health psychology is a new kid on the block and developed in the 1980s.

Psychoneuroimmunology added the immune system to the psychology-physiological relationship. Yet later research focussed on other parts of the body, such as the gut. The gut has been described as the 'second brain' as the gut contains more nerves than the spinal cord, and the gut is also the primary site of immune learning. A happy gut makes a happy mind and vice versa. Because the health of the gut is associated with the gut biome (the gut microflora) the gut biome of bacteria and viruses also has an effect on psychological state (Ridaura & Belkaid, 2015). Other mind-body interactions such as kinaesthetic feedback also feature in modern thinking so that the overall effect of these new developments is that the psychology-physiology relationship should be considered in terms of the mind and body, not the mind and brain.

Reductionism

If one had perfect understanding of the physiology of the whole of the body, would it then be possible to explain psychology in terms of physiology? And if so, is it possible to replace psychology with physiology? Can psychology be reduced to physiology? Reductionism is a type of relationship between two sciences. The most commonly accepted definition of reductionism is that provided by Nagel:

> A reduction is effected when the experimental laws of the secondary science (and if it has an adequate theory, its theory as well) are shown to be the logical consequences of the theoretical assumptions (inclusive of the coordinating definitions) of the primary science.
>
> (Nagel, 1961, p. 352)

In practical terms, this means that reductionism is not about finding correlations between physiological and psychological events. It is not about finding that drugs have psychological effects. Reductionism concerns the relationship between *theories* from two different disciplines, what Nagel refers to as the primary and secondary science. Finding that a particular part of the brain lights up when a person has a particular thought does not constitute reductionism. However, if *all* the theories of psychology can be shown to be *the logical consequences* of theories of physiology, with the addition of some 'bridging theories,' then psychology can be reduced to physiology. Note that the requirement for reduction is not that psychological theories should be the logical consequence of physiological theories, but rather that they should be the logical consequence with the addition of some additional theories that link them together. For reduction to occur psychological theories must be capable of *deduction* from physiological theories with the addition of a few extra bridging theories (Nagel, 1998).

Reductionism is a metatheoretical assumption, an assumption that, when applied to all science, is referred to as 'the unity of science' (Kemeny & Oppenheim, 1956). The unity of science concept is based on the assumption that

People as biological machines.

sciences occur in levels: atomic physics, chemistry, biology, psychology, sociology, and that each discipline at a higher level can be reduced to the theory at the lower level. So, taken to its extreme, humans are simply machines made out of bundles of atoms and everything we do can, ultimately, be explained by the way those atoms interact.

If humans are simply a bundle of atoms that obey the laws of physics, one interpretation is that psychology should be replaced by physiology and physiology should be replaced by chemistry and chemistry by physics. However, even if one accepts a reductionist position, not all reductionists share the view that reduction eventually leads to replacement.

The counter-argument that reduction does not necessarily mean elimination is given by Hilary Putnam (1973), who compares macro and micro accounts of the same phenomenon. Imagine a board with a square hole and a round hole and a square peg that fits into the square hole but not the round hole. We can explain why the peg fits into the square hole. The reason is that the peg is also square. Now imagine, that this phenomenon is reduced to the atomic level. There are three clouds of atoms whose shape is determined by forces of varying kinds, the round and square holes and the peg. A full understanding of the forces between atoms at the micro level will enable us to know what the shape of the atomic clouds are, and therefore be able to deduce the shapes the clouds will take and therefore that the square shaped cloud will go into the square shaped hole but not into the round shaped hole. The macro level can be logically deduced from the micro level. The micro-level account explains why the square peg behaves as it does but does not add anything more than is provided by the macro level. Putnam's argument is that even if reduction occurs, it may be better to *explain* things at a macro level, even though the same things can be *deduced* from the micro level.

Although reduction does not necessarily mean the elimination of psychology, the question still remains: is it possible to reduce psychology and physiology? The question is important because if psychology can be reduced to physiology, but not eliminated, then it becomes unnecessary to test psychological theories. All that is needed is to establish the veracity of the physiological theory and then the veracity of psychological theories that are deduced from the physiological theory is established by default. So, although Putnam's argument provides a justification for the continuation of psychology, if reductionism occurs, as proponents of the unity of science would suggest, then the status of psychology and psychological research is very much diminished.

There are several arguments against the possibility of reductionism between psychology and physiology, and they fall into two categories. One argument is that although reduction is possible in principle, it will not happen in practice. The other is that reductionism is neither possible in principle nor practice. The next section examines why reductionism is not possible in principle.

Arguments against reductionism in principle

There are three linked arguments against reductionism in principle between psychology and physiology: (a) complementarity, (b) functional versus structural description, and (c) emergentism.

Complementarity

Complementarity is a philosophical principle that owes its origins to quantum mechanics. The basic idea is that *it is the nature of reality* that phenomena can be explained only by using more than one *incompatible* theory. This principle has been demonstrated in quantum mechanics in several ways that need not concern us, but one that can be accepted as true. It is also possible to apply the same principle of complementarity to the relationship between psychology and physiology – even though neither are quantum theories. Methodological complementarity was proposed by Kirsch and Hyland (1987) as a way of understanding the relationship between biological and psychological theories.

Methodological complementarity is based on the following argument. When discussing reductionism, what matters is the relationship between the two types of theory. The exact nature of consciousness and of physical reality can be put on one side. Psychological theories and biological theories describe different types of entities, entities that have a different ontological status. 'Ontological status' refers to the way something exists. So mind states and physiological states exist in different ways.

Multiple uses of the same word can lead to confusion. The word *cause* is used in more than one way. When used informally, the word cause simply refers to the temporal sequence of events. If A is always preceded by B, then it is possible to say that B causes A. This informal sense is used when events are described as opposed to explained (as in inductive generalisations, see Chapter 1). By contrast, if *cause* is used in an explanatory sense (i.e., in terms of a theoretical mechanism that explains the observed events), then the term cause also has the requirement of connectivity. Connectivity means that there is some sort of connection that links the two events. For example, if ball A hits ball B so that ball B rolls away, then it is the physical contact between the two balls that is the connection. In the case of mental events, ideas can be connected in content when one idea leads to another. So both physiological and psychological mechanisms involve connectivity, though each has a different kind of connectivity. When used as part of an explanatory mechanism, causal relationships can exist only between entities that have the same ontological status – because causality requires some form of connection between the causally connected events.

The conclusion from this is that, if the term *cause* is used in a formal explanatory sense, then minds do not cause bodies nor bodies cause minds. Although mind states and physiological status exist in different ways and cannot cause each other, they can be *identified* with each other. That is, whenever there is a mind state there is a unique and corresponding body state (note the opposite does not always occur – variation in physiology does not require variation in psychology). The statement that stress causes inflammation which then causes disease (as suggested earlier) is a description of a causal sequence, not an explanation. From a formal, explanatory perspective, psychological stress is identified with a biological state that causes biological illness. The authors of methodological complementarity argue that although 'mind causing body' and vice versa statements are commonplace, they confuse two different ways of using the word *cause* – cause used in the informal and formal senses.

Methodological complementarity paints a picture of the relationship between psychology and physiology that is very similar to Wundt's idea of psychophysical parallelism. Psychological events and physiological events occur in parallel. Methodological complementarity adds the idea of identity relations that occur from time to time in the mutual causal sequence of events. Every psychological event must, in principle, be identified with a physiological event as otherwise the assumption of materialism is broken. However, there may be physiological events that are not represented psychologically, so not every physiological event is identified with a psychological event.

Methodological complementarity (Kirsch & Hyland, 1987) was a simplification of an earlier proposal of complementarity (Hyland, 1985) where there were three parallel levels of explanation: physiological, mentalistic, and mechanistic. The mentalistic and mechanistic levels provide a distinction between two types of psychological explanation. The mechanistic level corresponds to the type of constructs used in cognitive psychology (see Chapter 4), whereas the mentalistic constructs are those used in humanistic psychology (see Chapter 8). Methodological complementarity focussed on the mentalistic and physiological relationship rather than considering the mechanistic concepts that were proposed originally by Craik (1943).

Kirsch and Hyland argue that psychological description (i.e., mentalistic description) cannot be reduced to physiological description, even if there is a one-to-one relationship between psychological events and physiological events. The reason is that a one-to-one relationship requires a bridging theory. A reduction is effected if the theories of the secondary science can be deduced from the primary science *with the addition of bridging theories*. Although one cannot

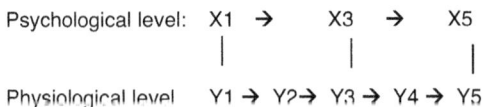

FIGURE 6.1 The idea of methodological complementarity.

A causal sequence of five events shown at the psychological (X) and physiological (Y) level with identity relationship between three of the events. Not all physiological states can be identified with a psychological state.

know what bridging theories are going to be discovered in the future, there are several possible reasons why bridging theories can never provide a logical (i.e., one-to-one) link between concepts in psychology and physiology. Two of these reasons are described in the next section.

Fodor's functional description

Fodor's argument is based on a difference between structure and function (Fodor, 1968). Physiology provides a description of the structure of the nervous system; psychology provides a description of its function. Physiologists might object to this characterisation, arguing that physiology describes the function of the nervous system whereas anatomy provides a description of its function, so Fodor's argument needs a little refinement: Psychology provides a description of the function of the nervous system in terms of behaviour.

Fodor states that although structure and function are linked, they are not logically related. As an example, consider the term *mousetrap*. A mousetrap is an object described in terms of its function: catching mice. There are several different types of mousetraps with different structures. There is the widely used 'little nipper' that kills the mouse with a mental bar. There is a 'humane mousetrap' that catches the mouse alive and allows the human to release it away from the house (at least that is the theory). There are other designs of mousetrap – an online search of images of mousetraps will illustrate how many there are. So it is not possible to know the exact structure of a mousetrap by the functional word, *mousetrap*. What about working in the other direction? Is it possible to look at the structure of a mousetrap and know, logically, that its function is to trap mice? The answer, again, is no. Looking at the objects of mousetraps viewed online, I am struck by their beauty. Why not have a mousetrap as a work of art? Or use a mousetrap as a paper weight? After all, there is no accounting for human taste, and someone somewhere might well use a mousetrap for something other than trapping mice.

Fodor (1968) argues that the brain has structures and these structures have functions. In a later work (Fodor, 1983), Fodor suggests how these functions can be represented as modules. Fodor developed his theory of the modularity of the mind to resolve two different approaches to perception, one where the stimulus has a direct link to perception and the other where perception depends on prior knowledge. Fodor's idea of a module is best expressed in his own words:

> One can conceptualize a module as a special purpose computer with a proprietary database, under the conditions that: (a) the operations that it performs have access only to the information in its database (together, of course, with specifications of currently impinging proximal stimulations); and (b) at least some information that is available to at least some cognitive process is not available to the module. It is a main thesis

of Modularity that perceptual integrations are typically performed by computational systems that are informationally encapsulated in this sense.

(Fodor, 1985, p. 3)

The word *computer* is revealing in this quote. The modularity approach to the mind is one that treats humans as a kind of information processing system. Computers are information processing systems. The underlying assumption of the modularity approach is that an understanding of the function of a computer aids the understanding of human cognitive function. It is not unusual for new theories to be influenced by new technology. Desktop computers started appearing in universities in the late 1970s and early 1980s, just at the time that Fodor developed his theory of modularity. Fodor's theory is influenced by the structure and function of a computer. A computer's hardware is related to its software, but the hardware of a computer is not logically related to its software. If physiology is equated with the hardware of a computer, psychology can be equated with its software. The importance of computers in the emergence of cognitive psychology was described in Chapter 4.

Sperry's theory of emergentism

Roger Sperry (1913–1994) received a Nobel Prize in 1981 for his work on split brains, that is, brains where the corpus callosum joining the two hemispheres of the brain were cut. Sperry examined the effect of 'splitting the brain' on consciousness, and it was these observations that led him to formulate a theory of consciousness.

The central idea of Sperry's theory of consciousness is that mind and body are at different levels of organisation. Note that the term *level* is not used in the sense of 'bigger or smaller than.' The mind isn't 'bigger' or smaller than the body. When the idea of levels is applied to minds and bodies, Sperry suggests that consciousness is an emergent property of a lower level of organisation, that of physiology or 'bodies.' That is, the central idea is that mind 'emerges' from bodies.

There are two important features to note about Sperry's theory of emergentism. The first is that the theory preserves the assumption that there is nothing in the world other than the material world. There is no 'mental substance' floating around. Sperry's theory adopts a materialist position (see previous sections). The second feature is that Sperry's theory rejects the unity of science hypothesis. The idea of emergent properties at the 'higher' level will always mean that the higher level cannot be reduced to the lower level.

So what are emergent properties and why do they occur? This topic will be returned to in the last chapter: The idea of emergent properties has a wider application than between psychology and physiology. Sperry, however, has a slightly different take on emergentism. A conventional view is that the emergent property at the higher level emerges from the lower level system, but that emergent property did not have a 'downward' effect on the properties of the lower level system. Sperry argued that emergent properties did have a downward effect. The consequence was that mind could 'cause the body,' even though the mind is not independent from the body.

Sperry illustrates this argument with the case of a wheel. A wheel has several parts – there are the spokes, the hub, and the rim. When all these parts are assembled in the correct way, then the wheel can roll along the ground. The property of 'rolling' is an emergent property of the parts of the wheel that is achieved only when the parts are in the right places. However, when the wheel rolls along, the position of the individual spokes are determined by the emergent property of rolling. The position of the parts is determined by the whole. Sperry argues that emergent properties such as the mind can have a downward effect on the physiology of the brain. Sperry's argument seems to make sense. If people engage in positive mental activities, such as meditation, then this leads to positive physiological changes, such as a reduction in stress.

Sperry's argument of cause between a higher and lower level – and more generally, between levels – is inconsistent with the argument, presented in methodological complementarity (see earlier) that, to avoid confusion, the term *cause* should be used in only in the formal sense, the sense where there is connectivity between events. In Sperry's example of a wheel, if the term *cause* is used in the formal sense, then the spokes of the wheel are caused to move by their two attachment points. In methodological complementarity, the idea that 'mind causes brain' is represented as identity relations, and this form of representation can easily accommodate the idea of emergent properties. The brain has emergent properties that are identified with psychological states. The state of the brain that generates those emergent properties has a causal effect within the brain. In summary, there is a compelling argument for treating emergent states at different levels as causally independent but connected by identify relations, even though the state at the lower level creates the emergent property that may defy description.

What can neuroscience add to psychology?

If one starts from the position that reductionism is not possible in principle, then an entirely different question arises. How are these two disciplines related and how does physiology in the form of modern neuroscience contribute to psychology? Before answering this question, here is a reminder of the meaning of *explanation*.

Explanation explained

There is a difference between description and explanation (see Chapter 1). A description of events is provided when an account of those events is given *only* by observation terms and words describing how those observations are related.

Description simply means describing what is observed and reporting on that observation. Explanation will always require description of those observations, but it includes something else. Explanation provides an account of *why* the observable events happen in terms of some kind of 'other' event. These other events are described in terms of non-observables, i.e., through the use of theoretical terms. The explanation therefore provides an account of what is happening using the theoretical terms plus observation terms plus the terms connecting them. The explanation provides a story using theoretical terms.

Psychology, physiology, and explanation

When someone asks you to explain something, a possible reply is "what kind of explanation would you find acceptable?" The reason is that there are different kinds of explanations. Explanations consist of theoretical terms, observation terms, and the words connecting them, and together they provide a kind of story. Explanations can be considered a type of story, a story of how something happens using an additional narrative that is not found in the observation terms themselves.

Novelists sometimes write a story using the following format: Events are described, but in each chapter the events are described by a different person. The novel therefore becomes a series of stories about the same events, each story being valid in its own way, but each story being different because it comes from a different perspective. The same can happen with explanations. There can be different stories, using different sorts of theoretical terms. There are (at least) two kinds of story to explain behaviour, one type of story being psychological and the other biological.

One idea (hinted at earlier in this chapter), is that biological explanations have some kind of precedence over psychological explanations in terms of 'goodness' of explanation. That is, if a psychological explanation and a biological explanation were both offered, then the biological one appears to be better. The biological is the better story because it is based on something tangible, namely biology. Is this true? Research does show that, whatever the truth of the matter, people have a preference for biological explanations. In a paper entitled "Superfluous Neuroscience Information Makes Explanations of Psychological Phenomena More Appealing," the researchers demonstrated exactly what is described in the title of the paper. Adding irrelevant neuroscience into a story helps the psychological story seem real to ordinary people (Fernandez-Duque, Evans, Christian, & Hodges, 2015).

The bias towards biological explanation is a psychological phenomenon. It has no basis in logic. One theory is better than another only if it is more useful than the other, for example, by making more powerful or more useful theories.

If biology provides a better kind of explanation than psychology, then it must be able to provide superior predictions. As psychology cannot be reduced to biology, a working hypothesis is that neither psychological nor biological explanations are intrinsically better than the other one. Instead, they provide different types of explanation – stories from different perspectives – and their usefulness depends on the context in which they are used. The question that needs addressing is this: How do biological explanations add to psychological ones?

There are several ways in which biology can be useful to psychological understanding. Here are three examples.

Example 1. Although there is no logical relationship between structure and function, they are statistically related. Suppose that psychologists are interested in determining what psychological mechanisms are responsible for two cognitive tasks. If different parts of the brain are active for the different tasks, then it is reasonable to infer that the tasks involve different psychological mechanisms. On the other hand, if the same part of the brain is active for the two tasks, then this leads to the possibility that the same psychological mechanism is responsible for both tasks. An example of this is found in research demonstrating the independence of short-term and long-term memory using neuroimaging techniques (Jonides et al., 2008).

Example 2. Psychological interventions can be assessed with physiological outcome measures. When a psychological therapy is used to reduce distress, it may be that people report less distress because of the demand characteristics of the intervention. A biological assessment of stress can provide greater certainty that the intervention was effective. An example of this type of research is the considerable evidence that meditation can reduce the shortening of telomeres that are associated with aging (Le Nguyen et al. 2019), a finding which shows the biological advantages of a psychological technique.

Example 3. More controversially, neuroscience can aid judgements when combined with non-biological evidence. Research shows that, on average, people who commit crimes have biological features that differ, on average, from those who do not commit crimes, with an estimate of up to 60% of criminal and anti-social behaviour being heritable (Fox, 2017) – but see caution about this kind of estimation discussed in Chapter 7. Although crime-disposing biological features may be used as part of the evidence in criminal cases, the use of evidence in this way is controversial (Greely & Farahany, 2019; Vincent, 2010).

Biopsychosocial interactionism

The term *biopsychosocial* was introduced by George Engel in 1978 (Engel, 1978). Engel's use of the term was purely practical and was aimed at medical education. Medical doctors are trained in biomedicine – also referred to as the medical model. Disease is understood and treated in terms of pathophysiology. Engel worked within that medical model but wanted to alert physicians and surgeons to the psychological needs of patients. Put simply, his message was this: Think also about patients as people and think about their psychological and social circumstances. Engel suggested several levels that were relevant to treating the patient – levels that are different from but bear some relation to the levels cited in the unity of science hypothesis. Engel's levels were community, family, two-person, person, nervous system, organ system, tissue, cell, and molecule.

Psychological care has always featured in good treatment by doctors and nurses, but its recognition was certainly stimulated by Engel's use of a catchy word. Subsequent to Engel, the term *biopsychosocial interactionism* has been used to describe a theory where psychosocial and biological elements are included. Several biopsychosocial theories have been proposed, and in each case the end state, typically some form of health variable, is affected by both biological and psychological variables.

This idea of applying different types of theory to the same context is also not new. It is an application of the idea of methodological complementarity described earlier in this chapter. Using this approach, there are two separate types of theory, one biological and one psychological, and each provides information about the treatment of the patient. One of the criticisms of biopsychosocial interaction is that it is *not* a theory (Pilgrim, 2015). It does not integrate biology and psychology at a theoretical level. It is simply the combination of two different theories in the same context. In biopsychosocial interactionist theories, psychological and biological processes add, they do not interact.

Biopsychosocial interactionism suffers from a theoretical problem. At an empirical level, it is clear that mind variables and body variables interact statistically. The effect of psychological stress on the body depends on the state of the body. A body that is stressed (high autonomic arousal) will exhibit a greater reaction to stress than a body that is not stressed. So, at an empirical level, minds and bodies are interactive rather than additive. However, if mind states do not cause body states or vice versa then it is not possible to represent the observed statistical interaction in terms of theory.

The solution to this problem is to propose another theoretical level, a level that intervenes between the biological and psychological levels of description (Hyland, 2017). This intervening level can be described in different ways but most usefully as a level of information. Both psychological and biological events can be identified with the events in the information level. So, events that *cannot* be causally connected because they are different levels of description and exist in different ways, *can* be connected once those events are represented in a common level of description.

The intermediary level in Figure 6.2 is similar in many respects to the type of theoretical construct that is characteristic of cognitive psychology, that is, the mechanistic level of person variables (see Chapter 4) (Hyland, 1985). There are, however, two differences between the way mechanistic concepts are commonly used in cognitive psychology and how they should be used in

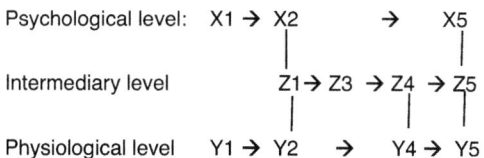

FIGURE 6.2 The intermediary or computational level of information that is between the psychological and physiological levels. The intermediary level provides theoretical concepts (Z3) that are unique to that level.

terms of biopsychosocial interactionism. First, the mechanistic concepts used in cognitive psychology are informational, but informational only in relation to inputs that are mediated psychologically – i.e., through the five senses. The information is 'psychological information.' In the intermediary level, information is encoded from both biological and psychological inputs. The intermediary level *combines* psychological information and biological information. The second difference is that the information level is assumed to have the property of intelligent adaptation (discussed further in Chapter 10) and therefore has the properties of connectionist rather than modular cognitive psychology (discussed in Chapter 10).

The idea that the body is capable of intelligent adaptation (i.e., intelligence is not a property only of the brain) has been proposed under the heading of 'body intelligence.' The concept of body intelligence has been proposed in several different ways, both in the context of conventional medicine (Hyland, 2001, 2002, 2011) and complementary medicine (Adelman, 2006; Rangel, 2005). A theory of biopsychosocial interactionism that combines inputs from psychology and biology can therefore be achieved so long as one makes the (reasonable) assumption that biological events are capable of encoding information, and that the biologically encoded information is then combined with the information processing that forms part of cognitive psychology. It is only by treating biological inputs as a form of encoded information that biopsychosocial interactionism becomes an interaction rather than an addition of biology and psychology.

Summary

Physiology plays an important part in the history of psychology. Modern psychology emerged from individuals who were trained in physiology, and the relationship between these two disciplines has continued and expanded to the present day. Scientists working on the relationship between psychology and physiology can focus on different aspects of this relationship. Some focus on measurement, some on intervention, some on only the brain, and some on the brain, immune system, and other parts of the body.

The unity of science hypothesis suggests that psychology can be reduced to physiology and that, ultimately, psychological phenomena can be reduced to clouds of atoms, because the ultimate reality is that humans are merely clouds of atoms. There are several arguments against reductionism: methodological complementarity, Fodor's functional modularity, and Sperry's emergent properties. Physiology adds to the story of psychology in a number of different ways, but it does not replace it. The contribution of a biological perspective to psychology (or vice versa) is reflected in the practical application of biopsychosocial interactionism to modern medicine. Although biopsychosocial interactionism provides a useful way of combining psychological and biological factors to affect outcome, there is a theoretical challenge in representing a mechanism where causality occurs between psychological and biological events, but this can be done by treating biological inputs as providing information to an intelligent system.

Essay questions

1   What does neuroscience add to psychology?
2   What evidence is there for and against the claim that drugs will one day replace the need for psychotherapy for mental illness?
3   Compare and contrast the different meanings of the term *biopsychosocial interactionism*.

7

How has the heredity-environment controversy been represented in the history of psychology and how is it informed by the person-situation debate and modern understanding of epigenetics?

The heredity-environment controversy is often presented to students as an argument based on data. Although data are undoubtedly relevant to this controversy, the controversy is underpinned by differing underlying assumptions. These different assumptions support different political systems. The term *political systems* means methods of organising and regulating society. The methodology and assumptions of the heredity-environment controversy are discussed in this chapter.

Social systems and the heredity-environment controversy

Nineteenth-century Europe was a class-based society in which people were born into different stations in life. The Indian system of caste is based on the assumption that heredity determines the kind of work a person is fit to do. Class and caste systems are based on the assumption that special people, such as kings, dukes, earls etc. have some special inherited characteristic that makes them fit and deserving for their particular station in life. The idea of being born to a 'station in life' is based on assumptions about the importance of heredity. In 19th-century Europe, marrying above or below your station was considered undesirable. Even today in India, some people have strong views that people from one caste should not marry into another caste. Belief in the importance of heredity is also part of a system of differentiating different groups of people, for example, people of African heritage or Jews, and forms the basis of racial and other forms of discrimination.

Although many political systems are based on assumptions of heredity, others assume that it is the environment that is important. John Ball's sermons in 1381 provide an early example of the rejection of heredity entitlement. Ball is reported to have preached "when Adam delved and Eve span, who was then a gentleman" (O'Brien, 2004: iv). Karl Marx's manifesto of communism was based on the assumption that all people were born equal, and therefore do not have privileges by virtue of birth. Socialist and communist political systems are antagonistic to the idea of inherited inequality. The rich don't deserve to be rich just because they have rich parents. If environment determines outcome, then poor people are not destined always to be poor because of their heredity, and their lot can be improved by exposure to a better environment. The American Head Start and the British Sure Start programmes (Glass, 1999) were based on the assumption that the early environment of children is important to their development and so providing a better environment for poorer children would help society overall. If madness is not hereditary, mad people should not be locked away in lunatic asylums but instead treated in a caring environment. In sum, politics and social policy are based on assumptions of heredity and environment. The heredity-environment controversy is relevant to psychology but has far wider implications.

Nature

The idea of heredity is not new. Since recorded history, people have noted that children resemble their parents, as do the offspring of cattle, dogs, and cats. It takes only a small leap of imagination from the observation that body type is inherited to the conclusion that psychological characteristics are inherited. Madness is a psychological characteristic. The concept of madness as a hereditary characteristic appears in several works of literature. For example, in Charlotte Brontë's novel, *Jane Eyre*, Mr Rochester marries Bertha Mason but is unaware that there was 'madness in the family.' Bertha becomes mad and is hidden away and confined to her room. The story revolves round this hidden secret of Mr Rochester – that he is married but wants to marry Jane. Madness in families was often hidden because it affected the marriage prospects of other family members. It comes as no surprise that scientists in the 19th century assumed that psychological characteristics were influenced by heredity.

Francis Galton (1822–1911) was born in Birmingham, England, and was related to Charles Darwin – his mother was the half-sister of Charles Darwin's father. Like William James, Galton was profoundly influenced by Darwin's *The Origin of Species* (Pearson, 1914, 1924). Darwin's theory is based on an assumption of heredity. Natural selection occurs because offspring resemble their parents. Galton wrote a book entitled *Hereditary Genius* in 1869 (Galton, 1869), some ten years after Darwin had published his *Origin of Species*. Galton put forward the argument that genius, like any other human or animal characteristic, was inherited. Consequently, if genius was an inherited characteristic, then genius should run in families. In order to demonstrate that genius was inherited Galton showed that the people who achieved eminence (i.e., whose contributions were recognised by others) tended to come from about 300 families. Galton established an *anthropometric laboratory* in 1884 at the International Health Exhibition in London where, for a small fee, people could have their ability measured. This very early type of intelligence test relied on some simple tests such as reaction time and sensory acuity, as Galton assumed a simple physiological basis underlying all ability.

Paying participants

Nowadays, psychologist pay the participants or provide some other form of inducement for participants to take part in studies. Galton actually charged people. Why did that work then and would it work now?

Galton introduced the idea of measuring differences between people, and also helped in the creation of a statistical methodology for individual differences (Galton, 1883). Galton plotted the relationship between the height or weight of parents with the height or weight of their children, using scatter plots. He realised by looking at these scatter plots that the children's heights and weights tended to be closer to the mean than their parents' – there was, as he put it, a regression towards the mean. Galton urged a follower of his, Karl Pearson, to develop a statistical formula for describing these scatter plots, and Pearson developed an index, called the Pearson product-moment correlation coefficient – a statistic that is well known to undergraduate students.

Galton introduced the terms *nature* and *nurture* (Galton, 1874, 1875). The phrase 'nature and nurture' is a convenient jingle of words, and in proposing his extreme nature viewpoint, Galton also recommended selective breeding or eugenics as a way of improving the human race, as well as sharing the widely held view at the time that Europeans were superior to 'the savage races.' Selective breeding of animals had been practised for centuries and was responsible for the breeds of farm animals known today. In suggesting eugenics, Galton applied what was appropriate for animals to humans. Whether humans should be treated like animals in this regard is another matter. Modern society takes a very different view towards both eugenics and racist assumptions. Both eugenics and racism are predicated on the assumption that inherited differences between humans are important.

Racism in psychology

Racism was commonplace in the 19th century. Slavery was abolished in Britain in 1833 and in the USA in 1865, but this does not prevent assumptions about racial differences. Racism is based on the assumption of genetic differences between races which confers superiority of one race over another. In Europe and America, racist beliefs were applied in particular to Jews and people of African heritage. Winston (1998, p. 28) writes that "The widespread antisemitism in the United States between the world wars is well documented . . . as are the discriminatory practices of universities in admissions and hiring." Edward G Boring (1889–1968) was one of a small number of people who helped place Jewish students and academics (not always successfully) into American Universities when the Nazi party in Germany banned Jews from universities. Boring had to certify that the Jews did not have 'Jewish characteristics' (Winston, 1998). However, feelings towards African Americans were considerably more negative to the extent that black psychologists were more or less non-existent until the 1960s. African Americans were segregated from European Americans in parts of the USA until the 1960s, and were subject to unequal treatment in many other ways.

African American psychologists

Robert Guthrie (1930–2005) wrote in 1976 (Guthrie, 1976) how when he enrolled for a master's course in Kentucky, USA in 1955 he was the only black face in a sea of white. The title of his book was *Even the Rat Was White*. Guthrie refuted the theory that was suggested then and subsequently that people of African heritage where less intelligent than those of European heritage, but his book also provides a revealing story about attitudes and behaviour towards African Americans in universities and elsewhere.

The race-intelligence controversy

The race-intelligence controversy was based on how to interpret data. The data was uncontroversial. The data showed that African Americans, as a group, had lower mean scores in IQ tests compared to white Americans. Some thought that the differences were genetic. Others thought that there was no genetic difference between races, and that differences in mean scores were due to two environmental factors. One reason for the lower scores in African Americans is that tests tend to favour the dominant culture, i.e., IQ tests are biased in favour of the cultural features that are found in white but not African Americans. The second (and possibly more important) factor is that the IQ is affected by environment, and that African Americans, as a group, were exposed to an environment that was less beneficial to development of the kind of skills measured in an intelligence test than whites. Even controlling for wealth or education, it can be argued that African Americans experienced problems not experienced by whites. The heredity and environment explanations of racial differences in IQ scores reflect deeper

Where do races come from?

The oldest skull of anatomically modern humans dates from 190,000 years ago, in North Africa. All non-Africans originate from a small band people who left Africa about 70,000 years ago, a band that would have numbered about 200 individuals. The light skin colour of some people is explained by evolutionary pressure. Light skin colour improves vitamin D production in northern regions, and having low levels of vitamin D produces rickets which reduces survival and reproduction – there is evidence of rickets in early European bones. However, many other physical features that distinguish races are difficult to explain – such as the almond shaped eyes of Chinese people.

assumptions about humanity and biases that are sometime implicit rather than explicit. It should be said, however, that the current consensus amongst psychologists is that there is no genetically conferred difference in intelligence between races of humans.

Nurture

Although some psychologists had racist views, many others took an entirely different approach and emphasised the importance of nurture. The strongest environmentalist view (i.e., supporting the nurture position) came from behaviourists.

The following quotation from J. B. Watson is repeated from Chapter 4.

> Give me a dozen healthy infants, well-formed, and my own specified world to bring them up in and I'll guarantee to take any one at random and train him to become any type of specialist I might select – a doctor, lawyer, artist, merchant-chief and, yes, even into beggarman and thief, regardless of his talents, penchants, tendencies, abilities, vocations and race of his ancestors.
>
> (Watson, 1924/1970, p. 10)

Watson and other behaviourists assumed there was no dividing line in terms of psychological processes between animals and humans. If there are no differences between animals and humans, then there can certainly be no differences between different humans, whether or not they come from different races.

Although behaviourists took an extreme nurture position, other early psychologists also favoured the effects of the environment over heredity. Witmer (1907) first assumed that mental illness was due to heredity, as did others at that time, but changed his mind, believing that mental illness had an environmental cause (see Chapter 3). The switch from a nature to nurture interpretation of mental illness had an impact on the way mentally ill patients were treated. If it is the nature of some people that they are mentally ill, then nothing can be done about it. However, if mental illness is caused by nurture, then there is the possibility that nurture can cure it.

What is inherited?

If a puff of air is blown into a person's eye, the person blinks. This is a reflex response. Everyone does it. It is inherited. Non-human animals inherit many complex patterns of behaviour, and these are called instinctive behaviours.

For example, when ducklings hatch out of the egg, they become imprinted on the first moving object. That is instinct. Every duckling behaves in this way. Humans differ from animals. Apart from reflexes, they do not exhibit instinctive stereotypical behaviour.

Rather than inheriting stereotypical behaviours, humans inherit capacities to behave in particular ways. Inherited capacities have evolutionary advantages in that they enhance the ability to adapt to changing environments – and humans evolved in a changing environment caused by periods of glaciation (the ice ages that started about six million years ago). Human capacities can be treated in two ways: capacities that are shared between all people and capacities that differ between people.

Capacities that are common to all people

The capacity for language is inherited and is common to all people. Just as the blink reflex is inherited and a feature of all people, so is the ability to learn language – a characteristic that is lacking in the rat. These common inherited characteristics and their evolutionary antecedents are studied under the heading of evolutionary psychology. For example, the tendency for people to prefer their own kin and members of their group (Smith, 1964; Wilson, 1975), altruism (Silk & House, 2016) and cognitive biases (Buss, 2015) can be explained in terms of their survival advantage to our human hunter-gatherer ancestors.

Evolutionary psychology contributes little to the heredity-environment controversy because of its focus on generalities, but it acts as a heuristic in two ways. First, genetic variety is important for evolution, so genetically conferred individual differences of one kind or another is to be expected. Seconds, humans evolved as hunter-gatherers in a Palaeolithic environment, and so it is likely that humans are adapted for that environment. Humans may be happiest when their psychological environment corresponds to that of the Palaeolithic – i.e., supported within a socially cohesive group. Anatomically modern humans (including those in the Palaeolithic) differ from their hominid ancestors in having a lengthy post-reproductive period, so what creates happiness in old age may therefore differ from what creates happiness in younger people. Evolutionary psychology provides useful heuristics for theory development, but the testing of those theories requires independent testing with modern people.

Capacities that differ between people

Everyone has the capacity to learn but some people may have a genetically conferred capacity to learn faster than others. People who have the capacity to learn faster will develop into people who are different from those who learn slower. The differences that arise from differences in capacity lead to differences in *disposition*. The dispositional differences are commonly described under two headings, intelligence and personality. Assumed differences in capacity lead to the linked questions such as these: How much is intelligence determined by heredity or environment? How much is personality determined by heredity or environment?

A problem

The following statement was in an earlier paragraph: People who have the capacity to learn faster will develop into people who are different from those who learn slower. Dig a little deeper and you will see that this statement is an over-simplification. People with different capacities to learn will develop into people who are different in a learning-rich environment. But what about a learning-poor environment? In a learning-poor environment, the ability of the genetic capacity to affect outcome will be reduced. Heredity and environment interact. The relative contribution of heredity and environment depends on the type of environment. More detail about this interaction will be provided later in this chapter under the topic of epigenetics.

Intelligence, heredity, and environment

How much is intelligence the result of heredity and how much environment? The question arises because different answers support different social and political systems. It seems reasonable, therefore, to answer the question using data, and twin studies form an important part of that data.

If one measures the intelligence of identical (monozygotic) twins raised together, the correlation between the scores of the two twins is high. This high correlation can be attributed to both heredity and environment. However, if one compares the correlation between identical twins raised together with the correlation of identical twins raised apart, then the difference between the two correlations must be due to the effect of the environment. So, the logic of this type of study is to compare two types of twin: (a) Those twins brought up together and who will have equal heredity and equal environments, and (b) those twins brought up separately who will have equal heredity but different environments. The closer the correlations are together, then the greater the impact of heredity. In Burt's study (see Chapter 1) (Burt, 1966), the correlation between the monozygotic twins reared apart was 0.77, which is a high correlation particularly if one considers that a correlation cannot be higher than the test-retest reliability of the test. It was so high that others questioned whether it was fake (Kamin, 1981). Nevertheless, later research shows that there is only a small decrease in the correlation between identical twins raised apart versus together, leading to the conclusion that the contribution of heredity is large.

What is the problem? Although the decrease in the correlation between twins raised together versus those raised apart is due to the environment, the environmental difference between the two pairs of twins may be very little. If the twins raised apart are raised in similar environments, then it is hardly surprising that the two correlations, between identical twins raised together and apart, are similar. There are two reasons why the environments of twins raised apart are similar. The first is that identical twins share the same placenta. Identical twins have the same environment at a crucial point of human development (see later section on epigenetics). The second reason is that adoptive parents are not randomly selected from the population. If adoptive parents have similar characteristics, then they will bring up their respective twins in a similar way. Just because two children are raised in different families, it does not follow that they differ in the environmental factors that affect intelligence. The estimate of the relative contribution of inheritance versus the environment is based on assumptions about the environments of both sets of twins. It is impossible to quantify how similar are the environments of twins raised apart versus together.

A second type of study examines the correlations between identical (monozygotic) twins and fraternal (dizygotic) twins raised together. The assumption underpinning these studies is that these two sets of twins have the same environment but different genes. Again, the assumption of this research runs into problems. Identical twins do not have the same environment as fraternal twins, even if they are brought up together. The reason is that identical twins share the same placenta, whereas fraternal twins have different placentas. As the nutrients received by the foetus depends on the state of the placenta, and because placentas vary, it follows that the early environment of the fraternal twins is not necessarily the same. There are also social reasons for doubting the assumption that the two sets of twins share the same environment. Identical twins can be treated (and dressed) differently from fraternal twins.

In conclusion, the underlying assumptions of the twin studies can be challenged in a way that would suggest a bias towards overestimating the contribution of inheritance. Although twin studies can be a useful way of examining the relative effects of inheritance and environment, this potential bias should lead to caution when interpreting results.

The person-situation debate

The heredity-environment controversy cannot be understood properly without an understanding of the person-situation debate. In the person-situation debate, the term *situation* can be treated as equivalent to the term *environment* in the heredity-environment controversy. The person, or personality is the result of a combination of heredity and environment. If the heredity-environment controversy is combined with the person-situation debate, then the causal sequence is that shown in Figure 7.1.

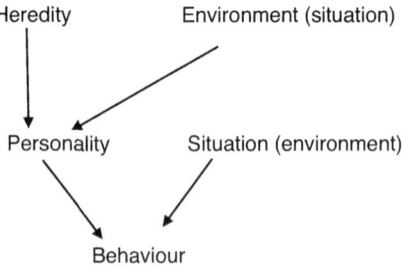

FIGURE 7.1 The antecedents of behaviour.

It can be seen from Figure 7.1 that behaviour is affected by the situation (or environment) in two ways. The situation affects behaviour indirectly through its past contribution to personality and the situation affects behaviour directly by its present influence on behaviour. It follows that the more behaviour is determined by events in the present, the less it can be affected by heredity, irrespective of the relative contributions of heredity and environment to dispositional factors such as personality or intelligence.

In 1957, Lee Cronbach (1957) wrote a paper with the title "The Two Disciplines of Scientific Psychology" in which he drew attention to a split between two types of psychological research. One type used correlational methods to examine differences in people's behaviour that were (assumed) consistent across situations. The other type used experimental methods to examine differences across situations that were (assumed) consistent across people. One focussed on the person; the other on the situation. This distinction remains to today. Social psychologists research the effects of different social environments on people and publish the research in social psychology journals. Personality psychologists research how people differ in the same environment and publish in personality journals.

Cronbach argued that this split in psychology was unhelpful and that a combination of the experimental and correlational methods was needed. For example, experimental methods will reveal that one treatment is better than another when people are considered as a group. However, it may be that some people respond better to one treatment and other people better to the other treatment. Cronbach – and others – argued the concept of the 'best treatment' was based on a false assumption and suggested instead that it is necessary to determine which treatment is best for whom. Cronbach's suggestion that correlational and experimental methods should be combined reflects earlier theoretical work by Kurt Lewin (1943a) who interpreted behaviour resulting from an interaction between the person and situation. The idea of integrating personality psychology and social psychology eventually became accepted. The *Journal of Personality and Social Psychology* was first published in 1965.

Personalised medicine

Despite Cronbach's logical argument against 'the best treatment' concept, that idea still dominates medicine, and to some extent clinical psychology. Recently, 'personalised medicine' provides an alternative to the assumption that there is a best treatment for any disease. Personalised medicine is defined as "treatments targeted to the needs of individual patients on the basis of genetic, biomarker, phenotypic, or psychosocial characteristics that distinguish a given patient from other patients with similar clinical presentations" (Agusti et al., 2016, p. 410).

If behaviour is influenced by both the situation and personality, then this leads to an obvious question: Which is more important? The person-situation debate arose over this question. Initially, there was an absence of consensus with personality theorists claiming that personality was more important, and social and experimental psychologists suggesting that the situation was more important. Consensus was reached by a position known as 'interactionism.' Behaviour is the result of an interaction between the person and the situation (Magnusson & Endler, 1977; Epstein & O'brien, 1985).

The consensus that persons and situations interacted – i.e., interactionism – has implications for the heredity-environment controversy. In both debates there is ambiguity about what exactly is being explained. In both debates it is behaviour that is being explained, but behaviour can be described in different ways. The behaviour under consideration is crucial to both debates.

The conclusion from the person-situation debate is that both the personality and psychologists and social psychologists were correct, but they were claiming different things and are therefore correct in different ways. They are correct depending on what is meant by behaviour. Does the word *behaviour* refer to a single instance of behaviour, or is it an aggregation of many behaviours? The consensus reached was that if one tries to explain a single behaviour, then in most cases that single behaviour is explained entirely by the situation, and personality plays only a minor role. However, if one tries to explain an average of several different behaviours across different situations, then personality does indeed explain that behaviour. So personality explains general trends in behaviour but is very poor at explaining individual behaviours. The situation explains individual behaviours but is poor at explaining trends in behaviour. If one considers that personality traits are defined in terms of 'behaviours that are consistent across situations and time' then it is not surprising that this is exactly what personality does. Some behaviours are consistent across situations and time, some are not. Those behaviours that are consistent across situations and time make up personality.

Not only does the answer to the person-situation debate depend on whether the behaviour is an aggregation or not, the result also depends on the particular behaviour. Consider how people respond when driving and they see traffic lights. Everyone stops at red, and goes at green. The behaviour at traffic lights is not determined by personality or intelligence. However, the results from a maths test result will differ between people as a function of mathematical ability, and behaviour at parties will differ as a function of sociability.

The non-linear interaction of person and situation (NIPS) model provides a theoretical framework for understanding whether situations and persons play a greater or lesser role in determining behaviour (Blum, Rauthmann, Göllner, Lischetzke, & Schmitt, 2018). According to this model, situations can be described as either strong or weak, where strong or weak refers to the affordance of the situation. In common sense language, the term *affordance* means the situation is 'telling' the person something. For example, a red traffic light has a strong affordance – it signals that you should stop. There is only one behaviour associated with the red traffic light, namely stopping. The red traffic light is a strong situation. A mouse that appears suddenly in front of you, on the other hand, can lead to a number of behavioural responses. You could jump on a chair, run away, try and catch it, or simply stand still and watch what it does. The mouse is a weak situation. According to the NIPS model, in strong situations, personality is unimportant in determining behaviour. Everyone stops at a traffic light irrespective of their personality. And if a person does not stop – for example, a bank robber fleeing from police – then it is not personality that is determining their behaviour at that particular moment in time. However, in weak situations, personality plays a much greater role. People high in neuroticism may behave differently to the mouse compared to those low in neuroticism.

The NIPS model also makes a distinction between strong and weak persons. Strong persons tend to behave in the same way irrespective of the situation. For example, some people are always aggressive or always non-aggressive whatever the situation. Such persons are described as strong. Others are sometimes aggressive or not depending on the situation. Such persons are described as weak. So, if a person exhibits cross-situationally consistent behaviour, then they are described as strong and for such people personality has a greater impact on behaviour that those weak persons whose behaviour varies with the situation. The conclusion from NIPS therefore is that it is meaningless to talk about the relative contribution of persons and situations to behaviour because it depends on the person and situation.

There is one more piece to the jigsaw that needs putting in place, and that is an explanation of the word *interactionism*. Interactionism is the resolution of the person-situation debate. The person and situation do not add to produce behaviour: They interact. What this means in practice can be illustrated by the following example of the interaction between neuroticism and stressors. A person high in neuroticism shows a large autonomic response to a mild stressor, but shows no autonomic response in the absence of any stressor. A person low in neuroticism has no autonomic response to either the mild or no stressor. Whether or not different situations affect behaviour depends on the person. It is precisely this point that was made by Cronbach in that early paper when he suggested that the two disciplines of scientific psychology should be working together. Interactionism provides a theoretical framework that is not provided by either personality psychology or social psychology (Fleeson, 2004)

Genetics and epigenetics

The heredity-environment controversy is based on an assumption. The assumption is that heredity and environment are independent contributors to the phenotype or behaviour of a person. The genes and environment *add* to produce the phenotype. This view is not correct: Genes and the environment interact. Genes can be switched on or off by the environment. Not only can genes be switched on during the lifetime of an individual, but switched on or switched off genes can also be inherited. *Epigenetics* is the term given to the study of how genes are switched on or off.

The following example illustrates how genes and environment interact. Let us suppose that there are genes for musical ability. A person with musical genes will develop musical skills only if exposed to music. A person may have tremendous genetic potential for playing the violin, but they will not play well if they have no access to a violin. It is only when musical genes are combined with musical education that musical skill develops. In families where there are genes for musical ability, then the parents of children are likely also to be strong in music and provide a musical environment for their children. If children with musical genes are not exposed to music, then their musical ability is limited. Thus, although it appears that 'music runs in families' and is due to genetics, in fact the environment is playing a role by interacting with genes.

Genes and environment do not simply add up to produce the phenotype. They interact. The same argument applies to the person-situation debate. Person factors and situational factors interact rather than add.

There is an additional factor that needs to be taken into account in an understanding of gene-environment interactions. If the environment of a group of people is very similar, then heredity is more important to outcome compared to an environment that differs between groups of people. If everyone is exposed to the same musical experience, then only musical genes will determine outcome. However, if some people are exposed to a musical environment and some not, then it is the interaction between genes and the environment that determines outcome. The proportion of variance attributable to heredity therefore depends on the variability of the situation.

The variability of the situation is relevant to an interesting phenomenon relating to the effect of age. The contribution of heredity to body weight decreases as people age. As people get older, their environment – i.e., what

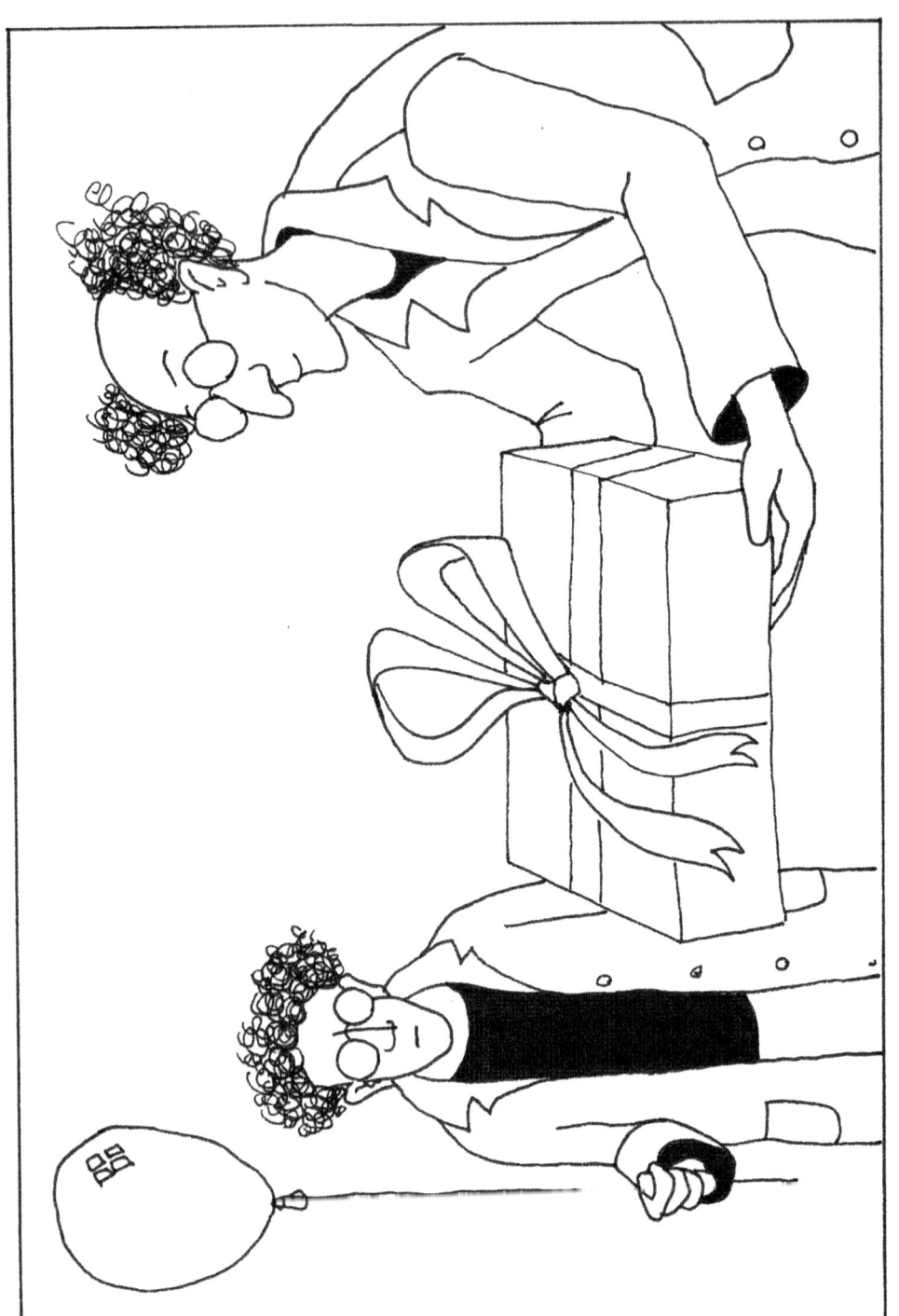

The gift of inher tance.

they eat – has a cumulative effect on their body mass. However, in the case of intelligence, the contribution of heredity *increases* with age. Results using twin studies show that the heritability of intelligence at age 5 years is estimated as 0.22, by age 16 it is 0.62, and at age 50 years it is 0.80 (Sauce & Matzel, 2018). The reason is that people high in cognitive ability seek situations of cognitive stimulation over the lifespan, and as they do so, more and more cognitively oriented genes become switched on. The environment is not random. People seek environments that are consistent with their genes, so the environment becomes more matched to their particular genotype. Gene-environment interactions are not only passive; they also are the consequence of an active process of behavioural choice.

Impact of the early environment on epigenetics

The prenatal environment is particularly important to the way genes are switched on or off. Some of the early research was conducted by David Barker (Barker, 1992) who used the records kept in India on birth weight to predict later health problems. The 'Barker hypothesis' is that low birth weight is associated with foetal stress and foetal stress switches on a variety of genes, including those associated with inflammation. The switched on genes then lead to later health problems 50 years later, because systemic inflammation increases diseases. (Many diseases have an inflammatory component, including mental illness.) Research supports the Barker hypothesis. Low birth weight is associated with mental health problems (Schlotz & Phillips, 2009) and attention deficit/hyperactivity disorder (ADHD) in children (Mick, Biederman, Prince, Fischer, & Faraone, 2002) and adults (Halmøy, Klungsøyr, Skjærven, & Haavik, 2012). Low birth weight is associated with greater hostility in the adult and greater adult weight (Rkkönen et al., 2008). The incidence of schizophrenia increases if, during pregnancy, the mother was exposed to psychological stress (particularly in the first trimester), including bereavement, war, famine, and natural disasters such as floods and earthquakes (Malaspina et al., 2008). There are critical periods when the genes are particularly prone to being switched on – such as the first trimester of pregnancy. These switched on genes then affect the person for the rest of their life, including psychological characteristics (Jones, Moore, & Kobor, 2018).

Trans-generational effects

One final factor must be added to the heredity-environment debate. There is evidence from animal models, and to some extent humans, that epigenetic effects – i.e., the switching on of genes – can be passed from one generation to the next. These effects are called trans-generational epigenetic effects. There is growing evidence that environmental influences can be passed from one generation to the next – a form of Lamarckian inheritance that was thought to be impossible. Not only are the foetus' genes affected by the maternal environment, but the maternal environment can also affect the eggs in a female foetus' ovum that then affects the maternal grandchildren. Although trans-generational epigenetic effects are well established (Bošković & Rando, 2018; Heard & Martienssen, 2014; Veenendaal et al., 2013), their impact on psychological factors is still at an early stage of understanding.

Summary

The heredity-environment controversy has been motivated by values and debate about the advantages or disadvantages of different political and social systems, and in particular privileges provided by inheritance.

How much is behaviour determined by heredity and how much by the environment? Percentage estimates of the relative contribution of heredity and environment to intelligence are based on twin studies, where the methodology creates a bias in favour of heredity. However, the main problem with heredity-environment controversy is not empirical but conceptual. The controversy is based on the assumption that a certain percentage of variance of behaviour is due to heredity and the remainder to the environment. This assumption is untrue as the relative contribution of heredity and environment depends on a variety of different factors. The correct conclusion of the heredity-environment controversy is that 'it depends' (Sauce & Matzel, 2018).

1   It depends on how behaviour is described. Single behaviours are largely determined by the current situation and therefore unaffected by heredity. Aggregated behaviours are determined by personality/intelligence, which result from an interaction between genes and the environment.
2   It depends on the type of aggregated behaviour. The aggregation of a person's response to traffic lights is unaffected by variation in heredity, whereas the aggregation of a person's responses to maths tests is.
3   It depends on the situation. Environments that are very different will have a greater impact on behaviour than environments that are very similar.
4   It depends on the person. The NIPS model shows that strong people are more likely to exhibit behaviours reflecting personality (and hence to some extent genetics) than weak people who are more likely to be influenced by the situation.
5   It depends on the interaction between heredity and environment. Some genes will not express themselves except in certain environments. The contribution of heredity depends on the environment.

The correct answer to the heredity-environment controversy is 'it depends' because the underlying question is based on a false premise – that heredity and environment are independent and additive contributors to behaviour. Why is this controversy important? Why is it that every undergraduate psychology student has heard of it? The reason is that the controversy is important to political debate, and about the role of inherited wealth and power. Do the data provide any insight that can help resolve that debate? Evolutionary psychologists argue that kinship preference had selective advantages (Smith, 1964), so it is not surprising that there should be a preference to allow children to inherit from their parents. Inheritance of wealth is a characteristic of almost all societies. At the same time, evidence supports the importance of the environment, particularly with regard to epigenetics – so there is a justification for an inheritance tax, a tax that tends to produce greater equality between citizens irrespective of the wealth of their parents. The level of inheritance tax and policies that affect the degree of equality in a society are not influenced by the findings of the heredity-environment controversy. They are based on values, and it is values that spurred the controversy in the first place. If there is anything to be learned from the debate it is the importance of improving the environment for everyone, not just those who are better off.

Essay questions

1   What is the person-debate and what are its implications for the heredity-environment controversy?
2   What are the advantages and disadvantages of twin studies in studying heritability?
3   What is epigenetics and what is its relevance to the heredity-environment controversy?

8

How do psychologists measure and explain the fact that in some ways everyone is unique?

In some ways everyone is the same. In some ways everyone is different but like some other people. In some ways everyone is unique.

Social and experimental psychology and many other branches of psychology provide an account of why people behave in the same way in different situations. Personality psychology and the psychology of individual differences provide an account of why people behave differently in the same situation. It is a self-evident truth that in some ways everyone is unique. Uniqueness is one of the ideas explored in humanistic psychology. Humanistic psychology developed in the late 1940s and 1950s (i.e., in the dying days of the empire of behaviourism and before the dominance of cognitive psychology) describing itself as 'the third force in psychology' – the other two forces being behaviourism and psychoanalysis. This chapter describes the methodology used by humanistic psychologists, some of their achievements, and its relevance today.

Humanistic, phenomenological, and existential

The terms *humanistic*, *phenomenological*, and *existential psychology* are sometimes used in different ways and sometimes interchangeably. The terms *phenomenological* and *existential* derive from philosophies, both of which share the idea that the mind provides important insights. The term *humanistic psychology* was the term used by USA psychologists in promoting phenomenological and existential psychology, and was the name given to Division 32 of the American Psychological Association when it was founded in 1971. Nowadays, the term *humanistic psychology* is used as a general category that includes almost all those approaches that focus on consciousness and the conscious mind.

Idiographic versus nomothetic science

The German philosopher, Wilhelm Windelband (1848–1915) distinguished two types of knowledge: nomothetic and idiographic (Lamiell, 1998). Nomothetic knowledge occurs where general laws can be formed about objects because those objects have common properties. Natural science is nomothetic. An atom of carbon is the same as any other atom of carbon. (Knowledgeable chemist: please do not split hairs about different atomic weights – the logic remains the same.) An atom of oxygen is the same as any other atom of oxygen. So, any theory about oxygen applies to any atom of oxygen, any theory of carbon applies to any atom of carbon, and any theory of carbon dioxide applies to any molecule of carbon dioxide. Most of psychology is nomothetic. If a theory does not apply to all people, at least it applies to some people. Theories of personality place individuals on a scale, a scale that applies to all people. Although people may fall at different places on that scale, given a large enough sample, some people must be at the same point on that scale as other people.

Windelband contrasted nomothetic science with idiographic science. Like nomothetic science, idiographic science has laws or theories, but different theories are needed for different situations. The idiographic approach lacks the universality of laws that is a feature of nomothetic science. Each event in history is unique, so it is possible to treat history idiographically as well as nomothetically where the latter describes general trends (Lyman & O'Brien, 2004). Equally, each person is unique so it is possible to treat psychology idiographically as well as nomothetically. Each person requires a unique form of description and explanation, but it is an explanation or theory that follows the rules of science in being falsifiable.

Humanistic psychology is not the only approach within psychology that assumes the uniqueness of the individual. Hermeneutical psychology is also predicated on the assumption that each person is unique. However, hermeneutical psychology rejects the scientific rational that is accepted by humanistic psychologists. The hermeneutical approach to uniqueness is discussed in Chapter 9.

Measuring uniqueness

The concept of a trait forms the basis of modern personality theories – hence the term *personality trait*. Neuroticism, extraversion, openness, conscientiousness and agreeableness are all traits. So are the traits of aggression, silliness, and laziness. Traits are almost invariably treated as a nomothetic concept in the sense that every trait applies to everyone. For example, everyone can be placed somewhere along a dimension of neuroticism. Everyone can be placed somewhere along a trait of aggression. Each trait dimension applies to everyone.

Personality traits from an idiographic perspective

Allport (1962) proposed that traits should be considered idiographic rather than nomothetic – he applied Windelband's distinction to personality theory. Allport's argument is as follows. A trait describes a pattern of behaviour that is consistent over different situations and over time. So, for example, if someone has an aggressive trait, then one would expect that person to be aggressive at work, at home, in the park, and on holiday. By contrast a person who has a non-aggressive trait would be non-aggressive at work, at home, in the park, and on holiday. In both cases the behaviour is consistent, and it would be reasonable to describe the two people as being aggressive and non-aggressive respectively.

Now consider another person who is aggressive at work and in the park but not at home or on holiday. Or another person who is aggressive at home but nowhere else. These individuals cannot be described as falling anywhere on the trait of aggressiveness, because their behaviour is inconsistent across situations. Allport argued that traits sometimes apply to a person and sometimes not. So, each person can be described by an array of traits that may differ from the array of traits used to describe someone else. Each person has their own unique (or reasonably unique) array of traits. When a trait applies to a person, then that person can be represented on that trait with a number. So Allport's approach is both idiographic and quantitative.

The idiographic approach to traits is based on the assumption that sometimes it is the situation rather than a trait that determines behaviour. A similar idea is found in the non-linear interaction of person and situation (NIPS) model that was described in Chapter 7. According to NIPS, strong people exhibit the same trait in different situations. Weak people vary their behaviour according to the situation. However, there is a difference between Allport's idiographic traits and NIPS. In the case of NIPS, the terms *strong* or *weak people* refer to a tendency that occurs across traits; it is a nomothetic concept. By contrast, in Allport's idiographic trait theory, a person can be weak in regard to one trait but strong with regard to another.

Despite being theoretically plausible, Allport's idiographic approach to traits never caught on. It is so much easier to explain personality in terms of dimensions shared by everyone rather than dimensions that are unique to each individual. In addition, personality theorists argue that people are in fact reasonably consistent across situations for the higher order traits, such as the big five traits of neuroticism, extraversion, openness, conscientiousness, and agreeableness, so it is meaningful to treat them nomothetically. Of course, they would say that wouldn't they! Personality theory is based on a nomothetic assumption. The NIPS model would suggest that consistency of behaviour across situations applies only to some people, namely, strong people. Perhaps both are correct to some degree. Students should come to their own conclusions.

Personal construct theory

Personal construct theory is an idiographic *and* quantitative approach to measuring personality that is still in use today. Proposed by George A. Kelly (1905–1967) the theory is based on the assumption that there is no objective reality. Instead, people *construct* a reality based on their experience. Reality is subjective and each person creates their own reality. Kelly suggests that people are naïve scientists: They form hypotheses about the world on the basis of observation, because ordinary people, like scientists, are trying to predict and anticipate events. (Kelly, 1955, 1963). Kelly is described by some as a humanistic psychologist; to others he is an early cognitive psychologist who focussed on perception. Kelly himself resisted being labelled with either category, considering his own work unique (Benjafield, 2008).

The personal construct

Kelly's theory of personality is based on the idea of a 'personal construct.' A personal construct is a way of construing or interpreting the world. People have different ways of construing or interpreting the world, that is, they have different personal constructs. By understanding personal constructs psychologists are able to understand how people function and how they differ between themselves.

A personal construct is a dichotomy that is used to make sense of the world. That is, it is a form of judgement that we make about the world. The dichotomy has two poles, a similarity pole and contrast pole. Any object is classified either in terms of the similarity pole or the contrast pole. This may sound complicated, so the easiest way to understand a personal construct is through an example of how they are discovered.

Imagine three objects:

A whale
A rat
A trout

In what way are two of these objects similar and one different? There are several possible answers, but suppose you replied with this:

"A whale and rat are mammals whereas a trout is a fish."

In this example, 'mammal' is the similarity pole of the construct and 'fish' the contrast pole. The construct is *mammal versus fish*.

However another possible answer is this:

"A whale and trout live in water, a rat lives on land."

In this second example, 'lives in water' is the similarity pole and 'lives on land' the contrast pole. The construct is *lives on water versus lives on land.'*

If students are asked to compare a whale, rat and trout, they usually create many more constructs, e.g.,

Smooth versus hairy
Big versus little
Eaten by people versus not normally eaten by people.

A construct is like a theory. It has a focus in the sense that it applies to a particular kind of context. For example, the construct *mammal versus fish* applies only to animals. When you see an animal, it is reasonable to classify it in terms of whether it is a mammal or not. When you see a plant, you are unlikely to ask yourself the question, "is this a mammal or not?"

Kelly's theory suggests that

◆ An individual's personality is their construct system
◆ People have different constructs: They construe the world in different ways.

◆ Finding out about someone's constructs tell us what that person is like and how they will respond to different situations.

Kelly provided a counselling service to students and school children, and to help in this he developed a method for understanding a person's construct system. He called this method the 'repertory grid test' or 'rep test' for short. Because many student problems arise from their interactions with others, constructs relating to the way a person views other people are particularly important.

Exercise to find out about your own constructs about people
The following procedure will allow students discover what constructs they use in their relations with other people

1 Write down a list of six people you know (i.e., six real people such as friends and relatives). For example, this might be Bob, Mary, Peter, Sue, Alison, and Roger.
2 Take the first three people in the list, and ask yourself in what way two are similar and one different? For example, you might say that Bob and Mary have a sense of humour and Peter hasn't.
3 Write down the similarity pole (the way two are similar) and the contrast pole (the way the third person is different). For example, this would be 'sense of humour versus no sense of humour.'
4 Now take another three people from the list. For example, this might be Peter, Sue, and Alison.
5 Ask yourself again, in what way are two similar and one different? You might say that Peter and Sue are old and Alison is young.
6 Write down the poles of the construct again, for example, 'old versus young.'
7 Now take a further three people and repeat the process. It doesn't matter which three people you compare as long as it is a different combination. Continue doing this until you have made at least ten comparisons, or until you are generating no new constructs.

Having created your list of constructs, now change roles and imagine you are the examining psychologist. The examining psychologist gains insight into the constructs that lie behind the words used by the client. The examining psychologist uses this insight to advise the client. If you are continuing with this exercise, you will be able to give yourself some sound advice.

First, the examining psychologist needs to find out how many constructs the client has. Sometimes the client uses different words for constructs that have similar meanings. For example, a client might present three sets of similarity and contrast poles: 'intelligent versus not intelligent' and 'educated versus not educated' and 'thick versus bright.' A moment's reflection will show that these different words refer to one underlying construct dealing with intelligence, so the examining psychologist should interpret these as one. The more constructs the person has, the more adaptable the person is in a complex world, so people who have many constructs usually do better in social contexts than those who have few.

Second, the examining psychologist interprets how the person construes the world in order to give advice. This involves the psychologist trying to interpret how the client views the world the world about them from the constructs that have been produced. Again, it is easiest to understand this with an example.

Imagine you are an examining psychologist and have been presented by the following constructs of a client:

Easy going – hypercritical.
Feels inferior – feels confident.
Socially skilled – unpleasant.
Tense – easy to be with.
Maladjusted – easy going.
Understanding – hypercritical.

The client's constructs relate to issues of perceived criticism and being criticised by others. The client has issues concerning self-confidence. The psychologist will also note that a therapist will be judged using exactly the same constructs as the client uses for other people. The psychologist will have to make a special effort not to appear critical and provide a way of helping the client become less defensive.

Kelly helped clients by advising them to try using other constructs. In practice, this meant asking clients to pretend to be someone else in a therapy session and try out what it feels like to take the role of someone else – hence, the name of his therapy, fixed role therapy. Kelly's method and theory show that it is possible to measure the mind, but at the same time accept there is an aspect of uniqueness to every person.

Modern use of personal constructs and comparison with nomothetic techniques

The rep test is used today, not necessarily by psychologists and not necessarily in a clinical context. It is a useful technique for understanding the constructs people use in different contexts. For example, the rep test has been used to find out how ordinary people attribute meaning to buildings. By finding out what constructs people use when they judge buildings, architects are able to take the perceptions of ordinary people into account in architectural design (Bannister & Fransella, 2019). The rep test has been used to find out how people construe meaning in different types of work-related organisations so that managers can better understand how workers respond to their decisions

(Bourne & Jankowicz, 2018). The rep test has been used to find out what constructs people use when they come to a museum, to help in the design and management of museums (Caldwell & Coshall, 2002). In these cases, the researchers refer to the 'rich meaning' that the technique provides, and in each case people, ordinary people, are presented with three buildings, three organisations, three museums, or whatever is the focus, and asked in what way two are similar and one different.

The use of the rep test in applied contexts can be contrasted with the equivalent use of the semantic differential (Osgood, Suci, & Tannenbaum, 1967). The semantic differential is based on the assumption that everyone uses the same dimensions of judgement. These dimensions are:

Evaluation (good versus bad).
Potency (strong versus weak).
Activity (active versus passive).

The semantic differential is based on the assumption that everyone uses the same constructs when judging objects, and uses the same constructs irrespective of the object being judged. Personal construct theory is based on the assumption that people use different constructs when judging objects. To some extent both views are true. To some extent people have common characteristics when judging objects. However, the ability of the rep test to find out how different types of constructs are used in different situations enables the technique to provide a more situation specific analysis of the attribution of meaning. It is the situational specificity of the rep test that makes it most attractive to those working in applied contexts. Furthermore, if different people use similar constructs to judge a particular type of object, then it is perfectly possible to use those constructs to develop a scale that is used nomothetically. Idiographic research can inform nomothetic research.

Being uniquely happy

Abraham Maslow (1908–1970) was one of the founders of the 'third force in psychology' (see introduction to this chapter), but died shortly before the founding of the humanistic psychology division (Division 32) of the American Psychological Association in 1971.

Maslow is known for his hierarchy of needs (Maslow, 1954, 1968), an idea that has been described as the best-known incorrect theory in psychology (Hoffman, 1980). The hierarchy is (from the top) self-actualisation, esteem, belongingness and love, safety, physiological needs. Maslow proposed that lower level needs require satisfaction in order for the higher level needs to emerge. In fact, the theory describes only a general trend. People who are struggling to keep family and home together can have little time for themselves, though

Self-actualisation.

an artist can self-actualise while starving in a garret. It is certainly possible to self-actualise when hungry.

It is Maslow's concept of self-actualisation, at the top of the hierarchy, that has had the wider impact. This concept features in the work of just about every humanist psychologist.

Self-actualisation means that you strive towards becoming the person you really are. There are two main characteristics of the concept of self-actualisation. The first is that it breaks with the *causal* tradition that characterises both psychoanalysis and behaviourism and replaces it with a *teleological* alternative. In the case of behaviourism and psychoanalysis, a person is thought to be caused to do things because of prior events. In the case of psychoanalysis these prior events are early childhood experiences. In the case of behaviourism they are previous patterns of reinforcement. In both cases the person is *driven* to behave by prior causes, that is, by things that have happened in the past. Maslow suggests that people behave in the way they do because they are trying to achieve something in the future. That is, people strive towards future states, rather than being driven by prior states. The use of a future state to explain behaviour is referred to as a teleological explanation. Teleological explanations (i.e., saying what someone is trying to achieve) are fundamentally different from the causal explanations. Only causal explanations are used in the physical sciences, and so the use of teleological explanation marks a distinct break with the natural science tradition on which much of psychology is predicated. The teleological explanation is a psychological explanation and not found in the physical sciences – one does not refer to atoms 'wanting to do something.' So, the first feature of self-actualisation is that this is something people are striving towards, rather than something people are driven to do.

The second feature of self-actualisation is the assumption that each individual is unique and different. Self-actualising is not a matter of becoming a better person, but rather becoming the person 'you are supposed to be.' This idea of 'supposed to be' assumes that *by nature* people have characteristics which make them unique. That is, the real you is genetically determined, rather than something that can be cultivated by nurture. Because people differ, any action is potentially self-actualising. Self-actualising behaviours can be defined only in relation to a particular person. What is self-actualising for one person may not be for another.

Maslow's emphasis on positive goal satisfaction is reflected in more recent works on goal satisfaction, including that of positive psychology (Csikszentmihalyi & Seligman, 2000), a movement that emphasises what is good in life rather than what needs to be changed because it is bad. Maslow even used the term *positive psychology* in the 1950s (Froh, 2004).

In his later works Maslow suggested that people self-actualise in two ways, one with and one without spiritualism or transcendence (Maslow, 1970). For some people spirituality is an important part of self-actualising, but for others

Origins of self-actualisation

Maslow was born in Brooklyn, New York, and was the eldest child in a large family of immigrant Russian Jews who lived close to the border with Poland. The following story is told of Rabbi Zusya (unknown–1800) of Hanipol, Poland: When he was dying he expressed concern about meeting God and said to those about him "When I reach the next world, God will not ask me, 'Why were you not Moses?' Instead, he will ask me, 'Why were you not Zusya?'" Why were you not the person you were meant to be? It is highly likely that Maslow would have known about Rabbi Zusya as well as the Hasidic tradition that Zusya represented. Hassidism includes two ideas that are common in humanistic psychology. One is the joy of living; the other is the acceptance of suffering.

it is not. Spirituality is not just a matter of spiritual religious or beliefs – but rather a sense of awareness of the ultimate. Maslow believed that Einstein was a spiritual self-actualiser because in thinking about physics Einstein had a concept of ultimate reality.

The idea that spirituality forms part of high level goals was developed independently by Viktor Frankl (1905–1997) who felt that this aspect of human existence was neglected by other humanistic psychologists (Pytell, 2006). Frankl was Jewish and living in Germany at the time of the Holocaust. He survived but his entire family did not. Frankl is the originator of 'logotherapy,' an approach to therapy based on understanding the clients' meaning of life (Frankl, 1959, 1967, 1969).

Frankl's personal experience

Pytell (2000) points out that although Frankl's book *Man's Search for Meaning* implied he was in Auschwitz for a good deal of time, in fact he was only in Auschwitz for three days. Nevertheless, his experiences as one of the few survivors of a concentration camp formed the basis for his theory.

Frankl suggested that the human super-ordinate goal was to find meaning in life. For him, self-actualisation meant meaning in life. Frankl distinguished three categories of the meaning of life.

◆ First, there is meaning that is based on what one accomplishes or gives to the world. Our work can give us a sense of meaning, whether it is paid employment, a hobby, being a parent or helping other people.

◆ Second, there is the meaning that comes from our experiences with the world. These experiences include things that are beautiful as well as the experience of love. The nature lover who looks from the top of a mountain, the gourmet who enjoys food, and the lover gazing into the loved one's eyes all gain a sense of meaning from those experiences.

◆ Third, there is the meaning that comes from our approach to suffering and those things that cannot be changed. This last meaning has particular resonance with Frankl's experience in a concentration camp where those who found meaning, including those who found meaning in future revenge, survived best. Frankl believed that there was meaning in demonstrating that one could suffer with dignity (Yalom, 1980).

Self-actualisation from a nomothetic perspective

Each person's meaning in life, or each person's self-actualisation, is unique. A common theme in humanistic psychologists is that finding meaning in life is important. Later authors have shown that it is possible to measure the degree of meaning or self-actualisation using nomothetic techniques. The 'meaning in life questionnaire' (Steger, Frazier, Oishi, & Kaler, 2006) asks people to rate their satisfaction with the meaning or purpose of their life. The scale produces a score that reflects a person's meaning of life, without that person having to define what that meaning is. The satisfaction with life scale measures a person's satisfaction with life (Diener, Emmons, Larsen, & Griffin, 1985). The 'sense of coherence scale' (Antonovsky, 1993) provides a similar sort of measure in that people are able to rate satisfaction with aspects of life that give it meaning. Research shows that people who feel that their lives have meaning, whatever that meaning is, are happier and healthier than those who do not. The silver lining questionnaire measures the extent to which people find meaning in illness (Sodergren, Hyland, Crawford, & Partridge, 2004). Research shows that finding meaning in illness promotes recovery (Hyland, Sodergren & Lewith, 2006).

Other recent authors have examined which goals, when satisfied, lead to happiness. Self-determination theory suggests that happiness is achieved through the satisfaction of three goals: autonomy, competence, and relatedness (Deci & Ryan, 1985). Self-determination theory is based on the nomothetic assumption that there are ways of achieving self-actualisation that are common to all people, but that they involve other subgoals, autonomy, competence, and relatedness.

In summary, the insights gained in humanistic psychology have influenced other areas of psychology. Ideas developed by humanistic psychologists that were developed originally within an idiographic framework have subsequently been used by other psychologists who used nomothetic measurement and research.

Treating people uniquely

Every psychotherapist would (or should) say that they treat each client as a unique person. The recognition of the uniqueness of the person is implicit in the talking therapy of Freud who suggested he was acting as an archaeologist in uncovering a person's past. Everyone has a unique past. Everyone has a unique present. When training a psychotherapist, it is impossible to prepare them in advance for all the different unique cases they will meet, but it is possible to train them in features that are common to all or some clients. Amongst the various humanistic contributors to advances in psychotherapy, Carl R. Rogers (1902–1987) stands out. Rogers is considered the founder of counselling psychology.

Rogers believed there were three types of knowing (Rogers, 1942, 1951):

Subjective knowing: The knowledge we have of our own consciousness and which is unique to us. Rogers referred to this as the phenomenal field. The term *phenomena* – meaning mental content – derives from the philosopher Husserl (1910/1965).

Objective knowing: The shared knowledge we have of the outside world, i.e., the kind of knowledge from observing things around us.

Interpersonal knowing: Interpersonal knowledge is the understanding of one person's phenomenal field by another person. Rogers' approach to psychotherapy focusses on interpersonal knowledge, how a therapist can understand the phenomenal field of a client. Rogers believed that it was possible to form and test hypotheses about the interpersonal field of a client, and so interpersonal knowledge is a falsifiable science and in that regard like any other science.

Rogers believed that humans are basically good. They are good when they are free or mature and they are only bad when they are neurotic. This idea of the fundamental goodness of Rogers' approach can be contrasted with that of Freud who thought people were driven by fundamentally bad instincts and only good because they were constrained to be good by society.

Rogers adopted the idea, proposed by Maslow, that people strive towards self-actualisation and believed that self-actualisation always manifested itself positively in one way or another. It is only when people are neurotic that they deviate from this pattern of goodness. Unkindness and cruelty are a deviation from the natural human state, not part of it.

Rogers noticed from his clinical practice that clients often referred to themselves. They would say things like, "I have not been feeling myself recently" or "I am not happy with the way I am." Rogers inferred that the self is something that is perceived. The self is an organised conceptual gestalt. It is not made up from lots of different bits and pieces, but is organised as a whole. Furthermore, this whole that is the self can grow and change and yet retain the same identity. The student applying to go to university is the same person when they graduate. The phenomenal field of the self remains the same.

Are humans good or bad?

The question of whether people are fundamentally good or naturally bad was debated long before the development of psychology. The Christian idea of 'original sin' suggests that people are basically bad (due to the fall of Adam) and are redeemed only through the mediation of Jesus Christ. By contrast, the philosopher Jean-Jacques Rousseau (1712–1778) supported the idea of 'the noble savage' who was pure and noble in the natural state. Rousseau believed that society corrupts what is otherwise a noble human. The Freudian view coincides with that of Christianity, whereas Rogers' view is consistent with that of Rousseau. The modern view is that humans have the capacity for good or evil, and that this capacity is influenced by environmental factors. There is evidence of a biological bias towards goodness or badness in some people (Fox, 2017), but the issue of heredity and environmental contributions to behaviour is complex (see Chapter 7).

Two types of self

Rogers distinguishes two types of self:

> *The self*, also known as the actual self or the real self, refers to the way clients describe themselves as they are now.
> *The ideal self* refers to the self clients would like to be.

One aim of Rogerian therapy is to reduce the discrepancy between the self and ideal self. The therapy is linked to the idea of uniqueness of people: The self that is right for one individual may be different from the self that is right for another. Rogers' aim in providing therapy was to help a person become the person they really are and be satisfied with the person they really are.

Measuring self-ideal–self-discrepancy

The Q-sort technique, used by Rogers, is based on 100 statements that describe a person, for example, the statements might be 'am generally happy' or 'get upset easily.' The statements are written on cards. The client is first asked to sort the statements into two piles, those that are 'like me' and those that are 'unlike me.' The cards are then shuffled and the client is asked to sort the statements into two more piles, those that are 'like the ideal me' and those that are 'unlike the ideal me.' The number of differences in the card allocations between the first sorting and second sorting determines the discrepancy between the self and ideal self.

Self-consistency or congruence

Rogers adds one more idea to the distinction of the self versus the ideal self. The client develops the concept of self on the basis of experiences about the self. For example, if whenever you met someone, they said to you 'you are amazingly beautiful,' you would begin to believe that you are amazingly beautiful. The concept of congruence is about the relationship between the perception of yourself, and the objective data with which you are presented. So, for example, if everyone says 'you are amazingly beautiful' and you believe that you are beautiful, then that is congruence. But if everyone says 'you are amazingly beautiful' and you believe that you are ugly, then that is incongruence. A modern and more easily understood example of incongruence is provided by anorexia. People with anorexia think they are fat, whereas the objective data – and what everyone else is saying – is that they are very thin.

Rogers believed that incongruence resulted from childhood experiences and was unhealthy because it creates a distorted sense of reality, a distorted sense that can lead to anxiety and depression. Rogers distinguished two ways of bringing up children: with unconditional positive regard and with conditional positive regard.

Children brought up with conditional positive regard are disciplined with the withdrawal of love as a means of punishment. That is, when the child is naughty, the parent becomes distant and unloving. Children brought up with unconditional positive regard are not disciplined with withdrawal of love as a means of punishment. When the children are naughty the children are disciplined in one way or another, but the children always believe that they as individuals are loved – it is the behaviour not the individual that is being punished. Rogers believed that conditional positive regard was very damaging as children brought up in this way would learn to believe a reality – the parent's reality – that is not their own. That is, in order to regain the parent's regard, the child learns to distort reality.

Other selves

Later authors have developed Rogers' theory further with additional self-related concepts. Higgins (1987) introduced the distinction between the ideal self (what you would like to be) and the ought self (what others would like you to be). The ought self is particularly relevant to feelings of dissatisfaction a person has that comes from social comparison. Higgins suggests that the discrepancy between the self and ideal self leads to depression whereas discrepancy between the self and ought self leads to anxiety. Another approach taken by Markus and Nurius (1986) is that there are several possible selves, including the past self and future self. Although people are free to create many sorts of possible self, the self they create is bound by their circumstances. Later authors have emphasised the malleability of the self concept. This idea of malleability is also found in the fixed role therapy of George Kelly (see earlier in this chapter). A person can become a different person by choosing to become a different person.

Therapy

Rogers (1957) suggested that six conditions were needed for therapy to be effective. This is how Rogers defined them:

1   Two persons are in psychological contact.
2   The first, whom we shall term the client, is in a state of incongruence, being vulnerable or anxious.
3   The second person, whom we shall term the therapist, is congruent or integrated in the relationship.
4   The therapist experiences unconditional positive regard for the client.
5   The therapist experiences an empathic understanding of the client's internal frame of reference and endeavors to communicate this experience to the client.
6   The communication to the client of the therapist's empathic understanding and unconditional positive regard is to a minimal degree achieved.

(Rogers, 1957, p. 96)

Note how Rogers' definition uses jargon in a way that gives the impression of a science. 'Two persons in psychological contact' simply means that two people are communicating in some way. Although Rogers presents his theory as scientific, he was aware of the tension between being scientific and a purely human sense of understanding other people, a tension he discussed in 1955 (Rogers, 1955). During its history, psychology has needed to present itself as a science in order to gain acceptability within a culture that is dominated by science. Humanistic psychologists maintained the scientific status of psychology despite the fact that each person is unique. The tension, between the purely intuitive and the scientific, is discussed in Chapter 9 in the context of hermeneutical psychology, an approach that rejects the scientific model entirely.

Rogers originally called his therapy non-directive therapy because he wanted to emphasise the fact that the therapist is not directing the client to a particular fixed goal. However, he found that other therapists were not as successful as he was, the reason being that non-directive was being interpreted as disinterested or even stand-offish. So, in his later writing, Rogers called his therapy client centred therapy to emphasise the unconditional positive regard and empathic understanding that was central to his therapy.

Rogers' client centred approach underpins the common factors or contextual model of psychotherapy (see Chapter 5). The description given by Rogers earlier about what is needed for effective psychotherapy is very similar to that described by Frank and Frank (1991) and quoted in Chapter 5. The underlying assumption shared by Rogers as well as the common factors model is that it is the therapeutic context that is therapeutic rather than anything specific that happens in the therapy session. Rogers stresses the importance of the relationship in psychotherapy. The common factors model includes other components, including the cognitive component of expectancy.

Given the evidence supporting the common factors or contextual model in contrast to specific models of psychotherapy (Wampold, 2013), one might wonder why specific models of psychotherapy, such as cognitive behaviour therapy (Beck, 1967) are more popular and more respected than contextual models. The reason has to do with one of the weaknesses of the contextual model, namely that it does not provide an explanation consistent with the dominant paradigm that symptoms are caused by faults and removed by the correction of faults.

The dominant paradigm owes its origins to modern western medicine, which is based on the assumption that symptoms are caused by diseases that are caused by specific faults (pathophysiology) in the body (see Chapter 5). The contextual model has difficulty answering this question: What is wrong with the client and how does the context help? Rogers explains that unconditional regard might have been lacking in the client's life, and that the therapist's unconditional positive regard helps. But why positive regard has this therapeutic function is never fully explained. In the case of response expectancy theory (Kirsch, 1985), which is one of the other components of the contextual model, expectancy fails to explain the underlying pathology even though it provides an explanation of benefit. The components of the contextual model provide only a partial account of fault and the correction of fault. By contrast, cognitive behaviour theory (Beck, 1967) explains symptoms as resulting from erroneous cognitions and that it is the change in these cognitions that then produces therapeutic benefit. The cognitive behaviour model is based on the assumption of a specific form of fault that is corrected by a specific intervention, and in this regard is consistent with the assumptions of modern western medicine, as are psychoanalytic explanations of psychopathology (see Chapter 5). The weakness of the contextual model, the model most associated with Rogers, is not that it doesn't work nor that it is inconsistent with the evidence. Its weakness – if it is a weakness – is that is inconsistent with the assumptions of a dominant paradigm.

Summary

Nomothetic science explains the generality of people and events. Idiographic science is the science of the uniqueness of people and events. Most of psychology is nomothetic. Experimental, social, developmental, health, and many other topics in psychology provide an account of the ways in which people respond in the same way to different situations, people respond differently to the same situation or some interaction of the two. However, every human is unique in some way and the uniqueness of humans is studied in humanistic psychology.

Allport reinterpreted the concept of a trait from an idiographic perspective. A trait applies to a person only if the person's behaviour is consistent with regard to that trait. Kelly's theory of personal constructs is based on the assumption that everyone construes the world in a different way. A person's constructs could be assessed through the rep test.

Several authors assume that people are motivated by a goal of self-actualisation or a search for meaning. People self-actualise in different ways, just as people can find meaning in their lives in different ways. Although there is uniqueness in self-actualisation, meaning, and life satisfaction, these concepts can be measured nomothetically by allowing people to provide their own definitions of meaning and life satisfaction.

The uniqueness of people is recognised in all psychotherapies, even though general principles of pathology and health also apply. The uniqueness of the therapeutic encounter is emphasised in Roger's psychotherapy, an approach that underpins modern counselling and the contextual model of psychotherapy.

Essay questions

1 How have psychologists assessed people from an idiographic perspective and what are the advantages and disadvantages compared with nomothetic assessment of individual differences?
2 What is self-actualisation, how can it be measured, and what are the consequences of achieving or not achieving self-actualisation?
3 How has Rogers contributed to the contextual model of psychotherapy and what are its advantages and disadvantages?

9

What are the assumptions of psychologists who use qualitative research methodology and what are the alternatives to treating psychology as a natural science?

> Whatever exists at all exists in some amount. To know it thoroughly
> involves knowing its quantity as well as its quality.
>
> (Thorndike, 1918, p. 16)

Much of psychology uses quantitative measurement of variables in the research process. Quantitative measurement means that a number can be assigned to the variable in question. The quote from Thorndike reflected his belief that psychology should employ quantitative measurement, like other natural sciences. At the same time, the quotation by Thorndike refers to quality. For him, the understanding of quality was taken for granted.

All quantitative variables differ in terms of quality. Theoretical terms and observation terms (see Chapter 4) need to be described in terms of qualities. There are many reasons why qualitative description is part of *all* sciences. However, *qualitative methods* are something more than the qualitative description of quantitative variables, however important that might be. Qualitative methods are one of the methods used in the discipline of psychology, but these methods can be used in different ways and with different underlying assumptions. The aim of this chapter is to (a) describe the different assumptions of the different types of use of qualitative methods and (b) describe approaches to psychology where psychology is treated as something that is different from a natural science.

The Romantics

The idea that there is a form of non-numeric meaning in the world is a feature of 19th-century German Romanticism exemplified in Goethean Science (Steiner, 1883/1988). Goethean science involves examining objects as they are and trying to intuit their essence. The essence cannot be ascribed a number. It is a purely intuitive process of feeling. In Goethean science, the colour white is a colour which has its own properties and 'feels' different from other colours. In Newtonian science, the colour white is simply a combination of all the colours of the rainbow and does not exist as a distinct colour.

The origin of qualitative research methods

Qualitative research methods do not originate in academic psychology. They were developed by psychologists who worked in a commercial setting in market research companies. In the 1950s there were two types of market research and two types of market research company: quantitative and qualitative. Quantitative market research involved questionnaires that were used to record people's quantitative response to particular questions. For example, a person might be asked how much they would like to buy a product, or whether they thought a product was useful, with the response recorded, quantitatively, on a numeric scale. Students may be familiar with quantitative market researchers who stop them in streets and shopping malls with a clipboard and who ask them if they could spare a few minutes to answer some questions.

The method used by qualitative market researchers was different from that of the quantitative researchers in that no questionnaires were used. Ernest Dichter (1907–1991) is credited with being the founder of qualitative market research (Stern, 2004). Dichter was trained in psychoanalysis in Vienna and obtained a doctorate in psychology in 1934. The Dichters were Jewish (at one time he lived across the street from Freud, their houses being 18 and 19 Bergasse, respectively) and Dichter originally planned to be a psychoanalyst. However, he was financially unsuccessful and started working for a market research company in Vienna. After he was arrested in 1937 (the market research company was accused by the Nazis of subversive activity), he and his wife fled to Paris in 1938 and then to America. In America, Dichter joined a market research company and developed his own unique and different way of finding 'motivational triggers.' He set up a consultancy business in 1939 and founded The Institute for Motivational Research in New York in 1946. Other institutes using his methods soon appeared.

Dichter was strongly influenced by Freudian theory and so he assumed that the reason why someone liked a product might not be available to that person's conscious. The reason why someone liked something had to be inferred from the way they talked about it, rather than asking the person directly, and in particular, how they talked to each other about it. Advertising could then be linked to the reason someone liked something. For example, Dichter analysed why people liked soup in order to advise soup manufacturers about advertising strategy. This is what he wrote:

> Soup is endowed with magic power. . . . It protects, heals, and gives strength, courage and the feeling of belonging. . . . Magic arises from the brewing together of special ingredients.
>
> (Dichter, 1964, pp. 67–68)

The Campbell soup manufacturing company developed a series of advertisements based on Dichter's advice. For example, they used the slogan "good for the body, good for the soul" to market their soups. They also used Dichter's interpretation in visual displays involving cherubic looking, rosy cheeked, happy toddlers where an emphasis was placed on the nourishing bond between mother and child, all of which was enhanced by the 'magic' of Campbell's soups (see examples in modern advertising at www.campbells.com).

Another example from more recent times illustrates the importance of hidden meaning in qualitative market research. In the 1960s coffee drinking was beginning to replace tea drinking in the UK as the socially upward mobile drink of choice, in part due to the convenience of instant coffee that had been developed by the company Nestlé. The instant coffee produced by Nestlé was a brown powder. Also in the 1960s, and in recognition of the popularity of instant coffee, Nestle developed a granular form of instant coffee that had a better flavour. However, some people continued to buy the original powder form and Nestlé wanted to find out why as there was a market for both types of coffee.

The market researchers used the same technique used by Dichter, namely, the focus group. The powder coffee drinkers described their coffee as being "not bitter" and that it "didn't upset my stomach," as well as other descriptives that were all about what the coffee did *not* do in comparison to the coffee granules. The researchers inferred from these focus groups that the powder coffee drinkers didn't really like coffee – they drank it because it was socially more acceptable to drink coffee rather than tea. The powder coffee drinkers did not refer to the social aspects of drinking, but this was inferred by the researchers. Nestlé used this research to reposition their powder coffee as 'mild coffee' and advertised it with pictures of women in nice, middle class kitchens drinking coffee with other nice women. The marketing pitch was "this coffee is a good social activity, rather than this coffee tastes nice."

Psychologists' earlier contribution to advertising

W. D. Scott was the first psychologist to develop the science of advertising, using direct suggestion as well as features of the target group (see Chapter 3). J. B. Watson (see Chapter 4) had a career in advertising after he was excluded from universities. Watson advertised products by associating them with other positive images (e.g., an attractive woman with a car). The motivational researchers went yet further by selecting objects to associate with the product that had the same motivational features as the product.

Dichter and other market researchers not only tried to understand the motivational basis for consumer objects, they also came up with slogans and strategies for improving sales. When he first moved to America, Dichter advised Proctor and Gamble on how to sell their soap. He came up with the slogan "wash your troubles away." A Proctor and Gamble executive acknowledged his creativity by writing "You s.o.b., you are really a copy writer" (Stern, 2004, p. 166).

Qualitative research as part of quantitative natural science

One of the arguments proposed by Karl Popper (Popper, 1963) (see Chapter 1) is that science proceeds through a series of conjectures and refutations. The conjectures are hypotheses about the world. Where do those conjectures come from? In part, conjectures come from observations. That observation can be accidental or it can be systematic. When Fleming discovered penicillin (see Chapter 1), his observation was accidental. However, it is perfectly possible to generate hypotheses by observing the world systematically, and qualitative methods can be used to assist that systematic observation. Used in this way, qualitative methods are part of the process of quantitative research and their only aim is to assist quantitative research.

A good way of understanding how qualitative research helps quantitative science is with an example. New pharmacological treatments had been developed to treat people with severe asthma. A quality of life questionnaire was needed to assess outcome in clinical trials of these new treatments, but a suitable questionnaire was not available.

In order to develop the questionnaire, the researchers needed to find out how severe asthma affected people's lives. One possibility was to guess, or to use clinical experience. Another possibility, and the one used by the authors, was to find out directly from patients using qualitative research. The authors recruited a number of people with severe asthma and interviewed them, asking about the various ways in which asthma affected their lives (Hyland, Whalley, Jones, & Masoli, 2015). The researchers then constructed a questionnaire on the basis of those interviews. In order to construct a questionnaire that was written in a way that patients would find most comfortable, the authors then asked patients to evaluate their questionnaire using focus groups (Hyland, Lanario, Pooler, Masoli, & Jones, 2018). In the focus groups, the patients read the questionnaire, commented on it and suggested modifications that were then adopted by the researchers. Finally, the patient-modified questionnaire was used to collect quantitative data validating the questionnaire. It was only after the qualitative and quantitative research that the questionnaire was ready for use for its original purpose as an outcome measure in clinical trials of new asthma treatments. So interviews and focus groups were used in the research process, but the qualitative methods were not an end in themselves, but only to help produce valid quantitative data.

There is an important difference between how qualitative research is being used in this example and how it was used in earlier qualitative market research. In the case of questionnaire construction, the statements of patients were taken at face value. If they said that their sleep was disturbed by asthma, then a question on sleep was added to the questionnaire. If they said that one word was difficult to understand and another was better, then the word was changed. Used in this way, the patients are simply acting to help the researchers carry out their

---

Qualitative research in drug regulation

The American Food and Drug Administration (FDA) published guidelines for the construction questionnaires measuring 'patient reported outcomes' in 2009 (U.S. Department of Health and Human Services Food and Drug Administration, 2009). These guidelines identify three stages. The first stage is concept definition. The second stage occurs when the domains of quality of life are discovered through qualitative research with patients. The third stage of quantitative research with patients establishes the reliability and validity of the questionnaire. Prior to that date, many researchers published questionnaires without either reporting or carrying out qualitative research. The FDA guidelines emphasised the importance of qualitative research in medicine.

---

research. In fact, many medical grant giving bodies require that patients *should* be involved in the design of the research. The technical term for this is *patient public involvement*, or PPI. However, psychologists who specialise in qualitative methods would draw a clear a distinction between this kind of informal use of qualitative research, such as PPI, and their own methodologically more rigorous use.

When used in questionnaire design there is no attempt to find hidden meaning in words. The term *thematic analysis* is used to describe an analysis of discourse that focusses on the surface meaning of words (Clark & Braun, 2013). The methodology of thematic analysis involves attention to detail and to coding of the detail. As the name suggests, thematic analysis is an analysis of themes in discourse, but without any *a priori* theoretical assumptions. Words reveal nothing more than the literal interpretation of what is said. Thematic analysis could also be described as an application of common sense to understanding the discourse of others.

Qualitative research can be used to develop methodology, as shown in the earlier example, but it can also be used in hypothesis generation. Talking to people can provide information that stimulates hypothesis generation. Of course, hypothesis generation comes not just from observation but also from the person doing the observation (see Chapter 1). The really difficult and important skill of scientific research, the skill that makes an immense difference to reputation, is in getting the right question. It takes experience to know what right questions to ask. The most impactful research questions are often not those that are being asked now, but those that will be important in a year or two when the data are collected, analysed, and the paper submitted. There is a purely intuitive process in developing research questions that depends on the person. Quantitative science depends on an intuitive process that involves qualitative understanding.

Social constructionism and the theoretical rationale for qualitative methodology in psychology

The use of qualitative methods in support of quantitative methods is based on the standard assumptions of quantitative science – if something exists it can be measured. However, there are those who believe that quantitative measurement destroys or at least obscures some of the essential meaning of something. Words spoken by people may reveal truths that could not be obtained by asking direct questions and recording the answers numerically. For these psychologists, qualitative research should be used as an end in itself, not in support of quantitative research.

Social constructionism provided a major impetus to the development of qualitative methods in academic psychology. It did so because of an explicit theoretical rationale that supports qualitative methods as an end in themselves. The term *social constructionism* is used in several different senses and is used by both psychologists and sociologists. The term first appears in the title of a book *The Social Construction of Reality: A Treatise in the Sociology of Knowledge* written in 1966 (Berger & Luckman, 1966), and, as the title of the book implies, it is used in the context of sociology. Social psychologists later used the term. The term *social constructivism* has been used to emphasise the development of an individual's meaning in a social context, and therefore to represent a psychological versus sociological interpretation, but the reality is that the terms are not used consistently. The term *social constructionism* was linked with psychology at least by the early 1980s (Gergen, 1985).

The underlying assumption of social constructionism is that the mind, by which is meant emotions and other conscious experiences, is constructed out of a social reality that involves other people. That social reality can be explored by examining people's conversations or discourses. Qualitative analysis provides an account of the deep meaning of reality which is not otherwise obtained by quantitative methods. The focus is on understanding the meaning of what people say.

Social constructionism represents a movement rather than a unified school of thought. Edley (2001) suggests that there are two forms of social constructionism, which he calls *ontological* and *epistemic*, each of which is based on a different set of assumptions. The term *ontology* refers to the study of how something exists – it refers to existence, becoming, or reality. The term *epistemology* refers to the study of how things acquire meaning. The difference between the ontological and epistemic forms of social constructionism depends on whether one believes social (or other) objects exist independently of the way they are socially constructed by people. The ontological interpretation is that social construction 'brings' objects into existence, and they would not exist without the people to construct them. The epistemic interpretation is that objects exist independently of people, but people give meaning to those objects by virtue of the social interactions between people. Edley argues that many of the criticisms of social constructionism are based on the assumption that social constructionists support the ontological form whereas he argues that few actually do. He writes:

> Contrary to the view of some critical realists, most social constructionists do not see language as the only reality. When they travel to conferences or go on holiday, for example, they consult their map books just like everybody else. They do not suppose that, say, Nottingham appears in the middle of the M1 motorway *because* it says so on the page and neither do they imagine that it somehow springs into existence at the moment it is mentioned. . . . Instead, a constructionist might point out that Nottingham is a city by virtue of a text (i.e., by royal decree) and that its boundaries – where it begins and ends – are also a matter of negotiation and argument. The argument is not, therefore that Nottingham doesn't really exist, but that it does so as a socially constructed reality.
>
> (Edley, 2001, p. 439)

Although social constructionism has its critics (sometimes of the ontological rather than epistemic type) the claims made by (the majority of) social constructionists are consistent with well-established ideas in the philosophy of science. The idea that meaning is theory laden is not new. Social constructionism can be seen as an extension of the 'theory ladenness of observables' proposal of Hanson (1958) (see Chapter 1), who argued that people interpret the world in terms of their theories. Social constructionism adds a social aspect to the idea of theory ladenness. People interpret or construct the world on the basis of social interaction. If socially acquired meaning is bound up with the description of humans, then an analysis of meaning should be central to any analysis of humans. Although meaning can be analysed through quantitative methods (e.g., the semantic differential, personal constructs), some would argue that a better way to understand meaning is by listening and hearing what people say in natural settings. Hence, a major contribution of social constructionism is that it promoted a form of methodology, qualitative methodology, that is now accepted as one of the methodologies available to psychologists.

Academic qualitative methodology versus commercial qualitative market research

The focus group method was developed by psychologists working as commercial market researchers. That and other methods of analysing talk was also available to psychologists who wanted to use qualitative methods as a research tool in an academic setting. The academic psychologists had a problem not experienced by those working in qualitative market research. In order to fit in with the presentation of psychology as a science, qualitative researchers had to show that the qualitative analysis of discourse was a science. (Note: discourse includes spoken and written speech.) There were three linked requirements to overcoming this hurdle. The first was to specify a methodology, a methodology that was accepted by consensus by other researchers. The second was that the methodology had to ensure the replication of results. Replicability is achieved when researchers follow the same methodology. The third was a consistent form of documentation. Documentation provides the basis for replication and evaluation by others. In order to be accepted and taken seriously by other psychologists – who had defined psychology as a science – qualitative researchers reinvented the earlier, commercial work as a rigorous qualitative methodology. The methodology of qualitative research became 'scientific' by virtue of its analysis and documentation (Willig, 2001).

The difference between academic qualitative research and commercial research is not only one of rigour. The difference is more complex. The basis of academic scientific research is that it is replicable. Two people in two different laboratories should get the same result. The attention to method is designed in part to achieve this replicability of results, so that different researchers produce the same results, despite those different researchers being different people with different skills. In commercial market research, however, there is recognition that the moderator can bring something unique to the focus group, such that some moderators and the companies they work for provide more insightful descriptions of products than others.

Qualitative research as a scientific end it itself

Two approaches can be distinguished in those using qualitative research as a scientific end in itself. First, there are those who use discourse as a way of making inferences about the content of the mind. This use is based on the same assumptions that guided the earlier qualitative market researchers. Discourse needs to be interpreted to reveal hidden meanings. Methodologies such as grounded theory (Glaser & Strauss, 1967) and interpretative phenomenological analysis (Smith, 1996) fall within this first category. Grounded theory is a theory that is inductive – i.e., induced from qualitative data by a detailed and systematic examination of the themes and ideas expressed in the discourse. Interpretational phenomenological analysis draws attention to the study of phenomenology, the role of the other, and the recognition that researchers should suspend their own beliefs so they can hear what the other person is saying. A key feature of both these approaches is that discourse can reveal the hidden meaning in what people say. This is particularly true of interpretative phenomenological analysis, though some, who describe their methodology as interpretive phenomenological analysis, do not in fact search for hidden meaning (Brocki & Wearden, 2006).

Second, there are those who study discourse as a form of behaviour where the detailed description of that behaviour provides insight into the ordinary interactions between people. In this second approach, the meaning is not assumed to be hidden in the minds of people. Conversational analysis provides an example of this second approach. Although there is no search for a person's inner meaning, conversational analysis can reveal meaning in the conversation that may not be apparent to those involved in the conversation. This meaning is revealed by a detailed analysis of the words themselves. This second approach is illustrated with the following example.

The mental capacity act of 2005 states that all people, whatever their intellectual impairment, should have the right to make their own decisions, and this is reflected in the policy of institutions caring for people with mental impairment. Antaki and colleagues (Antaki, Finlay, Walton, & Pate, 2008) wanted to examine how this was implemented in a particular residential home. In order to do this, they recorded the conversations between carers and residents and then analysed these conversations using the techniques of conversational analysis. The authors found that in some cases the carers provided choice in a way that the residents could understand and could make an informed choice, but in other cases staff presented choices in a way that the residents found confusing. For example, some staff repeated the choices after the resident had made a choice, which was interpreted by the resident as a criticism of the resident's first choice. The researchers were therefore able to advise the managers of the care home about training that would enable better interactions between carers and residents.

Conversational analysis requires training in a form of analysis that provides a detailed written representation of discourse. An example of text using this methodology taken from the research described is reproduced here (Antaki et al., 2008, p. 1172):

```
 8  → Kath [chicken, or beef, (1.0) [or (.) lamb.
 9  Vic: [°(beeh-)°
10  Kath: lamb.
11  → Vic: ((nodding)) lah.
12  (0.7)
13  Kath: lamb.
14  (0.5)
15  Kath: ((leaning head right)) or beef.
16  → Vic: ((nodding)) (beeh-) °lahm°,
17  Kath: ((leaning head left)) or chicken,
18  → Vic: ((moves hand forward to point to picture)) (mickeh).
19  Kath: which meat do you want.
20  Vic: ((points to a different picture)) (°mickeh°).
```

21 Kath: chicken.
22 Vic: ((leans back)) yeh ((nods))
23 Kath: °okay:° ((turns away from Vic)

This text illustrates three features of conversational analysis. The first is that this form of analysis provides the kind of methodological rigour one would expect from a science. The second is that discourse is being treated as a form of data without any attempt to find hidden meaning in the minds of those taking part. The third is that meaning can be found in the discourse itself that was not apparent to those taking part. The meaning that this analysis reveals is in the conversation, not in the minds of those taking part. The conclusions drawn by the researchers will be clear to anyone reading that extract. Although Kath wants to make sure Vic is making an informed choice, Vic is having difficulty negotiating what he is being asked to do because of the way it is being asked.

Psychology not as a science: hermeneutic psychology

The qualitative methods described earlier provide general statements about the world, statements that, as in the case of the aforementioned example, can be helpful in a practical sense. These statements are also falsifiable. The data are replicable, and any conclusions can, in principle, be falsified. The qualitative methodology used by the majority of psychologists therefore meets the criterion of a science, that of falsification. However, there are also those who believe that humans should not be understood in terms of falsifiable statements.

The word *hermeneutic* derives from the god Hermes, the messenger of the gods, who transmitted the thoughts – or meaning – of gods to humans. The central idea of hermeneutics is that meaning is transmitted between people, and it is possible to understand another person using intuition. Hermeneutics assumes that it is possible to take part in the inner life of another person through intuition. A shared understanding of the world makes intuition possible. It is a feature of being human that allows us humans to 'rethink' what the other person is thinking. The focus on intuition rather than method is something that makes hermeneutic psychology distinct.

> Hermeneutic philosophy does not aim at objective knowledge through the use of methodical procedures but at the explication and phenomenological description of [the] human.
>
> (Bleicher, 2017, p. 2)

Hermeneutic psychology owes its origins to hermeneutic philosophy developed by the German philosopher, Wilhelm Dilthey (1883–1911). Dilthey (1894/1977) provided an alternative to the historical analysis of the time where historians were trying to understand history in terms of general laws. Dilthey suggested

Hermes taking the thoughts of humans to gods.

instead that history should be understood by rethinking the thoughts of historical characters. He believed this is possible because humans share characteristics that enable them to have insight into each other's minds. The understanding that Dilthey proposed was not based on falsifiable statements, but on the intuitive understanding of others. It was based on the imaginative re-creation of the inner contents of a person's thoughts based on sympathy borne out of shared lived experiences (Bevir, 2007).

An important feature of this intuitive approach is that there is an explicit recognition that the context is important. The context includes the person who is trying to understand the other. So rather than thinking of 'understanding the other' as being something that can be objective and context free, there is recognition that it involves a relationship with an observer and the context in which the interaction take place. We cannot be dispassionate observers of each other (Slife & Christensen, 2013).

Hermeneutic enquiry accepts the relativism that characterises social constructionism, but adds one additional feature, sometimes called 'the criterion.' Although all interpretations are relative, they are not equally good. The criterion is the extent to which a person is able to gain hermeneutical insight of another. Characteristics that help hermeneutic enquiry include lack of self-ishness, open-mindedness, self-effacement, tolerance, and a sincere desire to understand another person. Harmful characteristics include self-righteousness and "conscious or unconscious resentment of ideas and positions which differ from the more common ones, and especially from those held by the observer" (Bleicher, 2017, p. 34). The quality of the intuitive understanding of the other depends on the observer, and the extent to which the observer meets the criterion, a criterion that involves a state of mind. All observers are not equal.

The idea of 'understanding the other' in an intuitive way is part of Rogers' approach to therapy (see Chapter 8). However, Rogers presented his work as part of the scientific tradition in psychology and his theories consist of general (nomothetic) statements that can apply to all people. Rogers was aware of the conflict between the intuitive and the scientific. This is what he wrote in one of his later works in what he described as a personal statement:

I have felt an increasing discomfort at the distance between the rigorous objectivity of myself as scientist and the almost mystical subjectivity of myself as therapist.

(Rogers, 1955, p. 267)

And

The essence of some of the deepest parts of therapy seems to be a unity of experiencing.

(Rogers, 1955, p. 267)

Rogers' description of the therapeutic process in this paper is the same as that found in hermeneutics – and is at odds with his earlier descriptions of the process of psychotherapy as a scientific endeavour. A unity of experiencing does not produce falsifiable theories. Rogers' recognition of the tension between the scientific and non-scientific was made possible because he inhabited both worlds, a world where psychology was justified to others in terms of science and an intuitive world of trying to understand the minds of his clients.

Psychology as politics: critical psychology

The term *critical psychology* is used to describe an approach to psychology that, as the word suggests, is strongly critical of the way psychology is practised. As the above sections of this chapter have shown, the dominant scientific and nomothetic approach to psychology has been criticised in a variety of ways. However, critical psychology is *very* critical of psychology.

Why is critical psychology critical of psychology? There are two reasons. The first and less important reason is the same as that given by those who use qualitative methods as ends in themselves. Psychology is following the path of a natural science and in so doing misses the deep meaning that is formed in social discourse. Critical psychologists therefore support the general criticism and solution provided by social constructionists – i.e., the rigorous, positivistic, quantitative methodology so beloved by many psychologists should be replaced by a more humane, qualitative methodology. The second reason is the one that really defines critical psychologists. They point out that the practice of psychology isn't some abstract activity that is carried out in an ivory tower. On the contrary, psychology is a *political activity*, and that psychologists, often unwittingly, play a political role in society.

There are two consequences of psychology's failure to appreciate its political role. First, psychologists contribute to an unfair and unequal relationship between groups of people, a relationship that can be exploitative. For example, occupational psychologists help capitalist masters make their workers work hard, thereby helping the profit of the capitalist masters but not helping workers themselves. There is at least some truth in this criticism. Work stress is undoubtedly bad for health, but stressed workers can, under some circumstances, produce more. The reference to capitalism reflects a tendency in critical psychology to support a Marxist view, or at the very least one that is collectivist rather than individualist. Other unequal power relations are found in the relationship between psychotherapists and their clients, between psychiatrists and their patients, between social workers and their clients, and between teachers and their pupils. Again, there is some truth in this sort of criticism, though it certainly does not apply to all therapeutic relationships. As pointed out in an earlier chapter, Rogerian therapy is based on an explicit rejection of the idea that the therapist is in control of the patient. Another unequal power relationship is found between men and women, and this forms part of the focus of criticism in feminist psychology (Wilkinson, 1996). Feminist psychology also draws attention to other gender imbalances in psychology – for example, that whereas the majority of psychology students are female, the lecturing staff in some universities are (or used to be) predominantly male. Feminist psychology is not only critical of the male bias in academic psychology, but also of a male bias in society which, as in the case of critical psychology, emphasises the unequal power between two groups of people.

The second consequence of psychology's failure to recognise its political role means that that political role is not properly studied. Critical psychologists therefore aim to remedy this deficit by providing an academic study of the political role psychologists play. The first issue of the journal *Annual Review of Critical Psychology* was published in 1999, and contains a manifesto for what critical psychology should do (Parker, 1999). The manifesto draws attention to four components that could be considered to form the subject matter of critical psychology:

1 How psychology operates to serve those in power.
2 How psychology is culturally constructed and operates within a historical context.
3 The way people are regulated, manipulated, and surveyed by others.
4 The study of ordinary, everyday practice by psychologists.

Critical psychology can itself be analysed from a political, cultural, and historical perspective. Critical psychology is primarily a UK and to a lesser extent European phenomenon. It became a recognised contributor to psychological thought at a time in history when there was a new type of political development in the UK, called Thacherism. Thacherism was named after the British Prime Minister 1979–1990, Margaret Thatcher who famously said "There is no such thing as society." Margaret Thatcher espoused a form of individualism that many, including the critical psychologists, felt was wrong. Some undergraduate psychology courses do not cover critical psychology, though the argument that psychologists are part of a political and historical context is as true now as it was in the past.

Summary

Qualitative research methods were first used by psychologists working in applied settings, not academia, who conducted motivational research to examine people's buying habits. Qualitative research can be used by academic psychologists in several ways with different types of assumptions. First, qualitative studies are used within the context of quantitative science where researchers use it for hypothesis generation and the refinement of the quantitative research process. When used in this way, i.e., as help in natural science, most researchers do not search for deep meaning in what people say.

Second, qualitative research is used as an end in itself to answer theoretical or practical questions. There are several different methodologies that can be adopted for this purpose, but they all rely on analysing the meaning of discourse rather than on quantitative assessment. The methodology selected is carefully selected and followed, and researchers provide a scientific study that is replicable by others. Discourse is analysed to discover meaning using a process of inference and hypothesis generation. Qualitative research used in this way meets the requirements of falsifiability and replicability that are the hallmarks of a science, but it is a different type of science to natural science. One difference between qualitative researchers is whether or not the discourse reveals hidden meanings in the minds of the participants, or whether the meaning of discourse when used in natural conversation can be inferred from detailed analysis of the words themselves.

Third, there are those whose approach to qualitative research is explicitly non-scientific and who rely on human intuition, using a hermeneutical approach that is not restricted to the discipline of psychology. In hermeneutic psychology there is an explicit recognition that their understanding of people should not be considered a science.

Finally, there are those whose qualitative methodology is part of a rejection of mainstream psychology in favour of a distinctly political agenda.

This chapter has provided examples to show that qualitative methods, however they are used, can provide information that cannot be obtained through quantitative methods. The inner meaning of soup is not revealed by a questionnaire asking people how much they like soup. The words of a questionnaire do not write themselves. Conversations can create problems of understanding that are not apparent to those taking part in the conversation. Quantitative research answers some types of questions; qualitative research answers other types of questions. Both are useful methods used in psychology.

Essay questions

1   When might it be useful to search for the hidden meaning in discourse and when might this not be useful?
2   In what ways is qualitative research useful?
3   What is the role of intuition in human understanding and research?

10

Is the whole greater than the sum of its parts? From gestalt psychology to artificial intelligence

The question addressed in this chapter, the last chapter in this book, is in some ways the most important question in psychology. It is important because an answer 'yes' can be used to justify the existence of psychology as a discipline separate from physiology. It is important because the difference between those assuming yes and those assuming no fuels a controversy that runs throughout the history of psychology. It is important because artificial intelligence and therefore the future of humans is linked to the assumption of 'yes.' It is important because artificial intelligence can act as heuristic for a new type of theory in psychology, a type of theory that would create a paradigm shift from the current neurocognitive paradigm – assuming that this *is* the current paradigm, which by now the reader will realise is not assumed by all psychologists!

There are two ways of understanding the world: analysis and synthesis. The process of analysis examines the different parts of something. After analysing something into its separate 'bits,' the whole is found by adding the separate bits together to make a whole. In the physical sciences this often involves micro-analysis – i.e., finding the smaller and smaller parts, for example, the genes in biology or fundamental particles in physics.

The process synthesis shows how the different parts of something interact and combine such that the whole cannot be understood by the separate contributions of the individual parts. Throughout the history of science, and in several different disciplines, there is a tension between those who want to analyse yet smaller and smaller parts of the jigsaw that is knowledge, and those who want to see the meaning of the jigsaw as a whole.

The coalescence versus brick wall hypothesis was introduced in Chapter 2. If the taste of lemonade can be understood as the combination of two separate tastes, lemon and sugar, then the sensation of lemonade can be analysed into its separate components. If, on the other hand, lemonade is a unique taste, different from lemon and sugar, then lemonade is a synthesis of sugar and lemon and must be understood as such. The brick wall versus coalescence controversy was a debate amongst philosophers in the 19th century, and it is a precursor to a much more important movement in psychology, the gestalt movement.

The gestalt movement

The gestalt movement was never associated exclusively with one university or person, nor was it associated with a particular type of psychology. Instead, the gestalt movement represents an idea that predates the beginning of academic psychology and continues to be important (Ellis, 1999). The assumption underlying the gestalt movement can be summed up in the phrase:

The whole is greater than the sum of its parts.

The word *Gestalt* is a German noun meaning shape or configuration – it does not translate easily into English. The use of this noun reflects the idea that psychological shapes or structures are more than the sum of their parts.

Phenomena that are now described as gestalt phenomena were discovered in the middle of the 19th century, long before the gestalt movement was recognised. The Necker cube was drawn by Necker in 1832 and the old woman/young girl illusion appeared on a German postcard in 1888. The significance of the gestalt movement is that an explanation was provided for phenomena that were previously interesting illusions. The gestalt movement provided theory.

The beginning of the gestalt movement is attributed to a chance observation made by Max Wertheimer (1880–1943). In 1910, Wertheimer was travelling by train from Vienna while on holiday, and noticed how an illusion of movement was created by telegraph wires along the track. This illusion is familiar to many train travellers – the wires seem to move up and down. The idea of apparent movement was not new. There was a 19th-century toy called a stroboscope that exploited this phenomenon, and Lumière invented the Cinématographe in 1895. Wertheimer realised that the phenomenon of apparent movement could not be explained by the then current theory of movement perception that had been proposed by Wundt (see Chapter 2) (Wertheimer, 1912). Wundt thought that apparent motion was caused by the summation of eye movements – i.e., you perceive movement because the eyes move. Wertheimer felt and was eventually able to show that movement perception was something that 'more than the sum of the parts' of any elements observed by the observer (Ash, 1995).

Wertheimer started to investigate this apparent movement, or the *Phi* phenomenon as it was called, using himself and two colleagues as observers. Along with Wertheimer, these two colleagues, Wolfgang Köhler (1887–1967) and Kurt Koffka (1886–1941), are looked on as the founders of the gestalt movement.

Wertheimer used an instrument called a tachistoscope that enabled images to be presented on a screen at precisely defined times and for precise durations. Tachistoscopes were standard psychology experimental equipment before the introduction of computers. As an example of an experiment done by Wertheimer, imagine lines placed at slightly different angles, and which we can call line A and line B, and which can be shown independently on a tachistoscope screen or on a computer (Figure 10.1).

First, line A is shown on the screen. Then line A disappears, and line B appears. Then line B disappears and line A reappears again, and so on.

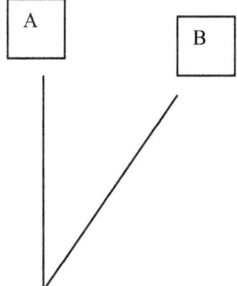

FIGURE 10.1 Line A appears and then disappears and is replaced by line B, then vice versa.

Wertheimer was able to vary the rate of alternation between line A and B. He found that as the rate increased, there came a point when it appeared that a line was moving between A and B and *something* was actually visible between them. The line appears to be rotating around the point where the two lines meet. In fact, the same experiment is more easily demonstrated by two lights in a dark room that are separated by a short distance. If the light alternates between A and B, it appears that the light is moving between A and B and *something* is visible between A and B. The demonstration of apparent motion is interesting but was not novel. Wertheimer's important contribution, which was published in 1912 (Wertheimer, 1912), was a modification of this type of *phi* experiment.

Wertheimer used three lines, two of which are called A, and one B (Figure 10.2).

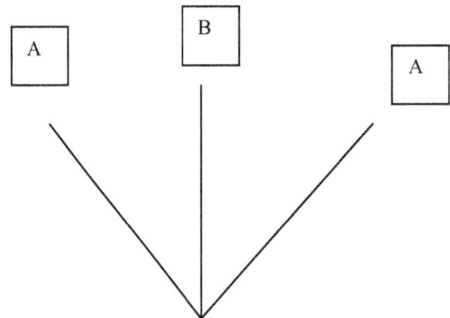

FIGURE 10.2 Line B appears then disappears and is followed by lines A and vice versa.

As before, the A and B lines alternate on the screen, but in this case the two A lines appear at the same time. The B line appears, then the two A lines appear as the B line disappears, then the A lines appear again and the B line disappears. This arrangement creates the peculiar impression that the B line moves in two directions at once – it looks as though the B line splits and moves outwards. Wertheimer realised that this impression could not be caused by eye movement, because *the eyes cannot move in two directions at the same time.* His demonstration therefore showed that Wundt's explanation of how we perceive motion was false. Motion is not perceived because of the way the eye moves, but is due the overall pattern of what we see. Why do we see movement from the overall pattern? The answer is that perception follows certain rules, so that when a pattern of a particular kind appears, then we perceive according to that rule.

The idea that perception follows rules or principles led over a short period of time to the discovery of several gestalt principles. Students studying psychology will already be familiar with these principles from the study of visual perception. They include:

Figure-ground: Several examples of these exist, including the face-vase illusion and young-old woman illusion.

Continuity: There is an assumption that lines that are interrupted are continuous (a principle exploited in the 'three rope trick' (search online and you will find videos showing you how to do this).
Proximity: Objects close together are assumed to be connected.
Similarity: Objects that are similar are assumed to be connected.

Gestalt principles also are used in colour perception. The colours of the rainbow are well known: red, orange, yellow, green, blue, and violet. So where is brown? Where is gold? Where is silver? Gold and silver are the easiest ones to explain. Gold is yellow and silver is light grey with particularly bright highlights (highlights are the reflections that come off shiny objects). If you examine a painting of a gold shield, you will see that from a distance the shield really looks gold, but when you come up close it is simply yellow. The trick is that artists puts in more highlights than are in the surrounding objects so that you assume that the object must be shiny gold. Colours such as gold and silver show that people infer colour not only from the colour impinging on the eye but from the whole of the visual array.

Brown is a little more difficult to understand. If you have paints that are red, orange, yellow, green, and blue next to each other, they look like those colours – i.e., red orange, yellow, etc. However, if you take a colour such as yellow, and reduce the amount of light that is emerging *relative to its surroundings*, then this 'yellow' looks brown. Brown (there are lots of different browns) is the colour that we infer from knowing that relatively little light is being reflected – of course, when no light is reflected, then we assume the colour is black. Colour perception shows that colour is not just a matter of an addition of signals from the cones in the eye but is an inference that is made from the total array of the visual image.

Gestalt learning phenomena and other gestalt psychologists
Although much of the early research and phenomena labelled as 'gestalt' was associated with perception, the idea of a gestalt obviously has a wider application than perception. The perceptual focus of the early gestalt psychologists was because most early psychology was perceptual, and the gestalt psychologists were proposing a new, holistic way of understanding the psychology of the time. Gestalt psychologists were also interested in learning.

Wolfgang Köhler was one of Wertheimer's collaborators in his early experiments (Henle, 1971). Köhler's later work focussed on additional topics including human values (Köhler, 1947, 1959, 1966). Köhler investigated insight learning in chimpanzees (Köhler, 1925), working on the island of Tenerife at the German Primate Research Centre. He conducted a famous study with chimpanzees. The study took various forms, but in one form there is banana outside the chimpanzee's cage which is just out of arm's reach. A stick is placed in the cage with the chimpanzee. After a time, the chimpanzee will pick up the stick and hook the banana inside. Repeated study shows, for example, that the chimpanzee picks up the stick faster if the stick is between the chimpanzee and the banana rather than at the other end of the cage. The significance of Köhler's studies was to show that learning happened in an 'all-or-nothing' fashion. At one point in time the chimpanzee did not know what to do and at the next point it did. This finding was important because it contradicted the more atomistic theories of learning that were being developed by animal psychologists working within the behaviourist tradition (see Chapter 4) where learning was believed to be a gradual process of the strengthening of stimulus-response bonds. Köhler's research showed that learning could be all or nothing.

America

Koffka moved to America in 1924. Wertheimer, who was Jewish, moved to America in 1933 when the German National Socialists dismissed all Jewish professors from German Universities – including Nobel prize winners such as Albert Einstein. Köhler published an article in 1933 strongly criticising German discrimination against Jews (Henle, 1978). Köhler left Germany for America in 1935. The three men were friends throughout their academic lives (Brett & Wertheimer, 2005).

Kurt Koffka moved to America before his German friends. He was proficient in English before he left (Koffka, 1922, 1924, 1935) and his proficiency in English enabled him to promote gestalt principles in the English-speaking world (Gibson, 1979). He influenced Tolman (see Chapter 4) and befriended James J. Gibson (1904–1979), whose book *The Ecological Approach to Visual Perception*, published in 1979, is viewed as an important culmination of the gestalt approach. One of Gibson's many ideas was that, when people look at a visual array, they immediately register what objects are *for*. So, for example, if a person sees something that has the structure of a path, that person will know that the path is for walking on. The shape of a hammer will indicate that the object is for hitting things with. Gibson described these 'what things are for' as affordances.

> A *path* affords pedestrian locomotion from one place to another. . . . An *obstacle* can be defined as an animal-sized object that affords collision and possible injury.
>
> (Gibson, 1979, p. 36)

So an affordance is a gestalt – it is the whole that is perceived directly.

Field theories

Many theories in psychology take the logical form of A causes B. The experimental method is suited for assessing such causal statements. Causal statements are important because they have practical implications. Does spaced learning help a student revise more than massed learning? Do adverse childhood experiences affect behaviour in later life? Does drinking alcohol on a regular basis lead to greater happiness? Causal theories of this kind take the form of

$$S \rightarrow O \rightarrow R$$

Or more generally

Situation/stimulus/environment $\rightarrow$ person variable/mechanism/processing $\rightarrow$ response/behaviour/mental state

However, any causal relationship is just one of many, many different causal relations that are happening at any one time. The assumption of the gestalt movement is that the whole is greater than the sum of its parts. That being the case, it also makes sense to consider how all the many, many different causal relations that are happening at one time interact to produce some kind of outcome. Not only is perception and learning holistic, it also may be that one needs holistic theories. Field theories are based on the assumption that theories should explore how all the different causal relations occur together. In this section two field theories are examined, the field theory of Lewin and inter-behaviourism.

Lewin (1890–1947) was Jewish and like Kofka moved to America in 1933, as did other Jews who had university careers and had to leave Germany. Lewin was familiar with gestalt psychology and refers to this in his field theory. The following quote sums up the essence of Lewin's field theory:

> Whether or not a certain type of behavior occurs depends not on the presence or absence of one fact or of a number of facts as viewed in isolation but upon the constellation (structure and forces) of the specific field as a whole.
>
> (Lewin, 1939, p. 889)

Lewin suggests that behaviour is the result of different forces that result from a person's "life space" where life space consists of all the different experiences and motives that make up a person. Lewin suggests that behaviour can be considered a path through this life space, and he gives a name to this space, *hodological space*. Lewin was influenced by newly developed mathematics of topology and he invented symbols to represent the various concepts in hodological space. In his most detailed publication of his theory (Lewin, 1938), he provides four pages of symbols that are used in the diagrams which he created to represent hodological space. This type of representation looks very scientific!

Although field theory naturally stems from gestalt principles, field theory was also developed by a behaviourist, Jacob Kantor (1888–1984). Kantor had worked with Skinner (see Chapter 4) whom he admired, but felt that the interactional nature of behaviourism was not sufficiently developed (Morris, 1984). Kantor proposed a form of behaviourism called inter-behaviourism (Kantor, 1970). Kantor suggested there was a bidirectional causal connection between stimulus and response, instead of the single-directional, stimulus-causes-response approach taken by other behaviourists. Kantor's approach is described as ecological behaviourism. He suggested that the stimulus-response interaction takes place in a context and it is the context that is neglected in other behaviourist approaches to understanding behaviour.

What these different field theories have in common is the idea that it is not possible to isolate the organism and study it separately from its natural environment. It is the interaction with the natural environment that is important. The idea of understanding behaviour in terms of a number of simultaneous causal interactions is found not only in field theories of psychology, it is the most basic assumption in the study of ecology. Ecologists study the mutual interactions of species in the total environment. Some argue that experimental studies fail to provide a true picture of the mechanism's underlying behaviour because they lack ecological validity. The term *ecological validity* is based on the assumption that a valid – i.e., true – account of human behaviour requires investigation in its natural setting, not in the laboratory

Field theories can be considered an extension of ideas first proposed by the gestalt psychologists. Sharps and Wertheimer sum up the contribution of the gestalt movement to modern psychology as follows:

> Several points for modern psychology emerge from the Gestalt perspective. Phenomena should be studied within their full context; there is a need to acknowledge the domain specificity of principles in experimental psychology; it is wise to study phenomena that either exist in the real world or have close real-world analogues; psychology must recognize interchanges between organisms and surroundings as determinants of behaviour.
>
> (Sharps & Wertheimer, 2000, p. 315)

Field theories in psychology are intuitively plausible. So why are they practically unknown? Students reading this book could ask fellow students whether they have heard of either Lewin or Kantor. Lewin and Kantor suggested *how* psychology theory should be constructed. The problem is they never demonstrated that this type of theory was able to solve problems that could not be solved by other existing theories – despite Lewin being committed to the practical use of psychology. The history of psychology is one where different people have advocated different types of psychology. If all that is done is to recommend a particular type of theory, then this advocacy eventually disappears. What is needed is a demonstration that the particular approach or theory can provide an answer not provided elsewhere. That is the reason this book has given examples of how particular approaches can be used in practice (for example, that of conversational analysis in the previous chapter). Field theories were never used in practice, despite their intuitive plausibility. They are important because the problem of multiple simultaneous causes was eventually solved with the development of connectionist psychology and artificial intelligence.

Why do emergent properties occur?

What is the difference between a living organism and a dead one? This question is at the root of why emergent properties occur. Several explanations were provided for the difference between living and inanimate objects during the 19th and early 20th centuries. A popular one was that living organisms have a 'vital force' that leaves them when dead. This idea of a vital force was used by Mary Shelley in her book *Frankenstein*. Shelley proposed that this vital force came from a newly discovered force, the force of electricity.

The psychologist William McDougall (1871–1938) had a number of interests outside psychology. In his last book, *The Riddle of Life* (McDougall, 1938), McDougall reviews several explanations for the difference between living and inanimate matter. These explanations included animistic ones (such as that used by Mary Shelley) which McDougall dismisses as being unscientific. One of the explanations favoured by McDougall is that put forward by Max Loewenthal in his book *Life and Soul*, which was published in 1934. Although Loewenthal strays into animistic theories, which McDougall rejects, Loewenthal makes the prescient suggestion that living organisms are different from non-living matter because of organisation. The reason for this hypothesis is that snails can be frozen to −120 °C when they appear dead but, if carefully thawed, come back to life. As a 'life force' or any form of energy cannot exist at such low temperature, Loewenthal suggests that life must have something to do with structure, a structure that is independent of temperature. The nature of this structure was not known.

It is now known that it is a particular type of structure that makes life possible. It is the same network structure that forms the basis for artificial intelligence (AI) and a type of structure that gives rise to a parallel distributed processing (PDP) system. A PDP system is one where processing is occurring over the whole network at the same time. It is the existence of network structure and parallel distributed processing that makes emergent properties possible, including the emergent property of life. Research and understanding of networks can therefore be seen as the solution to a problem that the gestalt psychologists failed to answer: How exactly are patterns recognised as a whole?

Artificial intelligence.

Artificial intelligence (AI)

There are a number of key steps in the discovery of AI, and two are described here, the work of the behavioural psychologist, Donal Hebb (1904–1985) and the collaboration between the neuropsychiatrist Warren McCulloch (1898–1969) and mathematician Walter Pitts (1923–1969).

Donald Hebb published his book, *Organization of Behaviour: A Neuro-psychological Theory* in 1948. Hebb was interested in discovering what happened in the brain when learning took place, in particular the type of learning known as classical conditioning. Hebb knew that the brain was a network of inter-connected neurones, and came up with a simple proposition, a proposition now known as the Hebbian learning rule. The Hebbian learning rule is that if two neurones fire simultaneously, then the connection between those two neurones strengthens. The rule is sometimes stated by the slogan:

Neurones that fire together get wired together.

Hebb showed that networks can adapt or learn if they follow rules. Several other rules were later developed to show how networks could learn.

Different types of leaning rule

A distinction is made between unsupervised and supervised learning rules. The Hebbian learning rule is unsupervised in that there is no external agent giving feedback. Other rules can explain 'supervised learning' where the network learns to recognise patterns on the basis of feedback from a 'teacher.' Supervised learning explanations are used in several applications of AI, including pattern recognition and behavioural adaptation.

McCulloch and Pitts developed their ideas through the inter-disciplinary collaboration of neuroscience and mathematics (Abraham, 2002). Inter-disciplinary developments can be some of the most important in the development of science. The McCulloch-Pitts model is based a simple assumption (McCulloch & Pitts, 1943). Suppose there is a network of neurones that are either 'on' or 'off.' Then assume that this on-off state of a neurone corresponds to true-false in a logical argument. McCulloch and Pitts showed that variation in the connection strengths between the neurones in a network could produce on-off or true-false states that followed the rules of logic. The contribution of their approach was to show that networks could *solve problems*, simply by the connection strengths of the neurones.

The two pieces of the jigsaw, from Hebb and from McCulloch-Pitts, were put together in what become known as connectionist psychology (Ellis & Humphreys, 1999). A network system can learn and in doing so solve problems. In adapting to their inputs, networks can learn to function better in their environment. Connectionist psychology and artificial intelligence are based on the same assumption. The assumption is that in order to understand or mimic the intelligence of a human, it is necessary to have a structure of a network where multiple, simultaneous causal connections occur. Pattern recognition is one of the achievements of AI, and the way an AI system recognises a pattern provides an answer to the question that the gestalt psychologists were never able to answer, how patterns are recognised.

How is a pattern recognised? How do we recognise the letter A when handwriting differs so much between people? One way would be to have a series of templates, of different kinds of A. For example, the following are the letter A using different fonts

A   𝓐   @   𝒜   A

Any new letter could be compared with a storage bank of letters A to see whether or not the letter was an A. The problem with the template approach is that it will recognise the letter A only if it has been seen in that format before. The templates here would fail to recognise a letter A that has never been written before, but which you, the student, will recognise as a letter A.

Humans – and machines that mimic humans – are able to recognise the letter A in a format that has not been seen before. Pattern recognition requires an understanding of the relationship between the elements of the pattern – the relationship between the lines that make up a letter A, for example.

Pattern recognition devices, i.e., devices capable of recognising a letter even if that form of the letter has not been seen before – use neural network structure similar to that shown in the Figure 10.3.

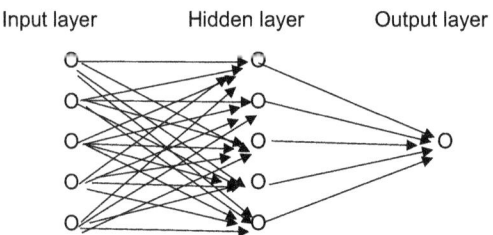

FIGURE 10.3 In this figure, there are three layers of neurones, input, hidden, and output.

The input layer receives inputs from the external environment. Each input node is either on or off depending on its input from the external environment. Figure 10.3 shows only five input nodes, but there can be many more. The input nodes could also be arranged in a two-dimensional array connected to detectors that detect whether a point in a pattern is either black (i.e., a line passes through that point) or white (a line does not pass through that point). Just one input layer is shown in the figure, but additional hidden layers can be added one after another, all connecting with each other.

The neurones in the output layer – just one is shown in the Figure 10.3, but there could be more – provide the answer, for example whether the pattern is an A or not. Figure 10.3 shows that information is processed in parallel – hence a parallel distributed processing system, rather than a linear system where one logical process is followed by another. The perceptive student will ask, "but how *exactly* does this parallel distributed processing system provide the correct answer?" It does it by getting the correct strengths of connection between the all three layers, input, hidden, and output. The strengths of connection can vary and once they are *exactly* right, then the system will correctly recognise patterns such as the letter A. The perceptive student will point out, "yes, but how do you get the connection strengths *exactly* correct? The diagram looks incredibly complicated and it looks like an impossible task." The answer is that a human does not work it out. Instead the answer is provided from a type of machine learning, called supervised learning.

Supervised learning occurs when a network adapts on the basis of feedback. First, the network needs to be trained. Training is achieved by presenting the network with letters of the alphabet in different fonts, some of them being As, and providing the network with information about whether the letter is an A or not. Then, if the network adapts using a 'supervised learning rule' or algorithm, then the connection strengths will gradually change so that eventually they are just right to be able to detect whether a letter is an A or not. There are several different possible supervised learning rules, but they all provide a way of gradually changing the connection weights until they provide the correct solution. So long as the network adapts – i.e., the connection strengths change – in accordance with the learning rule, then, after training, the network will be able to correctly identify the letter A, whatever form that A takes. This form of learning is also referred to as 'deep learning.'

Supervised learning or deep learning shows an important feature of artificial intelligence. After training, a machine will be able to perform tasks that it has not been programmed to perform. The human does not have to write the rules for task performance. The machine learns those rules by itself. The machine is capable of learning something that the human has not been able to make. The science of artificial intelligence was motivated by a desire to create a machine to do what humans are capable of doing. However, in creating artificial intelligence, scientists have been able to demonstrate *how* humans do what they are capable of doing.

Example of a learning rule

Supervised learning rules are based on mathematical rules and are beyond the scope of this book. Here is one example, called the back-propagation method. First, calculate the difference between the actual and desired output and multiply this by some function of the inputs to that output unit. This calculation creates an error term. Then, using that error term, adjust the weights of the connections from the penultimate layer in the network to the output unit. Repeat this procedure between the penultimate units and the layer behind them, and then repeat back through all the other network layers back to the input layer.

The human ability to recognise patterns, an ability demonstrated by the gestalt psychologists, is possible because the brain uses a network structure. Information is encoded in the connections between the nodes in the network – as Hebb originally suggested. When people see a hammer, they realise that it is used for hitting, and when they see a road, they realise that it is used for walking because actions – i.e., affordances – are just some of the many connections in the network of information that is encoded in the brain. It is the network structure of the brain that gives humans (and other animals) the capacity to process, understand, and respond to their environment in the way they do.

Parallel versus sequential processing machines

Artificial intelligence is now part of everyday life and will become more and more important as time passes. Phones and tablets provide predictive text, where each device learns its own user's use of language. Predictive text is made possible because of a network architecture. Life is made possible because of a network architecture. However, phones and tablets are not alive. As everyone knows, iPhones do not grow up and become iPads. What is going on?

Computers, tablets, and phones are sequential processing machines. They have the same basic structure that they have had since the very first computers. They perform tasks one after another. However, modern computers are very, very fast. Because of their incredible speed, they can do the calculations that are needed to *simulate* a parallel processing machine. Parallel processing is complex, but is simply a matter of mathematics. The sequential processing machine is sufficiently fast that it can give the appearance of doing the same tasks as a parallel processing machine.

Your phone, tablet, and computer are not alive, and if robots of the future are simply extensions of the same processing structure of modern computers, then the robots of the future will not be alive. If, however, it becomes possible to make a truly parallel processing machine in the way that humans are parallel processing, then one can certainly raise the question as to whether the machine is alive and should be granted the rights of 'wet' organisms. Who knows what the future will bring? As a student watching episodes of *Star Trek*, I thought the communication devices were an impossibility. Mobile phones are now taken for granted.

Modular versus connectionist psychology

Cognitive psychology, like any other part of psychology, developed on the basis of assumptions. The assumption of cognitive psychology is that the information is processed in the brain in the same way that it is processed in a computer – a sequential processing computer. This assumption forms the basis of Fodor's modularity approach to the mind. Information is processed in modules that have different functions (see Chapter 6). Each process is completed in a module before the next one takes place.

Connectionist psychology provides a challenge to the modularity theory of mind (Massaro, 1990). Examination of this challenge falls outside the remit of this book, but here is an example why connectionist psychology is a new conceptual approach to information processing.

Suppose I ask you the question, "what is big, red, and found in London?" You may guess straight away, "a London bus." How do you do this so quickly? What you do *not* do is search through a module of all big objects, a module of all red objects, a module of all things in London, and find the one object that is common to all three. A computer could do it this way because a computer is incredibly fast, but it would take a human too long. People immediately realise "a London bus" because information isn't organised in modules. Instead, information is organised as a network of concepts, where concepts are nodes connected to other concept nodes with connections of varying strengths. The word *red* is a node connected to everything that is red. The word *big* is connected to everything that is big, and the word *London* is connected with everything in London. When I ask you "what is big, red, and found in London?" what happens is that the connections from all three nodes become activated and the *combined activations* all link to one concept, that of a London bus.

Modern pattern recognition devices use the same logic. They look for connections not for templates in modules.

Networks, emergent properties, and the reduction of psychology to physiology

Networks are intuitively difficult to understand because so many causal relations are occurring at the same time. It is easy to understand A causes B causes C. But it is not easy to understand simultaneous cause between multiple nodes in a network. One way of getting an intuitive understanding of networks is to consider a flock of birds. Birds form flocks that fly through the air, often in beautiful patterns. Have you ever watched a flock of birds and wondered how it happens? How is it that different species of birds form flocks in different shapes? It looks magical. Magic is simply a mechanism that is not understood. If you don't want the magic taken out of flocks of birds, skip the next paragraph.

The shape of a flock of birds is an emergent property. It is achieved because each bird follows a rule. The rules are slightly different between species, but they all involve some kind of copying of the behaviour of neighbouring birds. The shape and behaviour of the flock are achieved by all the elements of the network following the same simple rule. The shape of the flock of the birds is an emergent property. It cannot be predicted from the behaviour of a single bird, only from the behaviour of the flock as a whole. If the brain (and body) is a network system, then there will be emergent properties that cannot be reduced to individual neurones. The network structure and its consequent emergent properties therefore provides an explanation for why psychology cannot be reduced to physiology. Psychology depends on physiology, in the same way that a flock of birds depends on the individual birds themselves, but there are psychological properties that cannot be predicted from physiology – assuming, of course, that the underlying structure is one of a network.

Clocks versus flocks

A mechanical clock (the sort with six cogwheels) is a sequential processing system. A flock of birds is a parallel processing system. If one cog in the clock is damaged or missing, then the entire clock stops functioning. If one bird in a flock of birds drops dead, then the flock continues without interruption. Sequential processing systems are sensitive to local error. Network systems are not. The fact that the brain has some, but not infinite, plasticity when damaged might suggest that there is some modularity and some connectionism in the way the brain works.

Robotics and psychology

There was a fundamental weakness of the field theories described earlier. These theories presented an intuitively correct idea about simultaneous multi-causality but did not develop useful theories, i.e., theories that were able to solve applied problems (see Chapter 3). What about psychology and robotics? Robots are particularly interesting because, unlike the computer that sits on your desk, robots can engage in spontaneous behaviour. Robots may be driven by AI and deep learning, but their ability to behave makes them more human-like than a computer. Psychologists have already made contributions to the understanding of human-robot interactions. The 'uncanny valley' hypothesis proposes that there is a non-linear relationship between the human realism of a robot and likeability (Mathur & Reichling, 2016). People prefer robots that are recognised as non-human or robots that can be mistaken for humans. Robots that are almost human (i.e., imperfect humans) are considered creepy.

Psychologists can contribute to the development and use of robotics, but what about the other way round? Can an understanding of robotics help in the development of psychology? The adaptive network theory is an example of how AI and robotics acts as a heuristic for a new type of theory, with practical application in helping people with somatic and psychological symptoms.

The adaptive network theory: an example of how AI can help theory development in psychology

The adaptive network theory is based on the assumption that symptoms are the result of biological symptom-causing mechanisms, but the mechanisms form a network of nodes with connections between the nodes. This network of nodes has emergent properties and so should be understood not in terms of biology but in terms of information in a network (Hyland, 2011, 2017). The information network is an adaptive system and receives inputs from information that is psychologically mediated and biologically mediated (as suggested by biopsychosocial interactionism, see Chapter 6).

In addition to having the structure of a theory consistent with biopsychosocial interactionism, the adaptive network theory assumes that symptoms and emotional states have the function of guiding behaviour. This additional assumption is not novel. William James suggested it over a hundred years ago (see Chapter 3). Symptoms adapt the body to the current environment and one of their functions is to inhibit behaviour. The following is a list of symptoms and how they are adaptive in inhibiting behaviour.

Pain – prevents injury.
Fatigue caused by infection or injury – enhances healing through resting.
Sadness – prevents continuation of unsuccessful activity.
Anxiety – prevents exposure to danger.

The novel part of the adaptive network theory is the proposal that the body adapts when symptoms fail to have their intended function, and it adapts by increasing the intensity of the symptom. If a person doesn't listen and respond to what the body is trying to tell them, then the body shouts louder. A similar idea had been presented some 30 years previously. The control theory of depression suggests that failing to disengage from unattainable goals leads to depression (Carver & Scheier, 1990; Hyland, 1987). The weakness of the control theory explanation of depression is that it did not explain *why* persistence in unattainable goals leads to depression. The science of AI shows how this is possible. Developments in AI show that if a control loop is part of an intelligent, adaptive system, then this is precisely what will happen. The parameters of the control loop will adapt if control is not being achieved.

The adaptive network theory provides a new paradigm for understanding symptoms. Instead of viewing symptoms as the result of a fault that is either psychological or biological, the theory presents symptoms as an adaptation which, from the patient's perspective, has gone wrong. The theory proposes that non-adaptive psychological and biological states creates 'stop signals' in an information network. The stop signals create symptoms that inhibit recurrence of the non-adaptive states, for example, by creating short-term symptoms of pain, fatigue, sadness, or state anxiety. The stop signal encodes the instruction to 'stop doing whatever you are doing' and the stop signal and symptom disappears once the behaviour stops. However, when stop signals and associated symptoms repeatedly fail to stop behaviour, doing so over a period of time, then the stop signals potentiate and become fixed to form a stop programme. The stop programme encodes the instruction 'whatever you are doing is unhelpful so stop doing things,' and the stop programme creates potentiated and persisting symptoms such as unexplained pain, severe fatigue, depression, and trait anxiety. The body has adapted in a way that inhibits any behaviour. A schematic representation of the theory is shown in Figure 10.4.

There are several reasons why people will persist in activities despite stop signals and symptoms that inhibit behaviour. People can 'keep going' despite

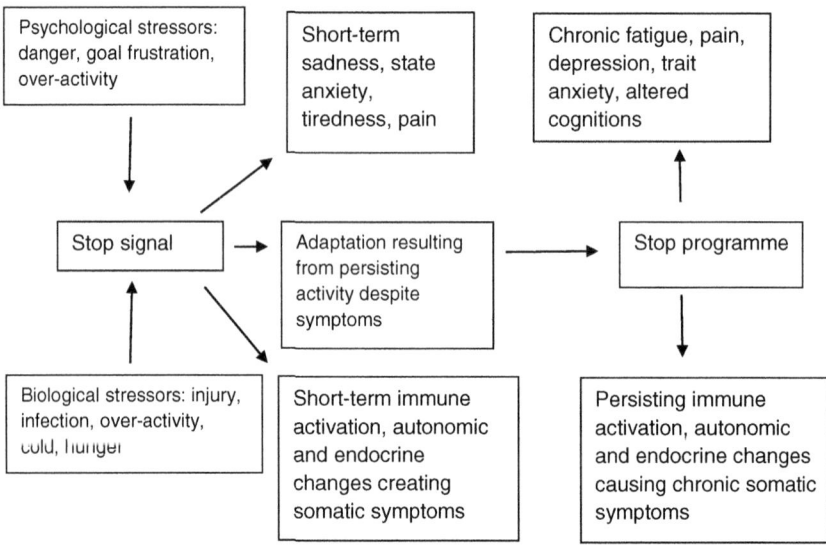

FIGURE 10.4 Schematic representation of the adaptive network theory. Stop signals encode the instruction to 'stop doing whatever it is that you are doing at the moment.' The stop programme encodes the instruction to 'stop everything that you are doing.'

pain and fatigue because of social obligations, because of work obligations, because of educational goals, because they find something very interesting, or because they find themselves in a situation where persistence is the only reasonable response to a difficult situation. The message to students is the same one that arises from the theory of reactive inhibition (see Chapter 4). Listen to what your bodies are telling you. Don't work too hard!

The theory can inform the treatment of any of the symptoms shown in Figure 10.4 (symptoms that tend to covary), but is currently being used only to treat unexplained symptoms of functional disorders (Hyland, 2017) where biological and psychological interventions have limited success (Henningsen, Zipfel, & Herzog, 2007).

Treatment

'Body reprogramming' is the name given to the educational intervention based on the adaptive network theory (Hyland et al., 2016). The aim is to explain to patients why they became ill and how they can help themselves by engaging in behaviours that do not create stop signals, see www.bodyreprogramming.org. Patients are taught how to teach their bodies that the world is a safe and rewarding place using evidence-based lifestyle change such as relaxation, stress avoidance, positive experiences, exercise, and nutrition.

The adaptive network theory provides a historical account of the development of symptoms in terms of past events, and therefore adds to existing models of illness. For example, Beck's theory of depression (Beck, 1967) is based on the hypothesis that depression is the consequence of erroneous cognitions, but does not explain the historical antecedents to those erroneous cognitions. The adaptive network theory shows how erroneous cognitions can be one of the outputs from a network that has adapted to a particular lifestyle. The adaptive network theory adds to the kindling hypothesis of depression and other stress-health theories as it predicts that the effects of stressors depend on how those stressors are interpreted within an intelligent system. Consequently, predictions based only on severity and frequency of stressors may be poor predictors of the health consequences of stress (Monroe & Harkness, 2005).

The adaptive network theory can be used to illustrate many of the principles covered in this book. First, science proceeds best by bold conjectures or hypotheses, but the hypotheses must be tested (see Chapter 1), because bold conjectures may be false. It is the lack of testing that was a problem with psychoanalytic theories (see Chapter 5). A therapy can be effective for any one of many possible reasons, so evidence that therapy is effective provides only weak evidence to support a theory on which the therapy is based (see Chapter 5).

There is evidence consistent with the predictions of the adaptive network theory that is separate from effectiveness of therapy (Hyland, Lanario, Wei, Jones, & Masoli, 2019; Melidis, Denham, & Hyland, 2018), but evidence merely corroborates and never proves a theory. The existing data may be explainable by another theory, and future data may falsify the theory. The adaptive network theory is an example of a theory being used to solve an applied problem (see Chapter 3), but its relative usefulness compared to other theories is yet to be evaluated. The theory combines the idea of adaptation and information processing (see Chapter 4) and provides a paradigm where humans are understood in terms of a mechanism similar to that found in robots. Some may argue that this paradigm is a travesty of what it means to be human, where humans have spiritual needs (Chapter 8) and where deep learning is no substitute for deep meaning (Chapter 9). Others may argue that in the long run developments in neuroscience will provide a better understanding (in what sense better?) of the phenomena explained by the adaptive network theory. The theory is a biopsychosocial theory in that symptoms result from an interaction between have psychological and biological causes. That interaction taking place in an information level consistent with the mechanistic explanations of cognitive psychology (see Chapters 4 and 6), but the usefulness of this approach in contrast to a purely physiological or purely psychological one may prove in the long term to be deceptive. The original hypothesis was informed by observation and qualitative information from patients (see Chapter 8), but failure to do a proper qualitative analysis is a shortcoming in any understanding of the phenomenon of functional disorders. Finally, any theory, however ardently supported by its inventor (as this one is) has a good potential for being wrong. Science advances only when conjectures are found to be false and new conjectures proposed.

Exam anxiety

Many students experience exam anxiety. According to the adaptive network theory, exam anxiety is caused by a history of exam taking. Each time a child takes an exam, they are engaging in a behaviour that creates anxiety. Their bodies are telling them to stop doing things that signal danger, but they keep on putting themselves in (what the body interprets as) danger by taking exams. Social and other pressures cause people to ignore what their bodies are telling them to do. The adaptive network theory predicts that the degree of exam anxiety in students should be correlated with the number of exams taken previously – a prediction consistent with observation (McDonald, 2001).

The history of psychology shows that new technologies can provide the opportunity for new paradigms in psychology. The original aim of AI was to create machines capable of simulating the intelligence of humans. Those machines can now do more than simulate what humans can do. The adaptive network theory uses AI to develop a new way of thinking about how the body functions as an adaptive system that is simultaneously biological and psychological. The original aim of AI is reversed. Instead of modelling machines on humans, theories to explain human behaviour can be modelled on what AI machines do. Whether this approach will lead to a new paradigm in the future is impossible to tell. One things that the history of science shows for certain: Paradigms do not last forever. Science changes as it advances. Psychology will change.

Summary

The idea that 'the whole is greater than the sum of its parts' was suggested by gestalt psychologists using perception as an example of this phenomenon. Later the idea was applied to learning to show that learning was (or could be) all or none rather than incremental. This idea of holism influences field theorists and underpins the idea of ecological validity. What happens in the laboratory may not happen in real life. Finally, the emergence of network theory in the 1940s and 1950s led to connectionist psychology in the 1980s and the start of the new technological revolution, that of artificial intelligence.

The development of factory production lines coincided with rise of behaviourism. The sequential processing computer coincided with the rise of cognitive psychology. Parallel processing, the basis of AI, is a new technology that could be more revolutionary than the other two technological revolutions. Connectionist psychology is based on the assumption that concepts form the nodes of a network and the psychological processes reflect an underlying network architecture. The adaptive network theory is based on the assumption that the body is a network with emergent properties and that particular patterns of lifestyle lead to adaptations that create symptoms.

The discipline of psychology has changed over the 150 years of its history, and will continue to change. When historians of psychology look back in 50 years' time, what will they see?

Essay questions

1 What were the main achievements of the gestalt movement?
2 What is machine learning and how has machine learning and artificial intelligence contributed to psychology?
3 Scientific paradigms change. Behaviourism lasted about 50 years, and cognitive psychology and humanistic psychology about the same length of time. What do you think the discipline of psychology will be like 50 years from now?

11

The changing assumptions of psychology

This chapter provides a summary of the different assumptions that psychologists have made during the history of psychology up to the present day and which have been described over the course of this book.

Science and psychology

Psychology is a science that makes quantitative predictions like physics or chemistry and is tested by the extent that quantitative data are consistent with the formulae that predict behaviour.

Psychology is a science that makes qualitative predictions like medicine and agriculture and is tested by statistical tests involving quantitative variables.

Psychology is a science but one that is fundamentally different from natural sciences. Qualitative methods provide a systematic and replicable way of interpreting discourse, in some cases finding the hidden meaning that lies behind what people say.

Psychology is not a science but is an intuitive way of understanding other people's minds, which is made possible by shared human experience.

Types of research

Humans are fundamentally the same as animals and so animal research advances our understanding of human psychology.

There are significant differences between humans and animals so animals cannot form a substitute for people in the study of psychology.

Psychology is a pure science whose aim is to understand basic processes.

Psychology is an applied and non-applied science where non-applied theories can have application following translational research.

Psychological research conducted in laboratories and on undergraduates generalises to the general population and everyday life.

Psychological research conducted in laboratories lacks ecological validity; to be valid, research needs to be carried out in the context to which it is being applied.

Aims of psychology

The aim of psychology is to document the elements of consciousness and the connections between those elements.

The aim of psychology is to explain how associations (operant and classical conditioning) lead to changes in behaviour and so enable humans to predict and control behaviour.

The aim of psychology is to understand the effects of the unconscious mind on mental health and behaviour.

The aim of psychology is to explain how information is processed, how memories are formed, and how decisions are made.

The aim of psychology is to understand how conscious experience ('phenomena') affects what people do.

The aim of psychology is to understand the meaning of what people say.

The aim of psychology is to create change in society.

The aim of psychology is to understand the relationship between physiology and psychological processes in order to predict behaviour.

The aim of psychology is to use the insights gained from the development of artificial intelligence in order to better understand psychological phenomena.

The aim of psychology is to provide solutions to one or more problems relating to mental health, somatic health, criminality, work experience, education, and any other of the many problems afflicting humans.

Essay question

1   What assumptions do you support and why?

References

Abraham, T. H. (2002). (Physio) logical circuits: The intellectual origins of the McCulloch-Pitts neural networks. *Journal of the History of the Behavioral Sciences, 38*(1), 3–25.

Abramson, L. Y., Seligman, M. E., & Teasdale, J. D. (1978). Learned helplessness in humans: Critique and reformulation. *Journal of Abnormal Psychology, 87*(1), 49–74.

Ach, N. (1910a). *Über den Willen* (On volition). Leipzig, Germany: Verlag von Quelle & Meyer.

Ach, N. (1910b). *Über den Willensakt und das Temperament* (On will and temperament). Leipzig, Germany: Verlag von Quelle & Meyer.

Adelman, E. M. (2006). Mind-body intelligence: A new perspective integrating Eastern and Western healing traditions. *Holistic Nursing Practice, 20*(3), 147–151.

Agusti, A., Bel, E., Thomas, M., Vogelmeier, C., Brusselle, G., Holgate, S., . . . Beasley, R. (2016). Treatable traits: Toward precision medicine of chronic airway diseases. *European Respiratory Journal, 47*(2), 410–419.

Albu, A. (1980). British attitudes to engineering education: A historical perspective. In *Technical innovation and British economic performance* (pp. 67–87). London, England: Palgrave Macmillan.

Allport, G. W. (1962). The general and the unique in psychological science 1. *Journal of Personality, 30*(3), 405–422.

Antaki, C., Finlay, W., Walton, C., & Pate, L. (2008). Offering choices to people with intellectual disabilities: An interactional study. *Journal of Intellectual Disability Research, 52*(12), 1165–1175.

Antonovsky, A. (1993). The structure and properties of the sense of coherence scale. *Social Science & Medicine, 36*(6), 725–733.

Ash, M. G. (1995). *Gestalt psychology in German culture, 1890–1967: Holism and the quest for objectivity.* Cambridge, England: Cambridge University Press.

Aulakh, R. (2016). Mandatory publication in India: Setting quotas for research output could encourage scientific fraud. *British Medical Journal, 354*, i5002.

Bannister, D., & Fransella, F. (2019). *Inquiring man: The psychology of personal constructs.* Abingdon, UK: Routledge.

Barker, D. J. P. (1992). The fetal origins of disease. *Journal of Hypertension, 10*(Suppl. 7), S39–S44.

Bartle, J. (2002). Market analogies, the marketing of labour and the origins of new labour. In N. O. O'Shaughnessy, N. J. O'Shaughnessy, S. C. Henneberg, S. Henneberg, & C. Henry (eds.), The idea of political marketing. Westport, CT: Greenwood Publishing Group.

Baumeister, A. A., Hawkins, M. F., & Uzelac, S. M. (2003). The myth of reserpine-induced depression: Role in the historical development of the monoamine hypothesis. *Journal of the History of the Neurosciences, 12*(2), 207–220.

Beck, A. T. (1967). *Depression: Clinical, experimental, and theoretical aspects*. Pennsylvania, PA: University of Pennsylvania Press.

Beck, H. P., Levinson, S., & Irons, G. (2009). Finding little Albert: A journey to John B. Watson's infant laboratory. *American Psychologist*, *64*(7), 605–614.

Benjafield, J. G. (2008). George Kelly: Cognitive psychologist, humanistic psychologist, or something else entirely? *History of Psychology*, *11*(4), 239–262.

Benjamin, L. T., Jr., & Nielsen-Gammon, E. (1999). B. F. Skinner and psychotechnology: The case of the heir conditioner. *Review of General Psychology*, *3*(3), 155–167.

Benjamin, L. T., Jr., Whitaker, J. L., Ramsey, R. M., & Zeve, D. R. (2007). John B. Watson's alleged sex research: An appraisal of the evidence. *American Psychologist*, *62*(2), 131–139.

Berger, P. L., & Luckmann, T. (1966). *The social construction of reality: A treatise in the sociology of knowledge*. New York, NY: Doubleday.

Bevir, M. (2007). Historical understanding and the human sciences. *Journal of the Philosophy of History*, *1*, 259–270.

Binet, A. (1903). *L'Étude experimental de l'intelligence* (The experimental study of intelligence). Paris, France: Schleicher.

Binet, A. (1909/1975). *Les Idées modernes sur les enfants* (Modern ideas about children). Albi, France: Presses de L'Atelier Graphique.

Bjork, D. W. (1993). *B. F. Skinner*. New York, NY: Basic Books.

Bleicher, J. (2017). *Contemporary hermeneutics: Hermeneutics as method, philosophy and critique*. Abingdon, UK: Routledge.

Blum, G. S., Rauthmann, J. F., Göllner, R., Lischetzke, T., & Schmitt, M. (2018). The non-linear interaction of person and situation (NIPS) model: Theory and empirical evidence. *European Journal of Personality*, *32*(3), 286–305.

Blumenthal, A. L. (1975). A reappraisal of Wilhelm Wundt. *American Psychologist*, *30*(11), 1081–1088.

Boor, M., & Hamill, R. B. (1978). Letters from Wundt's doctoral students. *American Psychologist*, *33*(2), 191.

Boring, E. G. (1929). *A history of experimental psychology*. New York, NY: Appleton-Century-Crofts, Inc.

Bošković, A., & Rando, O. J. (2018). Transgenerational epigenetic inheritance. *Annual Review of Genetics*, *52*, 21–41.

Bourne, D., & Jankowicz, D. A. (2018). The repertory grid technique. In M. Ciesielska & D. Jemielniak (eds.), *Qualitative methodologies in organization studies* (pp. 127–149). New York, NY: Palgrave Macmillan.

Brazier, M. A. B. (1961). *A history of the electrical activity of the brain: The first half-century*. New York, NY: Palgrave Macmillan.

Brett, K. D., & Wertheimer, M. (2005). *Max Wertheimer & Gestalt theory*. New Brunswick, NJ: Transaction Publishers.

Breuer, J., & Freud, S. (1893/1955). On the psychical mechanism of hysterical phenomena: Preliminary communication from studies on hysteria. In *The standard edition of the complete psychological works of Sigmund Freud, Vol. 2 (1893–1895): Studies on hysteria* (pp. 1–17). London, England: Hogarth Press.

Breuer, J., & Freud, S. (1895/1955). Fraulein Anna O. In J. Strachey (ed. and trans.), *The standard edition of the complete psychological works of Sigmund Freud, Vol. 2: Studies on hysteria* (pp. 21–47). London, England: Hogarth Press.

Bringmann, W. G. (1975). Wundt in Heidelberg: 1845–1874. *Canadian Psychological Review/Psychologie canadienne, 16*(2), 124–129.

Bringmann, W. G., & Tweney, R. D. (eds.) (1980). *Wundt studies: A centennial collection.* Toronto, Canada: Hogrefe.

Broadbent, D. E. (1958). *Perception and communication.* Oxford, England: Pergamon Press.

Brocki, J. M., & Wearden, A. J. (2006). A critical evaluation of the use of interpretative phenomenological analysis (IPA) in health psychology. *Psychology and Health, 21*(1), 87–108.

Bruce, D. (1998). The Lashley–Hull debate revisited. *History of Psychology, 1*(1), 69–84.

Buckley, K. W. (1982). The selling of a psychologist: John Broadus Watson and the application of behavioral techniques to advertising. *Journal of the History of the Behavioral Sciences, 18*(3), 207–221.

Buckley, K. W. (1989). *Mechanical man: John B Watson and the beginnings of behaviourism.* New York, NY: The Guilford Press.

Burnham, J. C. (1972). Thorndike's puzzle boxes. *Journal of the History of the Behavioral Sciences, 8*(2), 159–167.

Burt, C. (1966). The genetic determination of differences in intelligence: A study of monozygotic twins reared together and apart. *British Journal of Psychology, 57*(1–2), 137–153.

Bushman, B. J. (2002). Does venting anger feed or extinguish the flame? Catharsis, rumination, distraction, anger, and aggressive responding. *Personality and Social Psychology Bulletin, 28*(6), 724–731.

Bushman, B. J., Baumeister, R. F., & Stack, A. D. (1999). Catharsis, aggression, and persuasive influence: Self-fulfilling or self-defeating prophecies? *Journal of Personality and Social Psychology, 76*(3), 367.

Buss, D. (2015). *Evolutionary psychology: The new science of the mind.* Hove, England: Psychology Press.

Caldwell, N., & Coshall, J. (2002). Measuring brand associations for museums and galleries using repertory grid analysis. *Management Decision, 40*(4), 383–392.

Carver, C. S., & Scheier, M. F. (1982). Control theory: A useful conceptual framework for personality: Social, clinical, and health psychology. *Psychological Bulletin, 92*(1), 111–135.

Carver, C. S., & Scheier, M. F. (1990). Origins and functions of positive and negative affect: A control-process view. *Psychological Review, 97*(1), 19–35.

Catania, A. C. (1992). B. F. Skinner, organism. *American Psychologist, 47*(11), 1521–1530.

Caton, R. (1875). The electric currents of the brain. *British Medical Journal, 2,* 278.

Chomsky, N. (1959). A review of B. F. Skinner's verbal behavior. *Language, 35,* 26–58.

Clarke, V., & Braun, V. (2013). Teaching thematic analysis: Overcoming challenges and developing strategies for effective learning. *The Psychologist, 26*(2), 120–123.

Cohen, D. (1979). *J. B. Watson: The founder of behaviourism*. Boston, MA: Routledge and Kegan Paul.

Cohen, S., Janicki-Deverts, D., & Miller, G. E. (2007). Psychological stress and disease. *Jama*, *298*(14), 1685–1687.

Coon, D. J. (2000). Salvaging the self in a world without soul: William James's the principles of psychology. *History of Psychology*, *3*(2), 83–103.

Craik, K. J. (1943). *The nature of explanation*. Cambridge, England: Cambridge University Press.

Craik, K. J. (1948). Theory of the human operator in control systems: II. Man as an element in a control system. *British Journal of Psychology*, *38*(3), 142–148.

Croce, P. J. (1999). Physiology as the antechamber to metaphysics: The young William James's hope for a philosophical psychology. *History of Psychology*, *2*(4), 302.

Cronbach, L. J. (1957). The two disciplines of scientific psychology. *American Psychologist*, *12*(11), 671–684.

Cronbach, L. J., & Meehl, P. E. (1955). Construct validity in psychological tests. *Psychological Bulletin*, *52*(4), 281–302.

Csikszentmihalyi, M., & Seligman, M. E. (2000). Positive psychology: An introduction. *American Psychologist*, *55*(1), 5–14.

Danziger, K. (2001). The unknown Wundt: Drive, apperception and volition. In R. W. Rieber & D. K. Robinson (eds.), *Wilhelm Wundt in history: The making of a scientific psychology* (pp. 95–120). New York, NY: Kluwer Academic and Plenum Publishers.

Deci, E. L., & Ryan, R. M. (1985). *Intrinsic motivation and self-determination in human behavior*. New York, NY: Plenum.

Decker, H. S. (1991). *Freud, Dora and Vienna 1900*. New York, NY: Free Press.

De Marneffe, D. (1991). Looking and listening: The construction of clinical knowledge in Charcot and Freud. *Signs: Journal of Women in Culture and Society*, *17*(1), 71–111.

de Paula Ramos, S. (2003). Revisiting Anna O.: A case of chemical dependence. *History of Psychology*, *6*(3), 239–250.

Dichter, W. (1964). *Handbook of human motivations: The psychology of the world of objects*. New York, NY: McGraw-Hill.

Diener, E. D., Emmons, R. A., Larsen, R. J., & Griffin, S. (1985). The satisfaction with life scale. *Journal of Personality Assessment*, *49*(1), 71–75.

Digdon, N., Powell, R. A., & Harris, B. (2014). Little Albert's alleged neurological impairment: Watson, Rayner, and historical revision. *History of Psychology*, *17*(4), 312.

Dilthey, W. (1894/1977). Descriptive psychology and historical understanding. In R. M. Zaner & K. L. Heiges (trans.), *The Hague, the Netherlands: Martinus Nijhoff*. (Original work published 1894).

Dix, D. L. (1843–1852/1971). *On behalf of the insane poor: Selected reports*. New York, NY: Arno Press.

Edley, N. (2001). Unravelling social constructionism. *Theory & Psychology*, *11*(3), 433–441.

Ellenberger, H. F. (1972). The story of "Anna O": A critical review with new data. *Journal of the History of the Behavioral Sciences*, *8*(3), 267–279.

Ellis, R., & Humphreys, G. W. (1999). *Connectionist psychology: A text with readings*. Hove, England: Psychology Press.

Ellis, W. D. (ed.) (1999). *A source book of gestalt psychology*. London, England: Routledge and Kegan Paul.

Engel, G. L. (1978). The biopsychosocial model and the education of health professionals. *Annals of the New York Academy of Sciences, 310*(1), 169–181.

Epstein, S., & O'brien, E. J. (1985). The person: Situation debate in historical and current perspective. *Psychological Bulletin, 98*(3), 513.

Esterson, A. (2002a). The myth of Freud's ostracism by the medical community in 1896–1905: Jeffrey Masson's assault on truth. *History of Psychology, 5*(2), 115–134.

Esterson, A. (2002b). Misconceptions about Freud's seduction theory: Comment on Gleaves and Hernandez (1999). *History of Psychology, 5*(1), 85–91.

Evans, R. B., & Koelsch, W. A. (1985). Psychoanalysis arrives in America: The 1909 psychology conference at Clark University. *American Psychologist, 40*(8), 942–948.

Fang, F. C., Steen, R. G., & Casadevall, A. (2012). Misconduct accounts for the majority of retracted scientific publications. *Proceedings of the National Academy of Sciences, 109*(42), 17028–17033.

Farr, R. M. (1983). Wilhelm Wundt (1832–1920) and the origins of psychology as an experimental and social science. *British Journal of Social Psychology, 22*(4), 289–301.

Fechner, G. T. (1860/1966). *Elements of psychophysics*. New York, NY: Holt, Rinehart and Winston.

Fechner, G. T. (1865). Über die Frage des goldenen Schnittes (On the question of the golden section). *Archiv für die zeichnenden Künste, 11*, 100–112.

Fechner, G. T. (1871). *Zur experimentalen ästhetik* (On experimental aesthetics). Leipzig, Germany: Hirzel.

Fechner, G. T. (1904/2005). *The little book of life after death*. Boston, MA: Weisser Books.

Fernandez-Duque, D., Evans, J., Christian, C., & Hodges, S. D. (2015). Superfluous neuroscience information makes explanations of psychological phenomena more appealing. *Journal of Cognitive Neuroscience, 27*(5), 926–944.

Fleeson, W. (2004). Moving personality beyond the person-situation debate: The challenge and the opportunity of within-person variability. *Current Directions in Psychological Science, 13*(2), 83–87.

Fodor, J. A. (1968). *Psychological explanation: An introduction to the philosophy of psychology*. New York, NY: Random House.

Fodor, J. A. (1983). *The modularity of mind*. Cambridge, MA: MIT Press.

Fodor, J. A. (1985). Precis of the modularity of mind. *Behavioral and Brain Sciences, 8*(1), 1–5.

Forrester, J. (1986). The true story of Anna O. *Social Research, 53*(2), 327.

Fowler, R. D. (1990). In memoriam: Burrhus Frederic Skinner, 1904–1990. *American Psychologist, 45*(11), 1203.

Fox, B. (2017). It's nature and nurture: Integrating biology and genetics into the social learning theory of criminal behavior. *Journal of Criminal Justice, 49*, 22–31.

Frank, J. D., & Frank, J. B. (1991). *Persuasion and healing: A comparative study of psycho-therapy* (3rd ed.). Baltimore, MD: John Hopkins University Press.

Frankl, V. E. (1959). *Man's search for meaning*. Boston, MA: Beacon Press.

Frankl, V. E. (1967). *Psychotherapy and existentialism*. New York, NY: Washington Square Press.

Frankl, V. E. (1969). *The will to meaning*. New York, NY: The New American Library, Inc.

Freud, S. (1895a). Project for a scientific psychology. In *The standard edition of the complete works of Sigmund Freud* (Vol. 1). London, England: Hogarth Press.

Freud, S. (1895b). Studies in hysteria (with Joseph Breuer). In *The standard edition of the complete works of Sigmund Freud* (Vol. 2). London, England: Hogarth Press.

Freud, S. (1905/1955). Fragments of an analysis of a case of hysteria. In *The standard edition of the complete works of Sigmund Freud* (Vol. 7). London, England: Hogarth Press.

Freud, S. (1909/1955). Analysis of a phobia in a five-year-old boy. In *The standard edition of the complete works of Sigmund Freud* (Vol. 10). London, England: Hogarth Press.

Freud, S. (1918/1955). *From the history of an infantile neurosis*. The standard edition of the complete works of Sigmund Freud (Vol. 17). London, England: Hogarth Press.

Froh, J. J. (2004). The history of positive psychology: Truth be told. *NYS Psychologist*, *16*(3), 18–20.

Galton, F. (1869). *Hereditary genius: An inquiry into its laws and consequences*. London, England: Palgrave Macmillan.

Galton, F. (1874). *English men of science: Their nature and nurture*. London, England: Palgrave Macmillan.

Galton, F. (1875). The history of twins as a criterion of the relative powers of nature and nurture. *Fraser's Magazine*, *92*, 566–576.

Galton, F. (1883). *Inquiries into human faculty and its development*. London, England: Palgrave Macmillan.

Gergen, K. J. (1985). The social constructionist movement in modern psychology. *American Psychologist*, *40*(3), 266–275.

Gibson, J. J. (1979). *The ecological approach to visual perception*. Boston, MA: Houghton Mifflin.

Glaser, B. G., & Strauss, A. L. (1967). *Grounded theory: The discovery of grounded theory*. Rutgers, NJ: Transaction Publishers.

Glass, N. (1999). Sure start: The development of an early intervention programme for young children in the United Kingdom. *Children & Society*, *13*(4), 257–264.

Gorham, J. (1988). The relationship between verbal teacher immediacy behaviors and student learning. *Communication Education*, *37*(1), 40–53.

Graebner, W. (2006). "Back-fire to lust": G. Stanley Hall, sex-segregated schooling, and the engine of sublimation. *History of Psychology*, *9*(3), 236–246.

Greely, H. T., & Farahany, N. A. (2019). Neuroscience and the criminal justice system. *Annual Review of Criminology*, *2*, 451–471.

Greenwald, A. G. (1992). New Look 3: Unconscious cognition reclaimed. *American Psychologist*, *47*(6), 766–779.

Greenwood, J. D. (2003). Wundt, Völkerpsychologie, and experimental social psychology. *History of Psychology*, *6*(1), 70–88.

Gregory, R. L. (2007). Helmholtz's principle. *Perception*, *36*, 795–796.

Gross, C. (2016). Scientific misconduct. *Annual Review of Psychology*, *67*, 693–711.

Guthrie, R. V. (1976). *Even the rats were white*. New York, NY: Harper & Row.

Haas, L. F. (2003). Hans Berger (1873–1941), Richard Caton (1842–1926), and electroencephalography. *Journal of Neurology, Neurosurgery & Psychiatry*, *74*(1), 9.

Hall, G. S. (1904). *Adolescence: Its psychology and its relation to physiology, anthropology, sociology, sex, crime, religion and education* (Vols. 1 and 2). New York, NY: Appleton-Century-Crofts, Inc.

Hall, G. S. (1906). The question of coeducation. *Munsey's Magazine*, *34*, 588–592.

Halmøy, A., Klungsøyr, K., Skjærven, R., & Haavik, J. (2012). Pre-and perinatal risk factors in adults with attention-deficit/hyperactivity disorder. *Biological Psychiatry*, *71*(5), 474–481.

Hanson, N. R. (1958). *Patterns of discovery*. Cambridge, UK: Cambridge University Press.

Harris, B. (1979). Whatever happened to little Albert? *American Psychologist*, *34*(2), 151–160.

Hartley, D. (1749). *Observation on man: His frame, his duty and his expectations*. London, England: J. Leake & W. Frederick.

Heard, E., & Martienssen, R. A. (2014). Transgenerational epigenetic inheritance: Myths and mechanisms. *Cell*, *157*(1), 95–109.

Hearnshaw, L. (1979). *Cyril Burt: Psychologist*. Ithaca, NY: Cornell University Press.

Hebb, D. (1948). *Organization of behaviour: A neuropsychological theory*. New York, NY: Wiley.

Hempel, C. G. (1958). The theoretician's dilemma: A study in the logic of theory construction. In H. Feigl, M. Scriven & G Maxell (eds.), *Minnesota studies in the philosophy of science* (Vol. 2). Minneapolis, MN: University of Minnesota Press.

Henle, M. (ed.) (1971). *The selected papers of Wolfgang Köhler*. New York, NY: Liveright.

Henle, M. (1978). One man against the Nazis: Wolfgang Köhler. *American Psychologist*, *33*(10), 939.

Henningsen, P., Zipfel, S., & Herzog, W. (2007). Management of functional somatic syndromes. *The Lancet*, *369*(9565), 946–955.

Higgins, E. T. (1987). Self-discrepancy: A theory relating self and affect. *Psychological Review*, *94*(3), 319.

Hillhouse, T. M., & Porter, J. H. (2015). A brief history of the development of antidepressant drugs: From monoamines to glutamate. *Experimental and Clinical Psychopharmacology*, *23*(1), 1–21.

Hoffman, E. (1980). *The right to be human: A biography of Abraham Maslow*. Wellingborough, England: The Aquarian Press.

Höge, H. (1997). The golden section hypothesis: Its last funeral. *Empirical Studies of the Arts*, *15*(2), 233–255.

Hull, C. L. (1928). *Aptitude testing*. New York, NY: World Book.

Hull, C. L. (1929). A functional interpretation of the conditioned reflex. *Psychological Review*, *36*(6), 498.

Hull, C. L. (1930). Simple trial and error learning: A study in psychological theory. *Psychological Review, 37*(3), 241–256.

Hull, C. L. (1933). *Hypnosis and suggestibility*. New York, NY: Appleton-Century-Crofts, Inc.

Hull, C. L. (1945). *Principles of behaviour*. New York, NY: Appleton-Century-Crofts, Inc.

Hull, C. L. (1951). *Essentials of behaviour*. New York, NY: Appleton-Century-Crofts, Inc.

Hull, C. L. (1952). *A behaviour system*. New Haven, CT: Yale University Press.

Husserl, E. (1910/1965). Philosophy as rigorous science. In Q. Lauer (ed.), *Phenomenology and the crisis of philosophy*. New York, NY: Harper & Row.

Hussinger, K., & Pellens, M. (2019). Guilt by association: How scientific misconduct harms prior collaborators. *Research Policy, 48*(2), 516–530.

Huxley, A. (1932). *Brave new world*. London, England: Chatto & Windus.

Hyland, M. (1981). *Introduction to theoretical psychology*. London, England: Palgrave Macmillan.

Hyland, M. E. (1985). Do person variables exist in different ways? *American Psychologist, 40*(9), 1003–1010.

Hyland, M. E. (1987). Control theory interpretation of psychological mechanisms of depression: Comparison and integration of several theories. *Psychological Bulletin, 102*(1), 109–121.

Hyland, M. E. (2001). A two-phase network theory of atopy and asthma causation: A possible solution to the impact of genes, hygiene and air quality. *Clinical & Experimental Allergy, 31*(10), 1485–1492.

Hyland, M. E. (2002). The intelligent body and its discontents. *Journal of Health Psychology, 7*(1), 21–32.

Hyland, M. E. (2011). *The origins of health and disease*. Cambridge, England: Cambridge University Press.

Hyland, M. E. (2017). A new paradigm to explain functional disorders and the adaptive network theory of chronic fatigue syndrome and fibromyalgia syndrome. In G. B. Sullivan, J. Cresswell, B. Ellis, M. Morgan & E. Schraube (eds.), *Resistance and renewal in theoretical psychology* (pp. 21–31). Concord, Canada: Captus University Publications.

Hyland, M. E., Hinton, C., Hill, C., Whalley, B., Jones, R. C., & Davies, A. F. (2016). Explaining unexplained pain to fibromyalgia patients: Finding a narrative that is acceptable to patients and provides a rationale for evidence based interventions. *British Journal of Pain, 10*(3), 156–161.

Hyland, M. E., Lanario, J. W., Pooler, J., Masoli, M., & Jones, R. C. (2018). How patient participation was used to develop a questionnaire that is fit for purpose for assessing quality of life in severe asthma. *Health and Quality of Life Outcomes, 16*(1), 24.

Hyland, M. E., Lanario, J. W., Wei, Y., Jones, R. C., & Masoli, M. (2019). Evidence for similarity in symptoms and mechanism: The extra-pulmonary symptoms of severe asthma and polysymptomatic presentation of fibromyalgia. *Immunity, Inflammation and Disease* (in press).

Hyland, M. E., Whalley, B., Jones, R. C., & Masoli, M. (2015). A qualitative study of the impact of severe asthma and its treatment showing that treatment burden is neglected in existing asthma assessment scales. *Quality of Life Research, 24*(3), 631–639.

Hyland, M. E., Lanario, J. W., Pooler, J., Masoli, M., & Jones, R. C. (2018). How patient participation was used to develop a questionnaire that is fit for purpose for assessing quality of life in severe asthma. *Health and Quality of Life Outcomes*, *16*(1), 24.

Ivonin, L., Chang, H. M., Diaz, M., Catala, A., Chen, W., & Rauterberg, M. (2015). Traces of unconscious mental processes in introspective reports and physiological responses. *PloS One*, *10*(4), e0124519.

James, W. (1890). *The principles of psychology*. New York, NY: Holt.

James, W. (1895). Is life worth living? *International Journal of Ethics*, *6*(1), 1–24.

James, W. (1899/1922). *Talks to teachers on psychology*. London, England: Longmans, Green and Co.

Jones, M. B. (2003). Two early studies on learning theory and genetics. *Behavior Genetics*, *33*(6), 669–676.

Jones, M. J., Moore, S. R., & Kobor, M. S. (2018). Principles and challenges of applying epigenetic epidemiology to psychology. *Annual Review of Psychology*, *69*, 459–485.

Jonides, J., Lewis, R. L., Nee, D. E., Lustig, C. A., Berman, M. G., & Moore, K. S. (2008). The mind and brain of short-term memory. *Annual Review of Psychology*, *59*, 193–224.

Kahneman, D. (2011). *Thinking, fast and slow*. London, UK: Palgrave Macmillan.

Kamin, L. J. (1974). *The science and politics of IQ*. Potomac, MD: Lawrence Erlbaum Associates.

Kamin, L. J. (1981). The Cyril Burt affair. In H. J. Eysenk & L. Kamin (eds.), *Intelligence: The battle for the mind*. London, England: Pan.

Kantor, J. R. (1970). An analysis of the experimental analysis of behavior (TEAB). *Journal of the Experimental Analysis of Behavior*, *13*(1), 101.

Kelly, G. A. (1955). *The psychology of personal constructs* (Vols. 1–2). New York, NY: Norton & Co.

Kelly, G. A. (1963). *A theory of personality: The psychology of personal constructs*. New York, NY: Norton & Co.

Kemeny, J. G., & Oppenheim, P. (1956). On reduction. *Philosophical Studies*, *7*, 6–19.

Kirsch, I. (1985). Response expectancy as a determinant of experience and behavior. *American Psychologist*, *40*(11), 1189–1202.

Kirsch, I. (2010). *The emperor's new drugs: Exploding the antidepressant myth*. New York, NY: Basic Books.

Kirsch, I. (2014). The emperor's new drugs: Medication and placebo in the treatment of depression. In F. Benedetti, P. Enck, E. Frisaldi & M. Schedlowski (eds.), *Placebo* (pp. 291–303). Berlin, Germany: Springer.

Kirsch, I., & Hyland, M. E. (1987). How thoughts affect the body: A metatheoretical framework. *Journal of Mind and Behavior*, *8*, 417–434.

Kirsch, I., Moore, T. J., Scoboria, A., & Nicholls, S. S. (2002). The emperor's new drugs: An analysis of antidepressant medication data submitted to the US Food and Drug Administration. *Prevention & Treatment*, *5*(1), 23a.

Koffka, K. (1922). Perception: An introduction to the Gestalt-Theorie. *Psychological Bulletin*, *19*(10), 531.

Koffka, K. (1924). *The growth of the mind: An introduction to child psychology* (R. M. Ogden, trans.). New York, NY: Harcourt, Brace & World, Inc.

Koffka, K. (1935). *Principles of Gestalt psychology*. New York, NY: Harcourt, Brace & World, Inc.

Köhler, W. (1925). *The mentality of apes*. London, England: Routledge and Kegan Paul. (Original work published 1917).

Köhler, W. (1947). *Gestalt psychology: An introduction to new concepts in modern psychology*. New York, NY: Liveright. (Original work published 1929).

Köhler, W. (1959). Gestalt psychology today. *American Psychologist*, *14*(12), 727.

Köhler, W. (1966). *The place of value in a world of facts*. New York, NY: Liveright. (Original work published 1938).

Kuhn, T. S. (1962). *The structure of scientific revolutions*. Chicago, IL: The University of Chicago Press.

Lakatos, I. (1978). *Philosophical papers* (2 vols.). New York, NY: Cambridge University Press.

Lakatos, I., & Musgrave, A. (eds.) (1970). *Criticism and the growth of knowledge*. New York, NY: Cambridge University Press.

Lamiell, J. T. (1998). Nomothetic' and idiographic' contrasting Windelband's understanding with contemporary usage. *Theory & Psychology*, *8*(1), 23–38.

Landy, F. J. (1992). Hugo Münsterberg: Victim or visionary? *Journal of Applied Psychology*, *77*(6), 787–802.

Le Nguyen, K. D., Lin, J., Algoe, S. B., Brantley, M. M., Kim, S. L., Brantley, J., . . . Fredrickson, B. L. (2019). Loving-kindness meditation slows biological aging in novices: Evidence from a 12-week randomized controlled trial. *Psychoneuroendocrinology*, *108*, 20–27.

Lewin, K. (1938). The conceptual representation and measurement of psychological forces. In *Contributions to psychological theory* (Vol. 1, No. 4). Durham, NC: Duke University Press.

Lewin, K. (1939). Field theory and experiment in social psychology: Concepts and methods. *American Journal of Sociology*, *44*(6), 868–896.

Lewin, K. (1943a). Psychology and the process of group living. *The Journal of Social Psychology*, *17*(1), 113–131.

Lewin, K. (1943b). Defining the "field at a given time". *Psychological Review*, *50*(3), 292–310.

López-Muñoz, F., Alamo, C., Cuenca, E., Shen, W. W., Clervoy, P., & Rubio, G. (2005). History of the discovery and clinical introduction of chlorpromazine. *Annals of Clinical Psychiatry*, *17*(3), 113–135.

Lothane, Z. (1998). Freud's 1895 project: From mind to brain and back again. *Annals of the New York Academy of Sciences*, *843*(1), 43–65.

Luce, R. D. (1977). The choice axiom after twenty years. *Journal of Mathematical Psychology*, *15*(3), 215–233.

Lyman, R. L., & O'Brien, M. J. (2004). Nomothetic science and idiographic history in twentieth-century Americanist anthropology. *Journal of the History of the Behavioral Sciences*, *40*(1), 77–96.

MacCorquodale, K., & Meehl, P. E. (1948). On a distinction between hypothetical constructs and intervening variables. *Psychological Review, 55*(2), 95–107.

Magnusson, D., & Endler, N. S. (1977). *Personality at the crossroads: Current issues in interactional psychology.* Hillsdale, NJ: Erlbaum.

Malaspina, D., Corcoran, C., Kleinhaus, K. R., et al. (2008). Acute maternal stress in pregnancy and schizophrenia in offspring: A cohort prospective study. *BMC Psychiatry, 8*, 71. http://biomedcentral.com/1471-244X/8/71/.

Marbe, K. (1901). *Experimentell-psychologische Untersuchungen über das Urteil. Eine Einleitung in die Logik* (Experimental-psychological investigations of the judgement: An introduction into logic). Leipzig, Germany: Engelmann.

Marks, D. F. (2019). The Hans Eysenck affair: Time to correct the scientific record. *Journal of Health Psychology, 24*(4), 409–420.

Markus, H., & Nurius, P. (1986). Possible selves. *American Psychologist, 41*(9), 954–969.

Maslow, A. H. (1954). *Motivation and personality.* New York, NY: Harper & Row.

Maslow, A. H. (1968). *Toward a psychology of being.* New York, NY: van Nostrand Reinhold Company.

Maslow, A. H. (1970). *Religious, values and peak-experiences.* London, England: Viking Penguin Inc.

Massaro, D. W. (1990). The psychology of connectionism. *Behavioral and Brain Sciences, 13*(2), 403–406.

Masson, J. M. (1984). *The Assault on truth: Freud's suppression of the seduction theory.* New York, NY: Farrar Straus & Giroux.

Mathur, M. B., & Reichling, D. B. (2016). Navigating a social world with robot partners: A quantitative cartography of the Uncanny Valley. *Cognition, 146*, 22–32.

May, R. (1990). The idea of history in psychoanalysis: Freud and the "Wolf-Man". *Psychoanalytic Psychology, 7*(2), 163–183.

McCrae, R. R., & Costa, P. T., Jr. (1989). Reinterpreting the Myers-Briggs type indicator from the perspective of the five-factor model of personality. *Journal of Personality, 57*(1), 17–40.

McCulloch, W. S., & Pitts, W. (1943). A logical calculus of the ideas immanent in nervous activity. *The Bulletin of Mathematical Biophysics, 5*(4), 115–133.

McDonald, A. S. (2001). The prevalence and effects of test anxiety in school children. *Educational Psychology, 21*(1), 89–101.

McDougall, E. (1923). *Outline of psychology.* London, England: Methuen.

McDougall, W. (1938/1939). *The riddle of life: A survey of theories.* London, England: Methuen.

Melidis, C., Denham, S. L., & Hyland, M. E. (2018). A test of the adaptive network explanation of functional disorders using a machine learning analysis of symptoms. *Biosystems, 165*, 22–30.

Mick, E., Biederman, J., Prince, J., Fischer, M. J., & Faraone, S. V. (2002). Impact of low birth weight on attention-deficit hyperactivity disorder. *Journal of Developmental & Behavioral Pediatrics, 23*(1), 16–22.

Mill, J. S. (1829). *Analysis of the phenomena of the human mind.* London, England: Baldwin & Cradock.

Miller, G. A., Galanter, E., & Pribram, K. H. (1960). *Plans and the structure of behavior*. New York, NY: Henry Holt and Company.

Mills, J. A. (1978). Hull's theory of learning: II. A criticism of the theory and its relationship to the history of psychological thought. *Canadian Psychological Review/ Psychologie canadienne, 19*(2), 116–127.

Misiak, H., & Sexton, V. S. (1966). *History of psychology: An overview*. New York, NY: Grune & Stratton.

Monroe, S. M., & Harkness, K. L. (2005). Life stress, the "kindling" hypothesis, and the recurrence of depression: Considerations from a life stress perspective. *Psychological Review, 112*(2), 417–445.

Morris, E. K. (1984). Interbehavioral psychology and radical behaviorism: Some similarities and differences. *The Behavior Analyst, 7*(2), 197–204.

Münsterberg, H. (1908). *On the witness stand*. New York, NY: Clark Boardman.

Myers, G. E. (2001). *William James: His life and thought*. New Haven, CT: Yale University Press.

Myers, I. B. (1962). *Myers-Briggs type indicator manual*. Palo Alto, CA: Consulting Psychologists Press.

Nagel, E. (1961). *The structure of science: Problems in the logic of explanation*. New York, NY: Harcourt, Brace & World, Inc.

Nagel, T. (1998). Reductionism and antireductionism. In *The limits of reductionism in biology* (Novartis Foundation Symposium 213) (pp. 3–14). Chichester, England: Wiley.

O'Brien, M. (2004). *When Adam Delved and Eve Span: A history of the peasants' revolt of 1381*. Cheltenham, England: New Clarion Press.

O'Donnell, J. M. (1987). *The origins of behaviourism: American psychology, 1870–1920*. New York, NY: New York University Press.

Osgood, C. E., Suci, G., & Tannenbaum, P. (1967). *The measurement of meaning*. Champaign, IL: University of Illinois Press.

Parker, I. (1999). Critical psychology: Critical links. *Annual Review of Critical Psychology, 1*(1), 3–18.

Parsons, F. T. (1873). The art of questioning. *The Maine Journal of Education, 7*(8), 301–303.

Pearce, J. M. (2009). The ophthalmoscope: Helmholtz's augenspiegel. *European Neurology, 61*(4), 244–249.

Pearson, K. (1914). *The life, letters and labours of Francis Galton* (Vol. 1). London, England: Cambridge University Press.

Pearson, K. (1924). *The life, letters and labours of Francis Galton (vol 2): Researches of middle life*. London, England: Cambridge University Press.

Pelosi, A. J. (2019). Personality and fatal diseases: Revisiting a scientific scandal. *Journal of Health Psychology, 24*(4), 421–439.

Pilgrim, D. (2015). The biopsychosocial model in health research: Its strengths and limitations for critical realists. *Journal of Critical Realism, 14*(2), 164–180.

Plato (380BCE/1935). *The republic of Plato* (A. D. Lindsay, trans.). London, England: J.M. Dent.

Popper, K. (1935/1992). *The logic of scientific discovery*. Abingdon, England: Routledge.

Popper, K. R. (1963). *Conjectures and refutations*. London, England: Routledge and Kegan Paul.

Principe, G. F., & Schindewolf, E. (2012). Natural conversations as a source of false memories in children: Implications for the testimony of young witnesses. *Developmental Review*, *32*(3), 205–223.

Putnam, H. (1973). Reductionism and the nature of psychology. *Cognition*, *2*(1), 131–146.

Pytell, T. (2000). The missing pieces of the puzzle: A reflection on the odd career of Viktor Frankl. *Journal of Contemporary History*, *35*(2), 281–306.

Pytell, T. (2006). Transcending the angel beast: Viktor Frankl and humanistic psychology. *Psychoanalytic Psychology*, *23*(3), 490.

Rahula, W. (1959). *What the Buddha taught*. Oxford, England: Oneworld Publications.

Rangel, J. A. O. (2005). The systemic theory of living systems and relevance to CAM: The theory (Part II). *Evidence-Based Complementary and Alternative Medicine*, *2*(2), 129–137.

Reisman, J. M. (1991). *A history of clinical psychology*. Abingdon, England: Taylor & Francis.

Ridaura, V., & Belkaid, Y. (2015). Gut microbiota: The link to your second brain. *Cell*, *161*(2), 193–194.

Rkkönen, K., Pesonen, A. K., Heinonen, K., Lahti, J., Kajantie, E., Forsén, T., . . . Eriksson, J. G. (2008). Infant growth and hostility in adult life. *Psychosomatic Medicine*, *70*(3), 306–313.

Rogers, C. R. (1942). *Counseling and psychotherapy: Newer concepts in practice*. Boston, MA: Houghton Mifflin.

Rogers, C. R. (1951). *Client-centered therapy: Its current practice, implications, and theory*. Boston, MA: Houghton Mifflin.

Rogers, C. R. (1955). Persons or science? A philosophical question. *American Psychologist*, *10*(7), 267–278.

Rogers, C. R. (1957). The necessary and sufficient conditions of therapeutic personality change. *Journal of Consulting Psychology*, *21*(2), 95–103.

Rosen, D. H., Smith, S. M., Huston, H. L., & Gonzalez, G. (1991). Empirical study of associations between symbols and their meanings: Evidence of collective unconscious (archetypal) memory. *Journal of Analytical Psychology*, *36*(2), 211–228.

Royce, J. R., & Powell, A. (1983). *Theory of personality and individual differences: Factors, systems and processes*. Englewood Cliffs, NJ, US: Prentice Hall.

Rushton, J. P. (2002). New evidence on Sir Cyril Burt: His 1964 speech to the Association of Educational Psychologists. *Intelligence*, *30*(6), 555–567.

Rutherford, A. (2000). Radical behaviorism and psychology's public: BF Skinner in the popular press, 1934–1990. *History of Psychology*, *3*(4), 371–395.

Rutherford, A. (2003). BF Skinner and the auditory inkblot: The rise and fall of the verbal summator as a projective technique. *History of Psychology*, *6*(4), 362–378.

Sabat, S. R. (1979). Wundt's physiological psychology in retrospect. *American Psychologist*, *34*(7), 635–638.

Sagan, C. (1979). *Broca's brain*. New York, NY: Random House.

Sandford, S. (2006). Sexually ambiguous: Eros and sexuality in Plato and Freud. *Angelaki: Journal of the Theoretical Humanities, 11*(3), 43–59.

Sauce, B., & Matzel, L. D. (2018). The paradox of intelligence: Heritability and malleability coexist in hidden gene-environment interplay. *Psychological Bulletin, 144*(1), 26.

Schlotz, W., & Phillips, D. I. (2009). Fetal origins of mental health: Evidence and mechanisms. *Brain, Behavior, and Immunity, 23*(7), 905–916.

Schneider, S. M., & Morris, E. K. (1987). A history of the term radical behaviorism: From Watson to Skinner. *The Behavior Analyst, 10*(1), 27–39.

Schwitzgebel, E. (2004). Introspective training apprehensively defended: Reflections on Titchener's lab manual. *Journal of Consciousness Studies, 11*(7–8), 58–76.

Scott, W. D. (1911). *Influencing men in business: The psychology of argument and suggestion.* New Yok, NY: Ronald Press Co.

Segerstrom, S. C., & Miller, G. E. (2004). Psychological stress and the human immune system: A meta-analytic study of 30 years of inquiry. *Psychological Bulletin, 130*(4), 601.

Seligman, M. E. (1968). Chronic fear produced by unpredictable electric shock. *Journal of Comparative and Physiological Psychology, 66*(2), 402–411.

Seligman, M. E., & Maier, S. F. (1967). Failure to escape traumatic shock. *Journal of Experimental Psychology, 74*(1), 1–9.

Sharps, M. J., & Wertheimer, M. (2000). Gestalt perspectives on cognitive science and on experimental psychology. *Review of General Psychology, 4*(4), 315–336.

Shubla, H. C., Solomon, G. F., & Dosli, R. P. (1979). Psychoimmunology. *Journal of Holistic Health, 4,* 125–131.

Silk, J. B., & House, B. R. (2016). The evolution of altruistic social preferences in human groups. *Philosophical Transactions of the Royal Society B: Biological Sciences, 371*(1687), 20150097.

Skinner, B. F. (1935). Two types of conditioned reflex and a pseudo type. *The Journal of General Psychology, 12*(1), 66–77.

Skinner, B. F. (1938). *The behavior of organisms.* New York, NY: Appleton-Century-Crofts, Inc.

Skinner, B. F. (1948). *Walden Two.* New York, NY: Palgrave Macmillan.

Skinner, B. F. (1953). *Science and human behaviour.* Oxford, England: Macmillan.

Skinner, B. F. (1957). *Verbal behavior.* New York, NY: Appleton-Century-Crofts, Inc.

Skinner, B. F. (1971). *Beyond freedom and dignity.* New York, NY: Knopf.

Skinner, B. F. (1974). *About behaviourism.* New York, NY: Vintage Books.

Skinner, B. F. (1976). *Particulars of my life.* New York, NY: Knopf.

Skinner, B. F. (1984a). Behaviourism at fifty. *Behavioural and Brian Sciences, 7*(4), 615–667.

Skinner, B. F. (1984b). Reply to Catania. *Behavioral and Brain Sciences, 7*(4), 718–719.

Slife, B. D., & Christensen, T. R. (2013). Hermeneutic realism: Toward a truly meaningful psychology. *Review of General Psychology, 17*(2), 230–236.

Smith, J. A. (1996). Beyond the divide between cognition and discourse: Using interpretative phenomenological analysis in health psychology. *Psychology and Health, 11*(2), 261–271.

Smith, J. M. (1964). Group selection and kin selection. *Nature, 201*(4924), 1145.

Sodergren, S. C., Hyland, M. E., Crawford, A., & Partridge, M. R. (2004). Positivity in ill-ness: Self-delusion or existential growth? *British Journal of Health Psychology, 9*(2), 163–174.

Sodergren, S. C., & Lewith, G. T. (2006). Chronic fatigue syndrome: The role of positivity to illness in chronic fatigue syndrome patients. *Journal of Health Psychology, 11*(5), 731–741.

Spearman, C. (1927). *The abilities of man.* London, England: Palgrave Macmillan.

Steen, R. G. (2011). Retractions in the scientific literature: Do authors deliberately com-mit research fraud? *Journal of Medical Ethics, 37*(2), 113–117.

Steger, M. F., Frazier, P., Oishi, S., & Kaler, M. (2006). The meaning in life questionnaire: Assessing the presence of and search for meaning in life. *Journal of Counseling Psychology, 53*(1), 80–93.

Steiner, R. (1883/1988). *Goethean science* (Goethes Naturwissenschaftliche Schriften, Einleitungen). Liverpool, England: Mercury Press.

Stevenson, R. L. (1886). *Strange case of Dr Jekyll and Mr Hyde.* London, England: Long-mans, Green and Co.

Stern, B. B. (2004). The importance of being Ernest: Commemorating Dichter's con-tribution to advertising research. *Journal of Advertising Research, 44*(2), 165–169.

Stolt, C. M. (2001). Why did Freud never receive the Nobel Prize? *International Forum of Psychoanalysis, 10*(3–4), 221–226.

Tansley, A. G. (1920). *The new psychology.* London, England: George Allen & Unwin.

Taylor, E. (1995). An epistemological critique of experimentalism in psychology: Or, why G. Stanley Hall waited until William James was out of town to found the American Psychological Association. In H. E. Adler & R. W. Rieber (eds.), *Aspects of the history of psychology in America, 1892–1992* (Vol. 727, pp. 37–61). New York, NY: Annals of the New York Academy of Science.

Taylor, E. (1996). *William James on consciousness beyond the margin.* Princeton, MA: Princeton University Press.

Thorndike, E. (1899). A reply to "the nature of animal intelligence and the methods of investigating it". *Psychological Review, 6*(4), 412–420.

Thorndike, E. L. (1905). *The elements of psychology.* New York, NY: Mason Printing Cor-poration.

Thorndike, E. L. (1911). *Animal intelligence.* New York, NY: Palgrave Macmillan.

Thorndike, E. L. (1918). The nature, purposes, and general methods of measurements of educational products. In G. M. Wipple (ed.), *Seventeenth yearbook of the national society for the study of education* (Vol. 2, pp. 16–24). Bloomington, IL: Public School Publishing.

Thorndike, E. L. (1921). Measurement in education. *Teachers College Record, 22,* 371–379.

Thorndike, E. L. (1932). *The fundamentals of learning.* New York, NY: Teachers College.

Titchener, E. B. (1912). The schema of introspection. *American Journal of Psychology, 23*(4), 485–508.

Todorov, E., & Jordan, M. I. (2002). Optimal feedback control as a theory of motor coor-dination. *Nature Neuroscience, 5*(11), 1226–1235.

Tolman, E. C. (1922). A new formula for behaviorism. *Psychological Review, 29*(1), 44–53.

Tolman, E. C. (1932). *Purposive behavior in animals and men*. New York, NY: Appleton-Century-Crofts, Inc.

Tolman, E. C. (1945). A stimulus-expectancy need-cathexis psychology. *Science, 101*, 160–166.

Tolman, E. C. (1948). Cognitive maps in rats and men. *Psychological Review, 55*(4), 189–208.

Tolman, E. C. (1959). Principles of purposive behaviour. In S. Koch (ed.), *Psychologicaly: A study of a science* (Vol. 2, pp. 92–157). New York, NY: McGraw Book Company.

Tuke, S. (1813/1964). *Description of the retreat: An institution near York for insane persons of the Society of Friends*. London, England: Dawson.

U.S. Department of Health and Human Services Food and Drug Administration (2009). *Guidance for Industry Patient-Reported Outcome Measures: Use in Medical Product Development to Support Labeling Claims*. www.fda.gov/downloads/drugs/guidancecomplianceregulatoryinformation/guidances/ucm193282.pdf

Van Rappard, H. (2004). Wundt as an activity/process theorist. In A. C. Brock, J. Louw & W. van Hoorn (eds.), *Rediscovering the history of psychology: Essays inspired by the work of Kurt Danziger*. New York, NY: Kluwer Academic and Plenum Publishers.

Van Rappard, H., Sanders, C., & De Swart, J. H. (1980). Wilhelm Wundt and the cognitive shift. *Acta Psychologica, 46*(3), 235–255.

Veenendaal, M. V., Painter, R. C., de Rooij, S. R., Bossuyt, P. M., van der Post, J. A., Gluckman, P. D., . . . Roseboom, T. J. (2013). Transgenerational effects of prenatal exposure to the 1944–45 Dutch famine. *BJOG: An International Journal of Obstetrics & Gynaecology, 120*(5), 548–554.

Vincent, N. A. (2010). On the relevance of neuroscience to criminal responsibility. *Criminal Law and Philosophy, 4*(1), 77–98.

Virués-Ortega, J. (2006). The case against BF Skinner 45 years later: An encounter with N. Chomsky. *The Behavior Analyst, 29*(2), 243–251.

Wade, N. J. (1994). Guest editorial: Hermann von Helmholtz (1821–1894). *Perception, 23*, 961–989.

Wade, N. J., & Finger, S. (2001). The eye as an optical instrument: From camera obscura to Helmholtz's perspective. *Perception, 30*(10), 1157–1177.

Walach, H. (2020). Naturalising religion-spiritualising science: The role of consciousness research. *Journal of Consciousness Studies* (in press).

Walach, H., Horan, M., Hinterberger, T., & von Lucadou, W. (2019). Evidence for anomalistic correlations between human behavior and a random event generator: Result of an independent replication of a Micro-PK experiment. *Psychology of Consciousness: Theory, Research and Practice* (in press). https://psycnet.apa.org/search/results?id=6a953a86-f303-fb36-ff07-34e71663ce86

Walsh, V., & Cowey, A. (2000). Transcranial magnetic stimulation and cognitive neuroscience. *Nature Reviews Neuroscience, 1*(1), 73–80.

Wampold, B. E. (2013). *The great psychotherapy debate: Models, methods, and findings*. New York, NY: Routledge.

Watson, J. B. (1903). *Animal education*. Chicago, IL: The University of Chicago Press.

Watson, J. B. (1913). Psychology as the behaviorist views it. *Psychological Review*, *20*(2), 158–177.

Watson, J. B. (1914). *Behavior: An introduction to comparative psychology*. New York, NY: Henry Holt and Company.

Watson, J. B. (1916). The place of the conditioned-reflex in psychology. *Psychological Review*, *23*(2), 89–116.

Watson, J. B. (1919a). *Psychology from the standpoint of a behaviorist*. Pennsylvania, PA: Lippincott.

Watson, J. B. (1919b). A schematic outline of the emotions. *Psychological Review*, *26*(3), 165–196.

Watson, J. B. (1924/1970). *Behaviorism*. New York, NY: Norton & Co.

Watson, J. B. (1928/1972). *Psychological care of the infant and child*. New York, NY: Arno Press.

Watson, J. B., & Rayner, R. (1920). Conditioned emotional reactions. *Journal of Experimental Psychology*, *3*(1), 1–14.

Watt, H. J. (1913). The main principles of sensory integration. *British Journal of Psychology*, *6*(2), 239.

Weber, E. H. (1834/1978). *The sense of touch*. New York, NY: Academic Press.

Wertheimer, M. (1912). Experimental studies of the perception of movement. *Zeitschrift für Psychologie*, *61*, 161–265. Also available in W. S. Sahakian (ed.), *History of psychology: A source book in systematic psychology* (pp. 418–422), Itasca, IL: Peacock.

Weyant, R. G. (1968). Who's afraid of John B. Watson? Comments on behavior: An introduction to comparative psychology. [Review of the book Behavior: An introduction to comparative psychology. J. B. Watson & R. J. Herrnstein]. *Canadian Psychologist/Psychologie canadienne*, *9*(3), 360–368.

Wiener, D. N. (1996). *B.F. Skinner: Benign anarchist*. Boston, MA: Allyn & Bacon.

Wilkinson, S. (1996). *Feminist psychology: International perspectives*. Buckingham, England: Open University Press.

Williams, R. D. (1912). An investigation of the personal equation and reaction time. *Publication of the Pomona College Astronomical Society*, *1*(5), 1–59.

Willig, C. (2001). *Introducing qualitative research in psychology*. Buckingham, England: Open University Press.

Wilson, D. S. (1975). A theory of group selection. *Proceedings of the National Academy of Sciences*, *72*(1), 143–146.

Winston, A. S. (1998). "The defects of his race": EG Boring and antisemitism in American psychology, 1923–1953. *History of Psychology*, *1*(1), 27–51.

Winston, A. S. (2004). Controlling the metalanguage. In A. C. Brock, J. Louw & W. van Hoorn (eds.), *Rediscovering the history of psychology: Essays inspired by the work of Kurt Danziger* (pp. 53–73). New York, NY: Kluwer Academic and Plenum Publishers.

Winter, D. G., John, O. P., Stewart, A. J., Klohnen, E. C., & Duncan, L. E. (1998). Traits and motives: Toward an integration of two traditions in personality research. *Psychological Review*, *105*(2), 230–250.

Witmer, L. (1896). Practical work in psychology. *Pediatrics*, *2*, 462–471.

Witmer, L. (1907). Clinical psychology. *The Psychological Clinic*, *1*(1), 1–9.

Wong, W. C. (2009). Retracing the footsteps of Wilhelm Wundt: Explorations in the disciplinary frontiers of psychology and in *Völkerpsychologie*. *History of Psychology*, *12*, 229–265.

Worcester, E. (1932). *Life's adventure: The story of a varied career*. New York, NY: Charles Scriber's Sons.

Wundt, W. (1862). *Contributions to a theory of sense perception*. Leipzig, Germany: Winter.

Wundt, W. (1874/1969). *Principles of physiological psychology* (5th ed., Vol. 1, E. B. Titchener, trans.). New York, NY: Kraus Reprint Co.

Wundt, W. (1880–1883). *Logic: An investigation into the principles of knowledge and the methods of scientific research* (4th ed., 1919–1921, 3 vols.). Stuttgart, Germany: Enke.

Wundt, W. (1886). *Ethics: An examination of the facts and laws of moral life*. Stuttgart, Germany: Enke.

Wundt, W. (1904). *Völkerpsychologie. Eine Untersuchung der Entwicklungsgesetze von Sprache, Mythus und Sitte*, 10 volumes, Leipzig, Germany: Kröner. 3rd edition.

Yalom, I. D. (1980). *Existential psychotherapy*. New York, NY: Basic Books.

Zeaman, D., & House, B. J. (1951). The growth and decay of reactive inhibition as measured by alternation behavior. *Journal of Experimental Psychology*, *41*(3), 177.

Zucker, A., & Wiegand, D. (1988). Freud, Fliess, and the nasogenital reflex: Did a look into the nose let us see the mind? *Otolaryngology: Head and Neck Surgery*, *98*(4), 319–322.

Zwaan, R. A., Etz, A., Lucas, R. E., & Donnellan, M. B. (2018). Making replication mainstream. *Behavioral and Brain Sciences*, *41*, E120.

Index